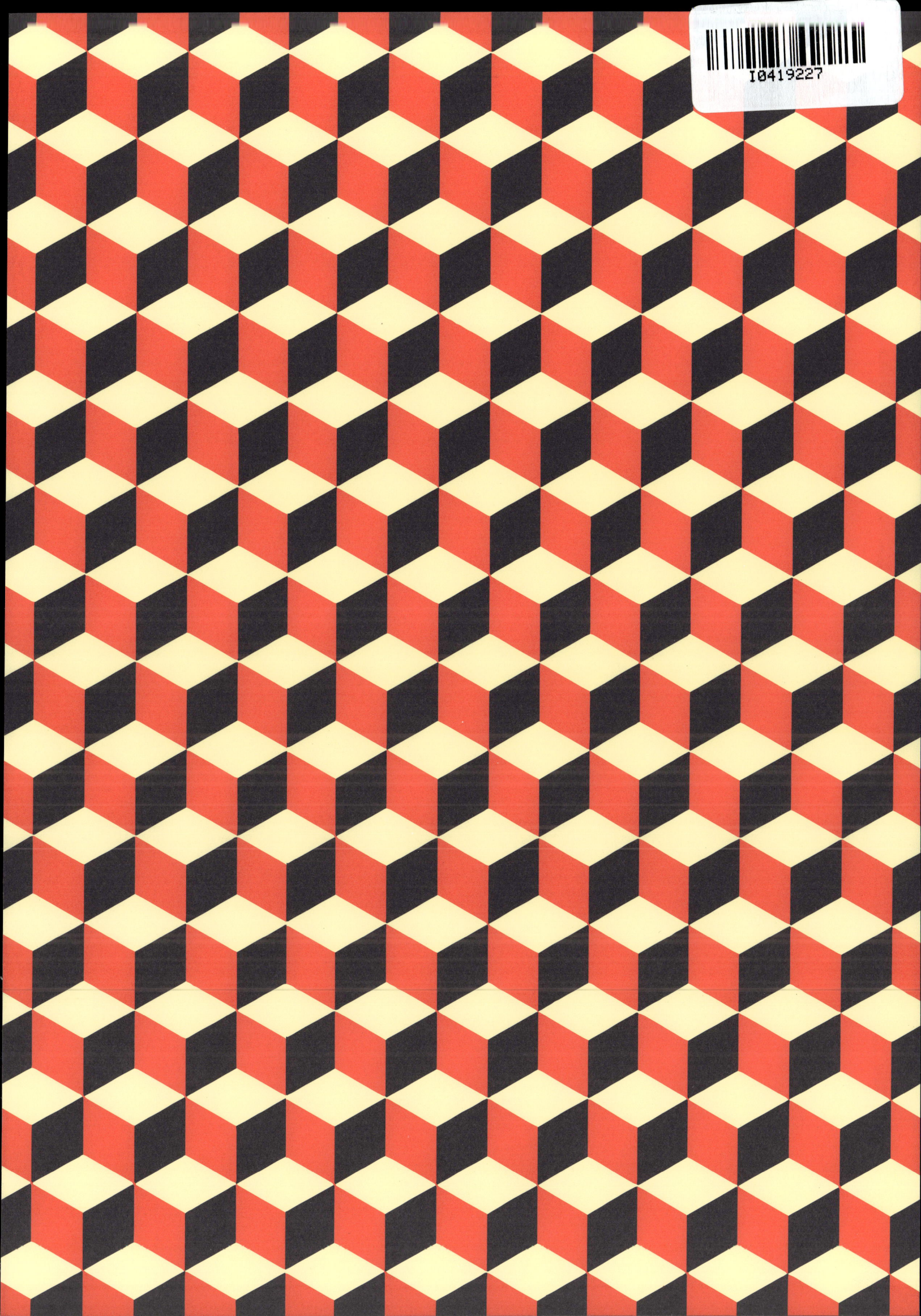

MARK RYDEN

YAKALINA SECRETS

PERROTIN

KASMIN

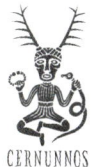

CERNUNNOS

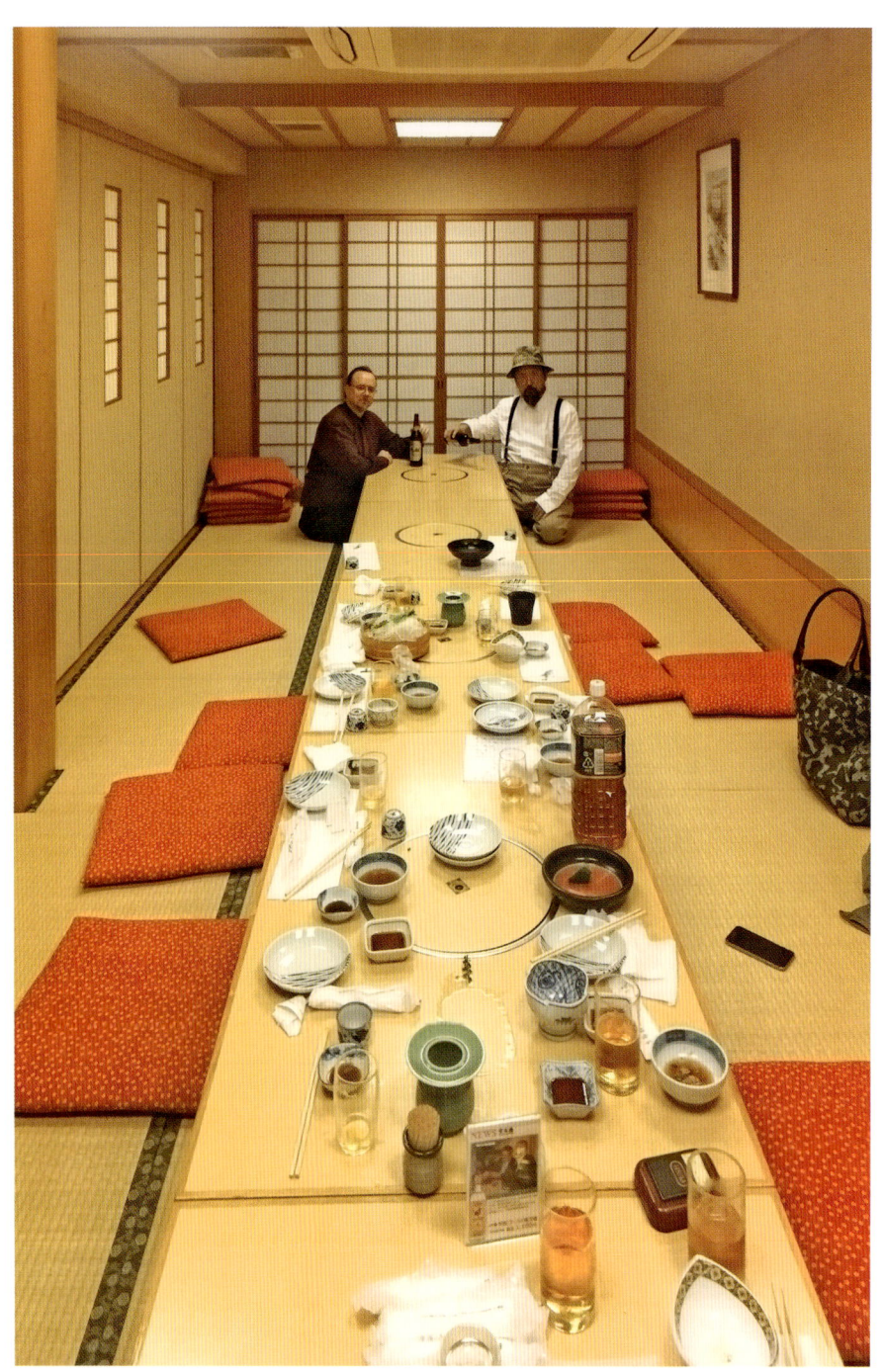

FOREWORD

My first in-person encounter with Mark Ryden's paintings was truly by chance, when I visited Leonardo DiCaprio's home in Los Angeles. Mr. DiCaprio himself was not there at the time, but his friend Tobey Maguire was living there for the time being and the latter invited me to come visit.

In the room I was received in, there were numerous paintings by the same artist on the wall, with Abraham Lincoln and animals staring at me with a tremendous presence, and a very ominous mood prevailed in the space. After looking at them for a while, I realized, "Oh! These are the works of the artist who painted Michael Jackson's album cover!" I relaxed at once and looked carefully at the works one by one.

Mark's works have an unmistakable, strong American West Coast flavor, with a slightly anachronistic style, blending a number of themes such as the founding of the United States, carnivorousness, and admiration for Japanese and Asian cultures. At the same time, their overall mood is tolerant and generous; they are painted with a solid oil-painting technique, and the paintings themselves are very powerful.

Mark also designed the set and costumes for the American Ballet Theatre's production of *Whipped Cream*, in which he created a unique cast of characters that brought a breath of fresh air to the world of ballet, inviting outcries of both approval and disapproval and asserting a strong presence.

Backtracking a little, I had an opportunity to hold a small solo exhibition of Mark's works at my own gallery in Tokyo in 2016. At that time, Mark was already very popular and his works were priced very high, so our gallery was not able to sell all of the exhibited works and ultimately had to return some of them. The following year or thereabouts, he moved on to Perrotin; I of course wish we could have kept working with him, but I do think he and Perrotin are a very good match.

When Perrotin first started out, the gallery represented artists who were completely unknown, including myself, Maurizio Cattelan, and Paola Pivi, ushering fresh possibilities into the industry. These were the first generation of artists at Perrotin. The second generation includes KAWS, JR, Mark Ryden, and Daniel Arsham, among others. I think that Mark symbolizes the new market of art that has developed over the last fifteen years.

The new trend in contemporary art over the past fifteen years has been the influx of collectors from non-Western countries, especially China. And the artists in their collections have been those mainly involved in art in the context of pop and street cultures rather than art history. This is where Mark's pop-candy-toys aesthetic mixed with horror-inspired style fits in perfectly and why he became extremely popular.

He let his core as an artist who lives on the boundary between fine art and commercial art encounter the young and inquisitive collectors and developed a new style of excitement, which values the shock itself, among the greater Chinese community and the countries of the Middle East. The harmony of his heavy oil painting, the light and darkness of America, and the lovely, unbalanced subject matters all fit together perfectly. He has become a sensation in such regions as a result, even more than in his home country of the United States.

I would be so happy if my gallery would gain sufficient power to sell his works someday and would be able to hold another exhibition of his works.

—Takashi Murakami

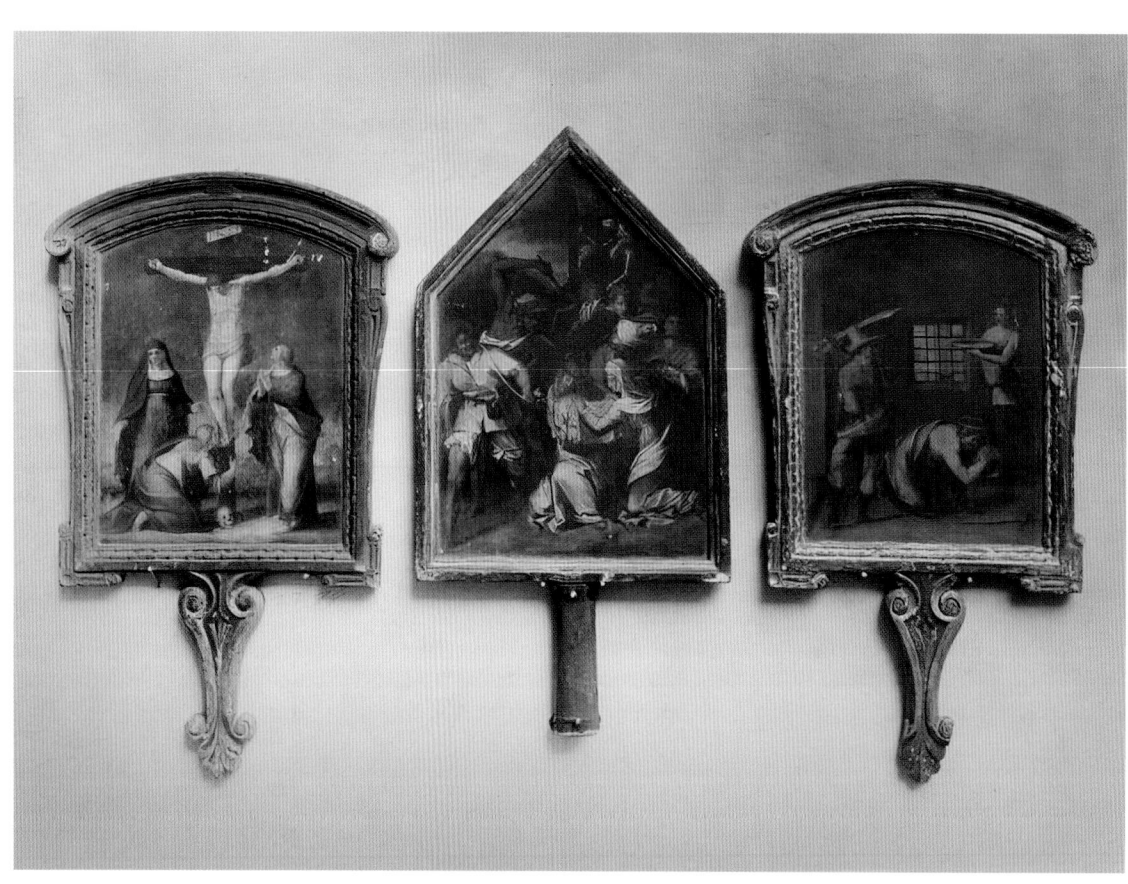

ARTIFACTS OF THE SACRED AND PROFANE

"It is not far—as the crow flies—from cloud to man; it is not far—
by images—from man to what he *sees*, from the nature of real
things to the nature of imagined things. They are of equal value."[1]
—Paul Éluard

If you feel the need for a companion to accompany you through Mark Ryden's mystical *Animal Secrets*, Ryden has painted a guide for you: the *Fratello della Tavoletta*. He is a pink-on-pink portrait of a brother of the Archconfraternity of San Giovanni Decollato. The *fratello* is clad in a hooded cassock. In one hand he grasps a strange painting on a paddle; in the other he holds a lantern to light the way. To where? In Ryden's work, viewers are always welcomed on a journey to an alternate reality, a numinous world where imagination coincides with nature.

Between the fourteenth and seventeenth centuries in Italy, the remit of the Archconfraternity of San Giovanni Decollato was to provide comfort and solace to those condemned to death. The monks did this, in part, by providing a sacred image for the *afflitto* to gaze upon in preparation for his/her demise. The friars were tasked to carry a *tavoletta* before the face of the *afflitto*—in the *afflitto*'s cell on the night before the execution, during the solemn march to the scaffold, and until the moment the soul departed this earth. The *tavolette* were painted on panels with a handle. On one side there would be a scene from the Passion of Christ; on the other side, a scene of martyrdom that more or less equaled the crime for which the *afflitto* would be punished. That's a formidable idea, isn't it? Not only to think that an entire *compagnia* would organize to ease the suffering of a person fated to such an end, but even more so the idea that a *picture* would be the primary tool of solace. This is the power of image: its potential to transmogrify into emotion.

The idea of the *tavoletta* piqued Ryden's interest as a trope to explore in several paintings in the *Animal Secrets* series. Why? Perhaps it is because Ryden has long explored the idea that a painting is an object—he frequently emphasizes this by designing elaborate frames for specific images, essentially employing sculpture to enrobe the central picture (the frame surrounding *Siren* is an excellent example of this). Ryden carefully designs these frames as assiduously as he crafts the central image, specifying the carving, polychroming, and gilding. But I think that the foil of the handled panel painting underscores the sacred nature of Ryden's image.

In *Animal Secrets*, Ryden has created four contemporary *tavolette*: *Tavoletta Rosa*, *Tavoletta Azzurri*, *Tavoletta Bionda*, and *Tavoletta Bruna*. The titles, of course, refer to the Italian roots of this ancient practice. The framework around Ryden's *tavolette* look remarkably similar to the Renaissance versions; original examples exist, and Ryden did a good job of evoking them. Ryden's icons are mounted into ornate frames, surrounded by egg-and-dart molding, rosettes, and spirals. The handles, here, are merely a decorative historical attribute—the contemporary viewer is unlikely to connect the format to the melancholic use of the Italian *tavoletta*. But I do think viewers will think of this: a handheld mirror. Today a mirror is a common household item, but throughout the distant past, in both Eastern and Western cultures, a mirror was believed to be magical; in fact, the English word derives from the Latin *mirare*, which is also the root of the word *miracle*. Symbolically, mirrors were believed to connect humans with the spirit realm, as either a portal or an aid for navigating the underworld. In this vein, Ryden's mirrorlike forms are held up to the viewer as an invitation into the subconscious. If Ryden's *tavolette* are simultaneously "mirrors," then whose likeness gazes back at the beholder?

The rosa, azzurri, bionda, and bruna portraits that stare back at us are polar opposite of dour images associated with death. In fact, the pink, blue, blonde, and brown busts depict gleefully happy creatures. Each figure has the face similar to Ryden's classic Yak character, with bright button eyes and rosy cheeks. Their faces are framed with shiny, gossamer hair arranged in flowing locks and bouncy curls accessorized by lustrous satin ribbon. Is it some version of us whom we see when we look into Ryden's fanciful "mirrors"? If so, Ryden imagines for us qualia of pure bliss.

Animal Secrets is populated by many other marvelous beings. The painting titled *163*[II] is another portrait housed in a highly decorative frame, in this case an architectural structure resembling a stand-alone reliquary. Again, the framework is as important as the picture. The black stanchion is sumptuously adorned with gold appointments—a bee, an all-seeing eye, and a column of the five Platonic solids, all symbols that frequently adorn Ryden's works. (On the verso of *163* is a painted merkaba, another sacred geometrical form.) Corinthian columns bracket the portrait, gilded spires rise from the Greek pediment, and the entire tabernacle rests atop golden lions paws.

This architectural fantasy celebrates the portrait of a gentle beast, whose disembodied head floats in the picture plane. (I am reminded of Saint Veronica and the image of Christ emblazoned on her veil.) Ryden's creature has a pale face, with enormous

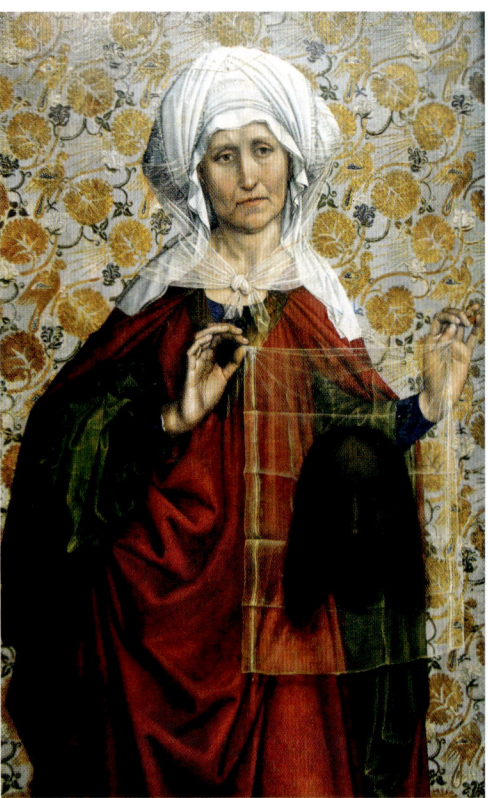

and reflective walleyes, wreathed by a wispy black mane. The creature recalls and continues Ryden's previous series of *Anima Animals*, here within a framework that emphasizes sanctity and ritual. Ryden is an artist who is fearlessly unselfconscious about quoting Christian attributes—as well as references to any of the world's religions. His work is gently pantheistic in reminding us that all things are sacred.

The painting *Red Siren (#156)* is a portrait of another being; unlike the *tavoletta* figures, its countenance is ambivalent—not cheerful, but neither is it malevolent. Its visage, pale white with smoky, smoldering eyes and a feline mouth, looks directly at the viewer with steely sangfroid. Its body is long and slinky, with short legs and a long tail. Except for its ghostly face, it is covered in shaggy carmine-pink fur, with long locks around the head, a tendril coquettishly drooping over one eye. Perched atop a rocky outcrop, this mysterious numen presides over a body of water. The horizon is as still and silent as the creature's calm bearing. The frame suggests that the scene is at oceanside, as the frame is a gilded cornucopia of shells, coral, sea stars, seaweed, and barnacles.

When I first saw *Red Siren (#156)*, I immediately thought of the Japanese mythological *kappa* and other watery *yokai* (spirits) that live near the shore and menace humans that come across their path. The title "siren" certainly implies peril. In Greek mythology, the beautiful siren is mermaid-like, with an alluring voice that harkens sailors to their death. Sirens appear in the lore of many cultures, but always with a propensity for danger. We all know that to follow a "siren's song" leads to a sorrowful end.

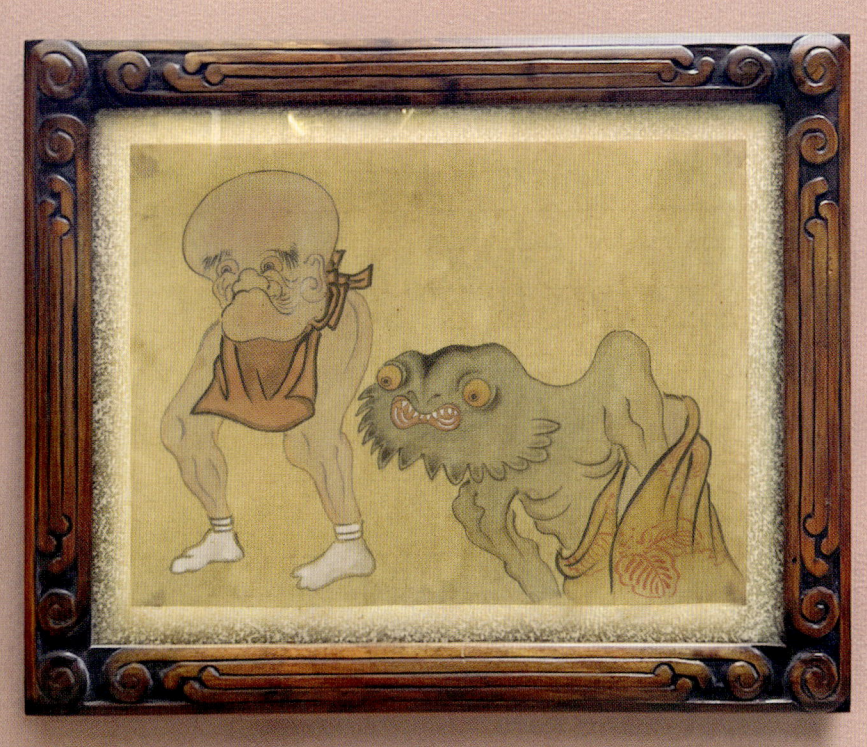
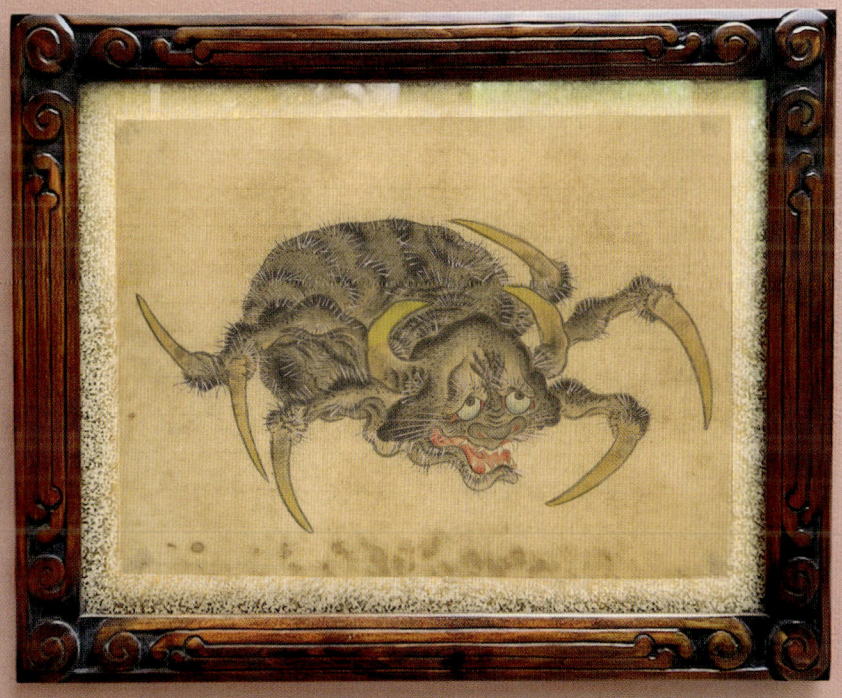

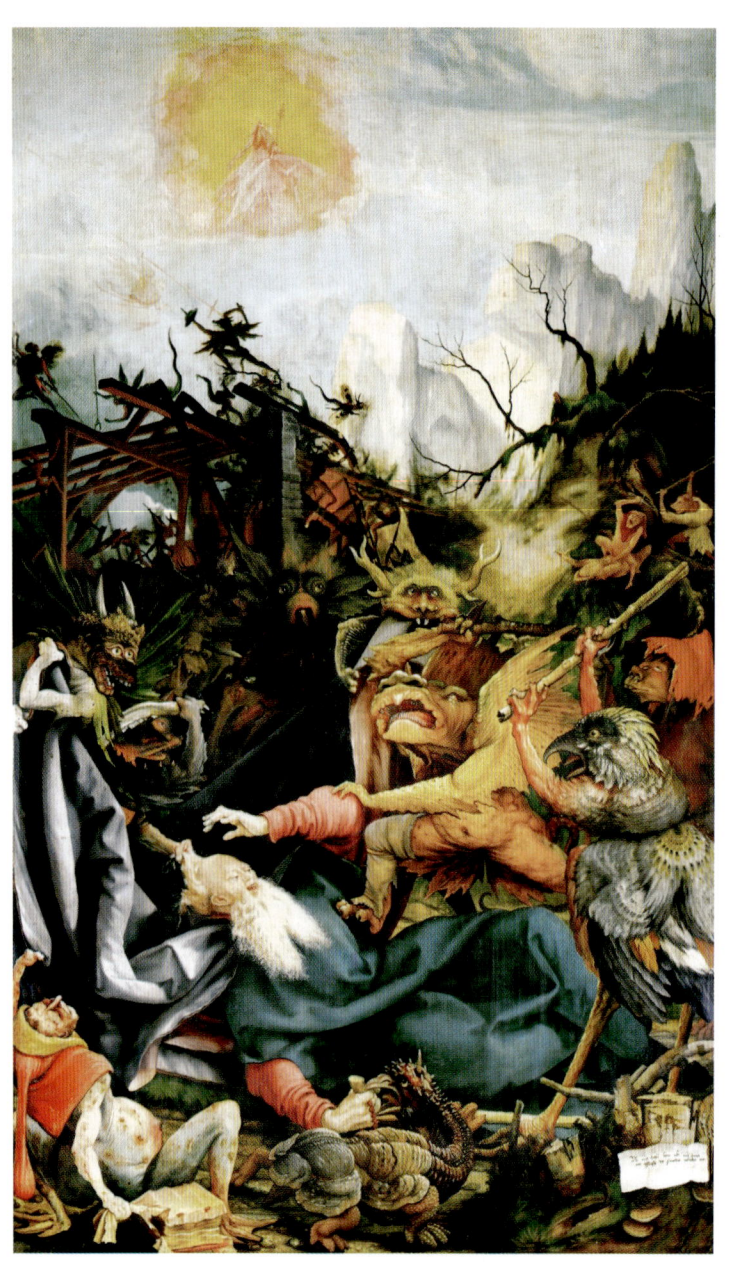
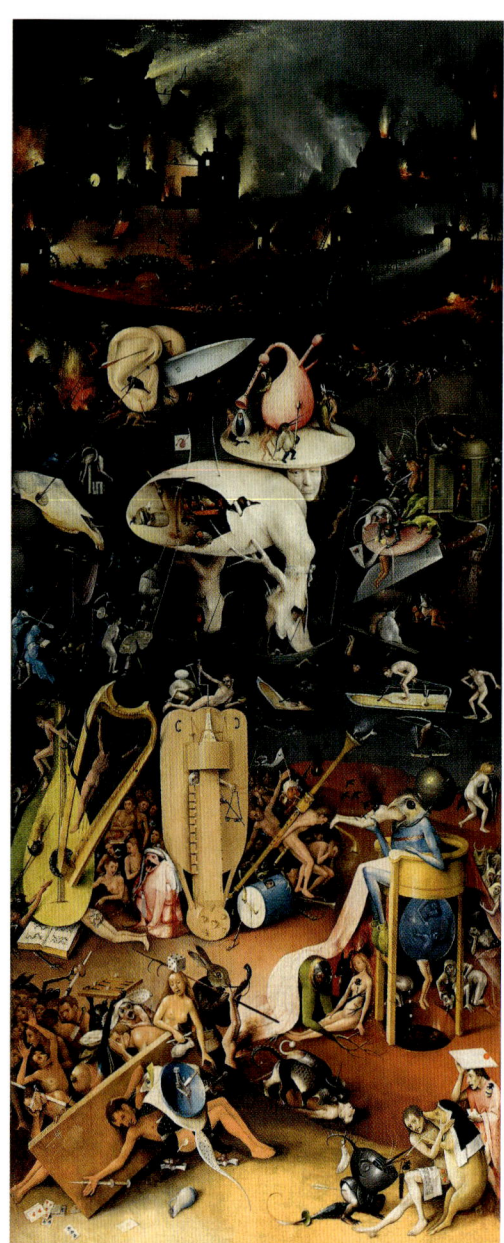

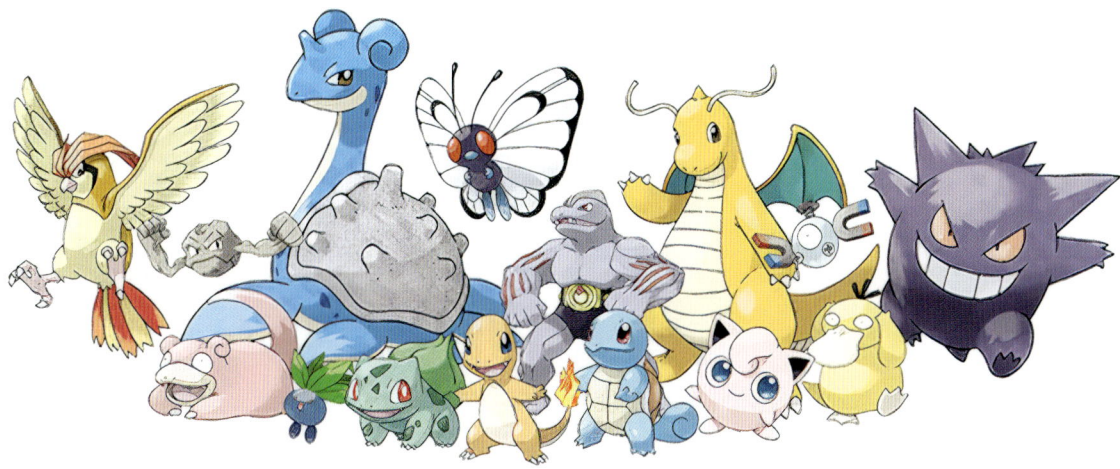

FROM WHENCE DO RYDEN'S MARVELOUS CREATURES COME?

On a wall in Ryden's house there are two vintage reproductions of nineteenth-century Japanese woodblock prints; the subjects in both are *yokai*, examples from the hundreds of supernatural sprites known in Japanese folklore. One is a representation of the *Ushi-oni*, the ox-headed *yokai* with upward-turned horns and a spider body.[III] The other print features *Gotaimen*, a *yokai* that has a huge head atop legs, with no arms or toro, next to *Iga bo*, a blue-bodied *yokai* who has distinct burrs along the lower edge of its jaw.[IV] During the Edo period of the nineteenth century, picture scrolls (*emaki*) illustrating all manner of monsters and spirits were printed to entertain and delight Japanese viewers. Is it too much of a stretch to imagine that Ryden's creatures are related?

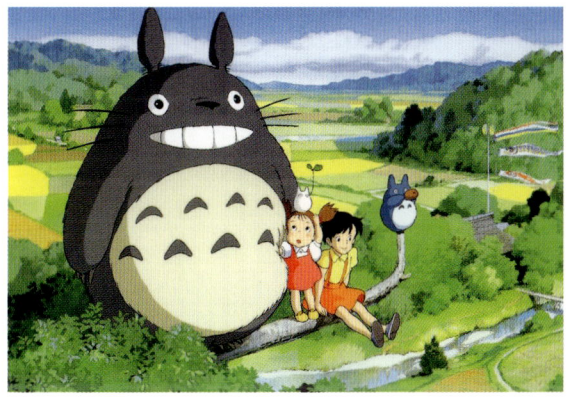

Ryden is not particularly unique in his proclivity for creating mystical creatures, nor would he claim to be. Indeed, the history of art, Asian and Eurocentric, includes a fantastic parade of selcouth and otherworldly beings. To note a few: Medieval bestiaries, the early Renaissance demons of Hieronymus Bosch and Matthias Grünewald, and mythical sea monsters signifying "ne plus ultra" on ancient maps. Hayao Miyazaki and Studio Ghibli, along with Pokémon, celebrate the netherworld of Japanese culture while the hybridized cryptozoological specimens of contemporary artists such as Alexis Rockman and Patricia Piccinini help us imagine a version of the anthropocene that is off-kilter and strange. But Ryden is an artist whose wit is entirely devoid of menace. While Ryden often dips into irony and humor, he never loses sight of the inherent beauty of the natural and the supernatural worlds. For Ryden, these fanciful creatures seem to exist to befriend us, to literally accompany us on the arduous adventure of being human.

On a practical level, an intrinsic aspect of Ryden's studio practice involves being surrounded by and immersed in visual stimuli. His home and studio are legendary for the innumerable books, collections, toys, specimens, and Eastern and Western art that Ryden loves. He maintains thick folders of collected pictures that might inform a composition someday, categorized by subject matter. An entire alcove of his home is curated into grids of what I call "rebus dioramas" (my term, not Ryden's) in which he has playfully, but very carefully, arranged various toys and other objects into thematic tableaus. Ryden's gamesome nature occasionally inspires him to craft his own playthings, too. On the occasion of the exhibition *Animal Secrets* at Perrotin in Paris in 2022, Ryden released *Yuki the Young Yak*, a collectible plush toy with a chirpy vinyl face and luxurious black or white fur.[V] Ryden's creative process is steeped in syncretism—he is uniquely curious about all cultures and eras—and he pulls from this vast universe of imagery to conceive his own mythopoeic world.

OPPOSITE, LEFT

Matthias Grünewald, inner right wing of the *Isenheim Altarpiece* depicting the Temptation of St. Anthony. Oil on panels, ca. 1512–1516

OPPOSITE, RIGHT

Hieronymus Bosch, *The Garden of Early Delights* (detail). Oil on oak panels, ca. 1490–1500

TOP

Pokémon, Gotta catch'em all! © 2024 Pokémon. © 1995–2024 Nintendo/Creatures Inc./ GAME FREAK inc. Pokémon.

ABOVE

My Neighbor Totoro © Studio Ghibli Inc.

There is something else to know about Ryden, this in the sphere of esoterica. But—for me—it is perhaps the most illuminating attribute to explain how Ryden's mind works. Astrologically speaking, Ryden was born with his sun in the twelfth house, that amorphous place of the collective unconscious; it is the house that rules the dream world and spiritual activity. Cazimi to his sun is Mercury, the god of communication, eloquence, divination. In the metaphoric language of astrology, this sun/Mercury placement means that Ryden's Mercury (expression) is seated in the lap of the king, exalted, exaggerated, and elemental to Ryden's life's work. In Ryden's chart, the sun and Mercury combination occur conjunct to the South Node, opposite the North Node. These lunar nodes describe one's life's purpose and patterning, one's karma and the lessons one is brought to Earth to learn. This is notable, as, again, in the pictorial interpretation of the stars, the North Node represents the head of a dragon, representing an individual's karmic path, the lessons a person is brought to Earth to learn. The South Node is the serpent's tail. When these parts come together, this "dragon" creates a portal, a tap from which the collective unconscious abundantly flows. Almost literally, it is in Ryden's nature to consume and absorb the cumulative images of the world—which he then processes and distills to disseminate back to the collective.

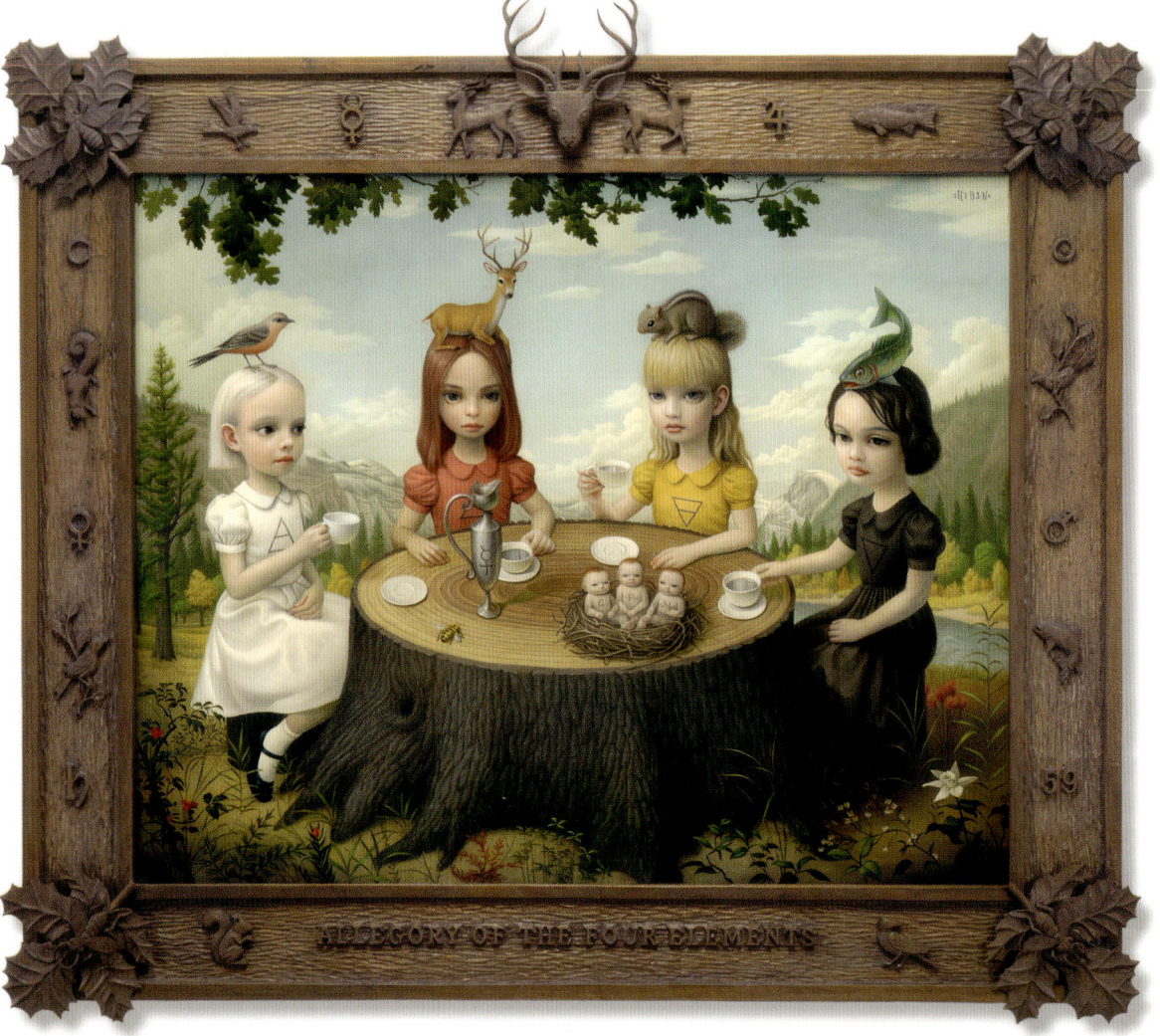

ABOVE

Mark Ryden, *Allegory of the Four Elements*. Oil on canvas, 2006.

OPPOSITE, TOP LEFT

Mark Ryden, *Dymaxion Principle*. Oil on canvas, 2014.

OPPOSITE, TOP RIGHT

Mark Ryden, *Saint Barbie*. Oil on panel, 1994.

OPPOSITE, BOTTOM

Mark Ryden, *Chroma Structure 113*. Oil on canvas, 2015.

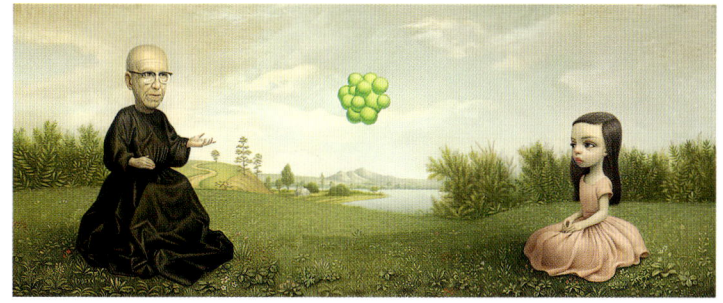

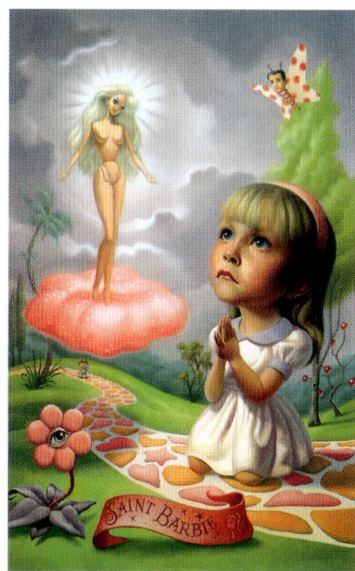

A GATHERING IN THE FOREST

The most narrative painting in *Animal Secrets* is *The Visitation*. Here, four figures congregate around a flattened stump in a foliated clearing. On top of the stump is a furry white being, not exactly Christlike, but its arms are outstretched in cruciform. Whether the children are idolizing this creature or learning from it is unclear, but there is a genuine sense of communion. This is a composition that appears occasionally in Ryden's œuvre, especially in the *Tree Show* painting, *Allegory of the Four Elements (#59)* (2006), in which four girls signifying air, fire, earth, and water gather around a tree stump tea party. This particular allegory—gathering around a table—has innumerable sacred and profane antecedents: the Last Supper, the Knights of the Round Table, *Alice in Wonderland*'s Mad Hatter tea party, even Norman Rockwell's *Freedom from Want* (1943). The theme conveys gravitas and a sense of metaphysical intercourse best described in imagery rather than words.

There are many other examples in Ryden's work in which the subject is humans venerating a supranatural form. Going all the way back to *Saint Barbie* (1994) where a little girl prays at an imagined vision of the Mattel doll, to *Dymaxion Principle (#110)* (2014) and *Chroma Structure 113* (2015) from Ryden's *Dodecahedron* series, Ryden suggests that there is always something outside of ourselves, beyond human culture, that we can learn from.

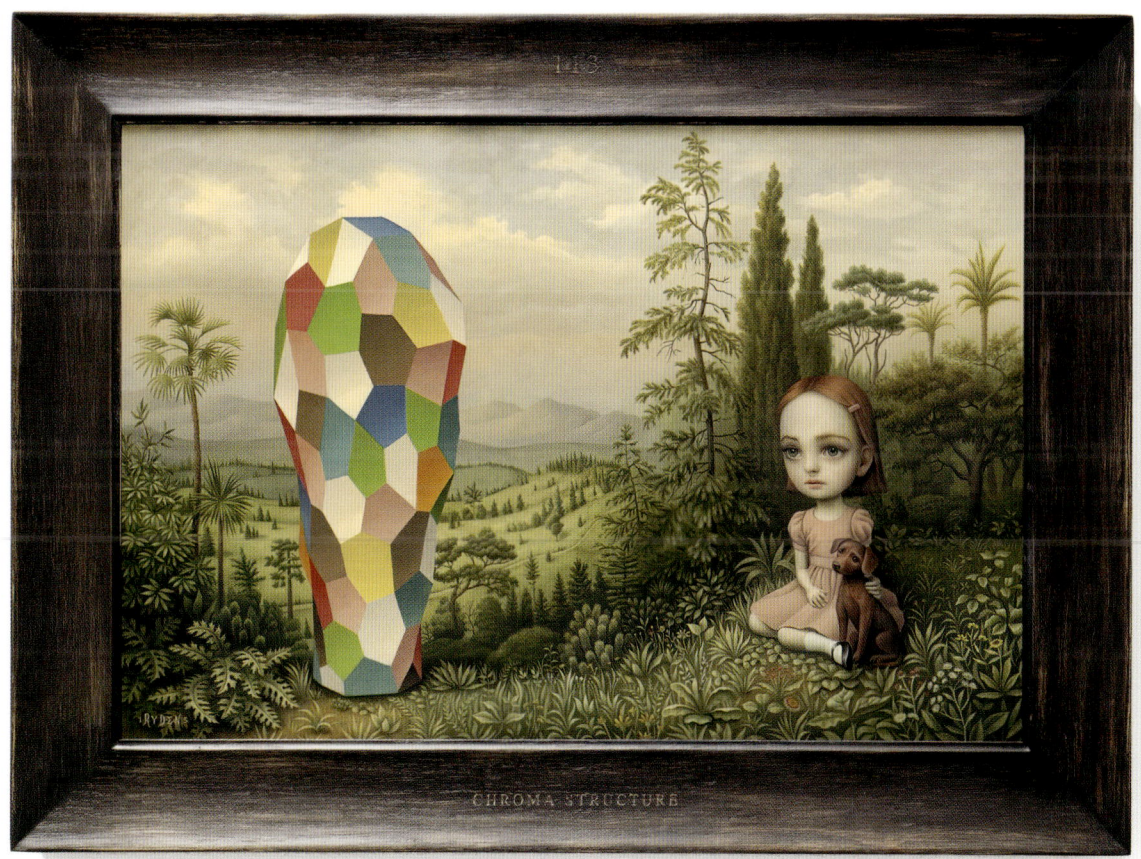

MERKABA MONKEYS

Animal Secrets includes a trio of drawings that offer another clue about Ryden's intentions. These works are *Merkaba Emerald*, *Merkaba Gamboge*, and *Merkaba Cerulean*; the titles identify the colors used for a merkaba form that hovers in space near each figure of a monkey. These drawings convey a sense of scientific verisimilitude reminiscent of the great naturalist illustrations of the nineteenth century; even the substrate that the *Merkabas* are drawn on resembles parchment, or the discolorations characteristic of ancient paper. One could easily imagine these drawings appearing alongside those of Charles D'Orbigny in the *Dictionnaire Universel d'Histoire Naturelle* (1837). Such stylistic considerations remind the viewer that there are other worlds to explore, other eras to experience.

Well, I call the figures "monkeys"—they resemble simians, but they are surely not portraits of actual primates. In my defense, the creature in *Merkaba Cerulean* reminds me of a snowy-white lemur, with its buggy, startled eyes and long tail. And I can't help but think of a capuchin monkey when I look at *Merkaba Gamboge*. The figure's squarish head and anthropomorphic posture recall the traditional companion to an organ-grinder. And it's worth remembering that a Magic Monkey lives in Ryden's studio; he comes out at night and helps Ryden paint.[VI]

There are so many rich, historically significant symbolic associations with monkeys that the *Merkaba* series piques innumerable threads of interpretation. It's easy to understand why these animals have been the object of human projection. Their appearance, intelligence, social habits, and behaviors are so like "ours." There's a reason that it's three wise monkeys in the Japanese maxim to "see no evil, hear no evil, speak no evil."[VII] Or that we commonly refer to the "monkey mind." Humans tend to romanticize their impishness and mischief-making, fascinated by the monkey's tendency to mimic human behavior. In the long history of both Eastern and Western art, it is the monkey who most often parodies and caricatures human pursuits—even to the point of standing in for the artist or art viewer (see Jean-Antoine Watteau's *The Monkey Sculptor*, ca. 1710, or Gabriel von Max's *A Visit to the Artist's Studio*, 1867—but there are many more examples).[VIII]

OPPOSITE

Jean-Antoine Watteau, *The Sculptor Monkey*. Oil on canvas, ca. 1710.

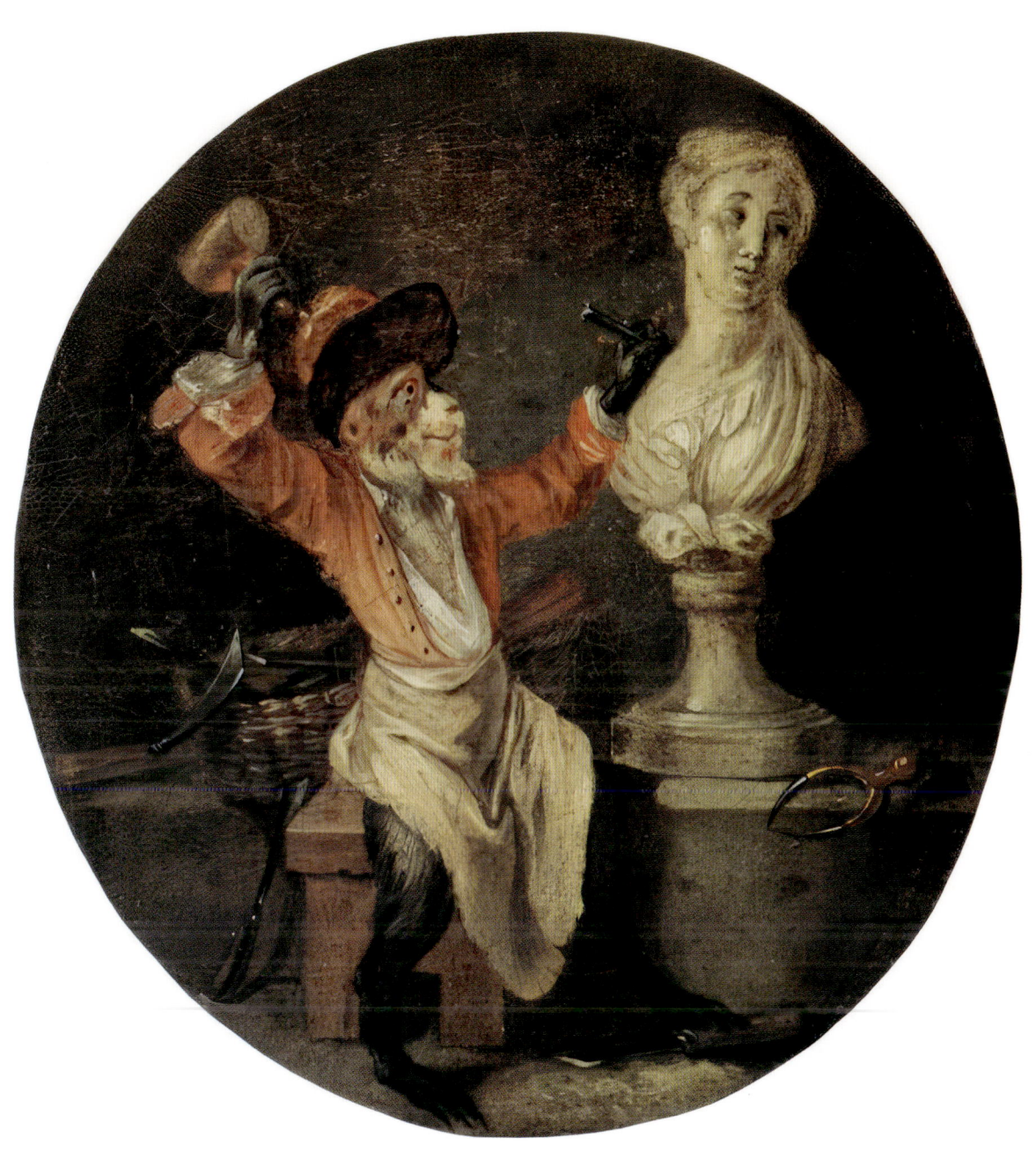

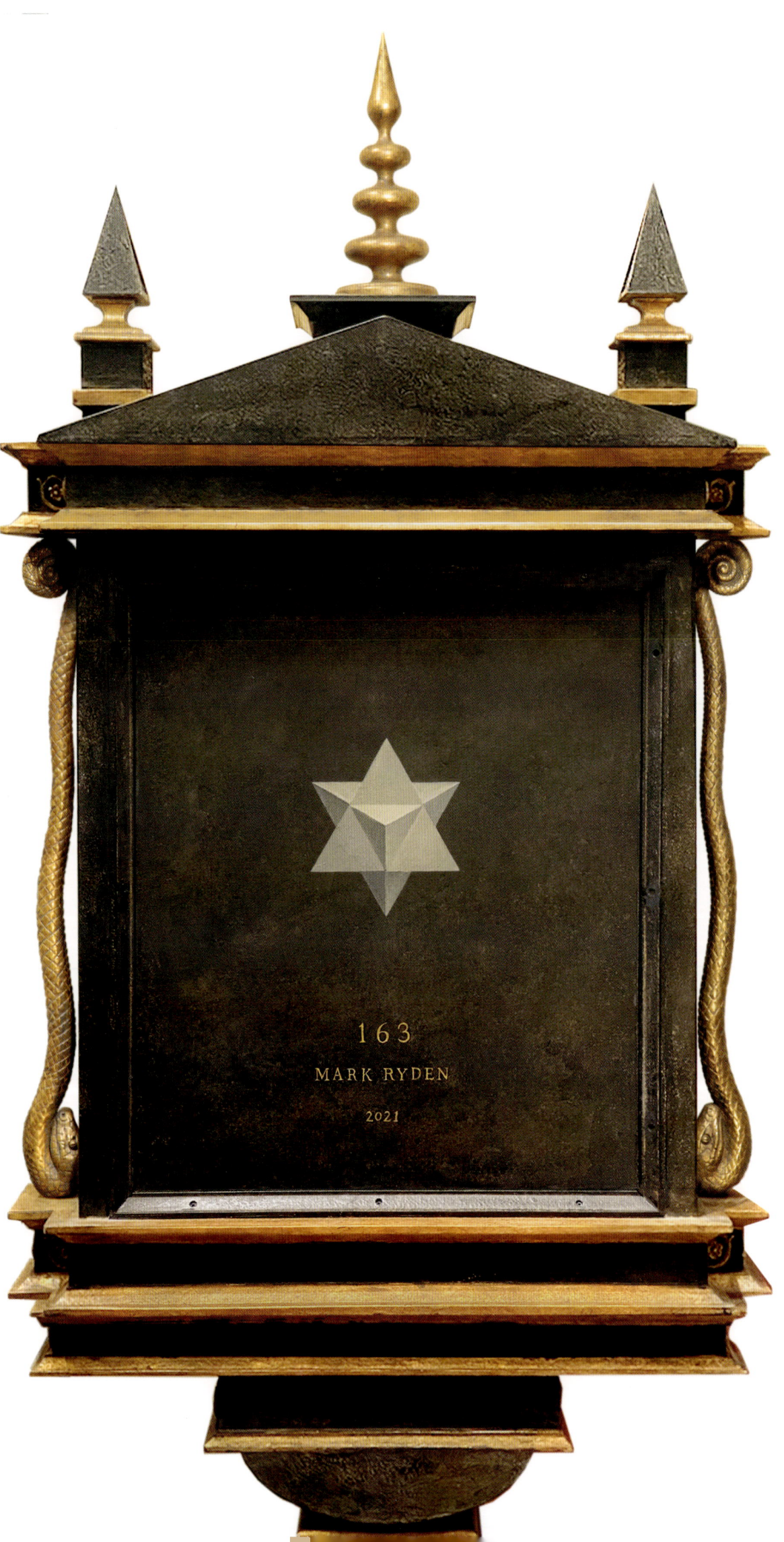

That said, Ryden would claim that he has no deliberate intentions to illustrate a parable, or let alone purposely frame a monkey-like figure as a surrogate for a person. I would argue, however, that virtually all of Ryden's made-up creatures are simulacra for sentient beings in the natural world, human and non-human: those that we recognize and those that exist in alternate universes. The monkey-like nature of the subjects in these drawings underscores, for me, how few degrees of separation exist between known and unknown beings.

Equal and opposite to the figures in these drawings is the merkaba itself. The merkaba is the geometric shape, composed of two intersecting tetrahedrons, that is suspended near the creature. The tetrahedron is one of the five Platonic solids; those familiar with Ryden's œuvre will recognize his use of another Platonic solid, the dodecahedron, in past works. He has an interest in sacred geometry and understands the potency of symbolic language. The word *merkaba* is a Hebrew word, with ancient Egyptian origins, that means chariot; the word is made up of three separate components that phonetically mean light, body, and spirit. The inclusion of the merkaba as a central theme of the drawings, and its primacy in the titles of these works emphasizes yet again the concept that virtually all of Ryden's works seek to convey: that art is a transport for the adventures of consciousness.

THE YAKALINAS

"Color = feeling."[IX]
—Carl Gustav Jung

Concurrent with Ryden's *Animal Secrets* is a sculptural series he calls the *Yakalina 9* (2022). The group consists of nine *Yakalina* figures, ethereal demigoddesses, cast in bronze and polychromed in symbolic colors.[X] By Ryden's own description, "Yakalina is a spiritual entity that originates from the divine realm through the luminiferous ether . . . Yakalina is sister to mermaids, fairies, and ghosts."[XI]

Yakalina's body is very simple: a sphere head attached to a conical body; in flattened form, her silhouette is a keyhole shape. Literally, she mimics the Phoenician anthropomorph for the moon goddess Tanit or the keyhole-shaped counterpoise *menat* of the sacred Egyptian necklace worn by priestesses of the goddess Hathor. Yakalina's contour is elemental; by shape alone, we know that she is a powerful being.

In terms of the lost wax casting of the nine Yakalinas, each figure is identical, the same shape and size, but—like humans—each is as unique as we are. Each Yakalina is imbued with her own special dominion, signified by her color chosen intuitively by Ryden. *Yakalina Brilliant* is gilded with resplendent gold, the color of the sun and daylight. *Yakalina Bombay* is ashen, like the moon, or smoke rising from incense, or the veil of fog on a cool beach. *Yakalina Buff* is the color of bleached bones or shells, whitened by the sun, quiet artifacts of past life. *Yakalina Blood* is a serious spirit, for she remembers old rituals and ceremonies long forgotten. *Yakalina Bronze* is the color of the forge, of tools and weapons; she sadly recalls wars and conflicts. *Yakalina Bistre* is the color of coal and smells like woods after a fire; she governs the mossy decay on the forest floor. *Yakalina Blush* is the least serious of the nine; she tends toward forgetfulness, but her color is reminiscent of the sunrise. *Yakalina Bianca* is the color of celestial light, bright white, so dazzling that it is hard to see. And *Yakalina Black* is the color of the subconscious, deep and dark, like the void between the stars.[XII] Together, the Yakalinas form an ennead, a grouping considered to have special spiritual significance. In the world of Ryden's creation, no detail is irrelevant.

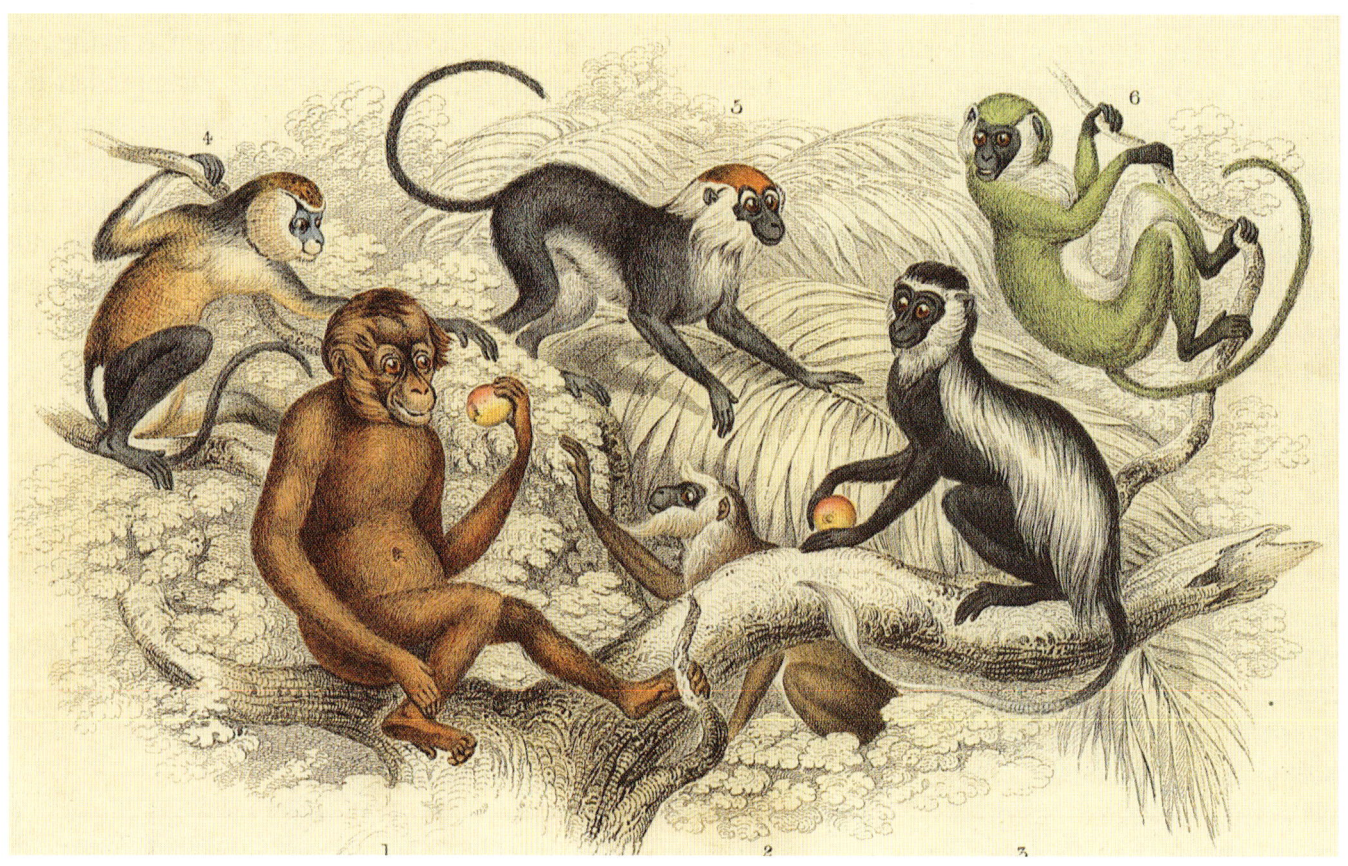

"To be authentic and to have sincere power, things have to come
first from the heart, and then from the brain. If an artist reverses
this, their art will be contrived and lifeless, soulless."
—Mark Ryden

Sometimes, when I consider Ryden's painted creatures, I am reminded of the great animalier of the early twentieth century, Franz Marc, now separated in time from Ryden by a century. Marc was an artist who knew a thing or two about the spiritual essence of non-humans. He considered animals to be more honest, more directly connected to the inner truths of nature; he, like Ryden, expressed this truth through his paintings. (Marc and his friend August Macke also wrote about the emotional and intuitive properties of color. Ryden shares deep kinship in this.) If visual art can do one thing besides delight the senses, it has the power to engender empathy—to quote Susan Sontag, "art is a form of consciousness"[XIII] that leads to greater communication and compassion. Can Ryden's art do this? I think so. To some, Ryden's work populates an enigmatic cosmos animated by spirits and souls that are fanciful and fun—but ultimately not part of the "real world." Instead, I posit, Ryden brings into perspective the essence of very real phenomena that are to be seen with the third eye and felt by a recondite sixth sense.

—Linda Tesner

TOP

Oliver Goldsmith, *Red Orang-Outang, Diana Monkey, Guereza Monkey, Varied Monkey, Collared White-Eyelid Monkey, and Green Monkey,* from *A History of the Earth and Animated Nature* (1820).

OPPOSITE

Gabriel von Max, *A Visit to the Artist's Studio.* Oil on canvas, ca. 1900.

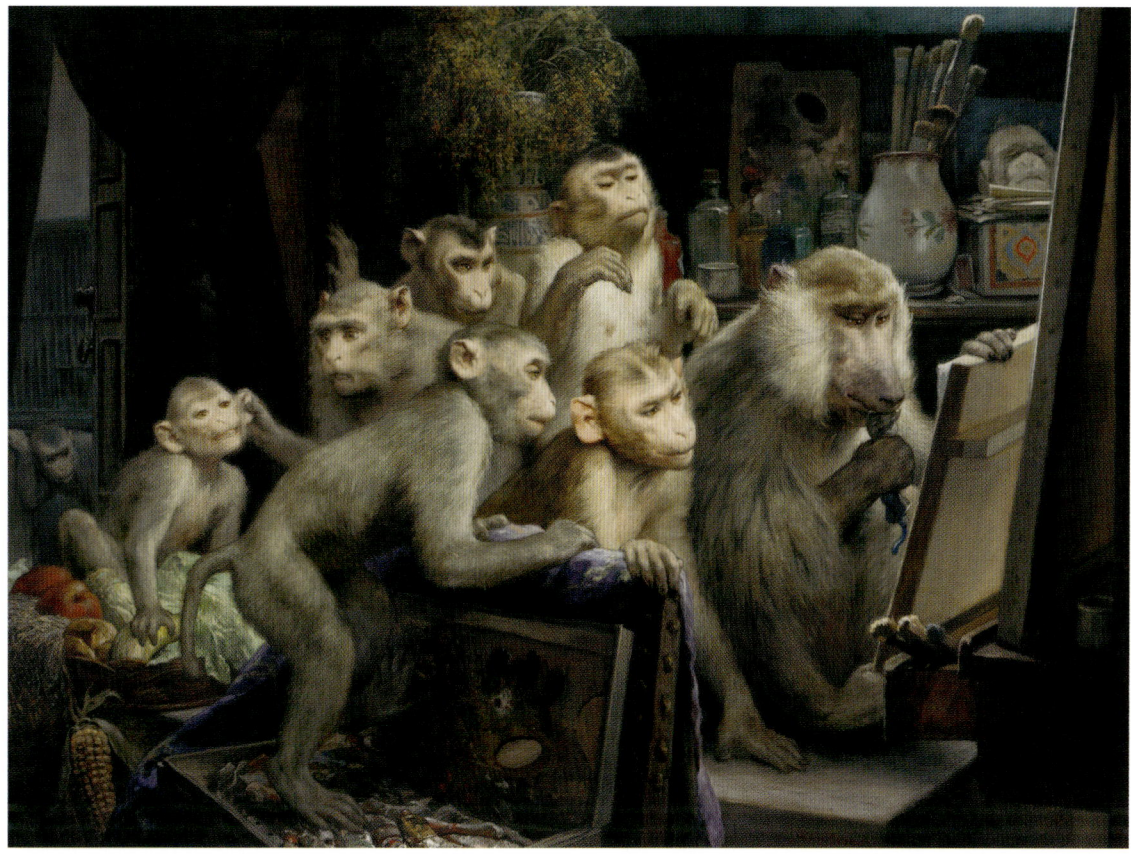

NOTES

I   Paul Éluard, "Food for Vision: 'Beyond Painting,'" in *Surrealists on Art*, edited by Lucy R. Lippard (Englewood Cliffs, New Jersey: Prentice-Hall, 1970), pp. 56–57.

II   Ryden started numbering his paintings during his first solo exhibition in 1998 as a means to distinguish his fine art career from his previous career in illustration. Thus, all major paintings and sculptural works are numbered consecutively and indicate where each work exists in the continuum of Ryden's œuvre.

III This version of the *Ushi-oni* is from *Hyakkai-Zukan (The Illustrated Volume of a Hundred Demons)* by Sawaki Suushi (1737).

IV   This version of the *Iga-bo* is from the *Hyaku monogatari bake-e (One Hundred Tales Monster Picture Scroll)* illustrated by Hoiku in 1780.

V   The urban vinyl toy *Yuki the Young Yak* was jointly designed by Mark Ryden and GOLEM (Artoyz) in an edition of 500 each of the black and white versions. The shape of *Yuki the Young Yak* reminds me of the wonderful forest spirits in Studio Ghibli's *My Neighbor Totoro* (1988).

VI   Linda Tesner, "Thoughts on Mark Ryden's Bestiary of Mystical Creatures," in *Mark Ryden: Anima Animals* (New York: Abrams, 2020), p. 22.

VII This well-known adage originates in visual art, from a seventeenth-century bas-relief over a door of the Tōshō-gū Shinto shrine located in Nikkō, Japan. The sculpture was carved by Hidari Jingoro.

VIII There is even a term for the genre of art in which monkeys are depicted aping human behavior. It is called "singerie," from the French for "monkey trick." See *The Public Domain Review*, "The Singerie: Monkeys Acting as Humans in Art," https://publicdomainreview.org/collection/the-singerie-monkeys-acting-as-humans-in-art/.

IX   Medea Hoch, *The Art of C. G. Jung* (New York: W. W. Norton & Company, 2019), p. 33.

X   For a short video documentary on the making of the *Yakalina 9*, see Mark Ryden's Instagram posts on April 18, 2022, https://www.instagram.com/p/Ccf1wMrlHax/, and May 3, 2022, https://www.instagram.com/p/CdGYAgLFxBF/.

XI   Mark Ryden, *Yakalina Part Two*, May 3, 2022, https://www.instagram.com/p/CdGYAgLFxBF/.

XII Ibid.

XIII Susan Sontag, *As Consciousness Is Harnessed to Flesh: Journals and Notebooks, 1964–1980* (New York: Farrar, Straus and Giroux, 2012), p. 42.

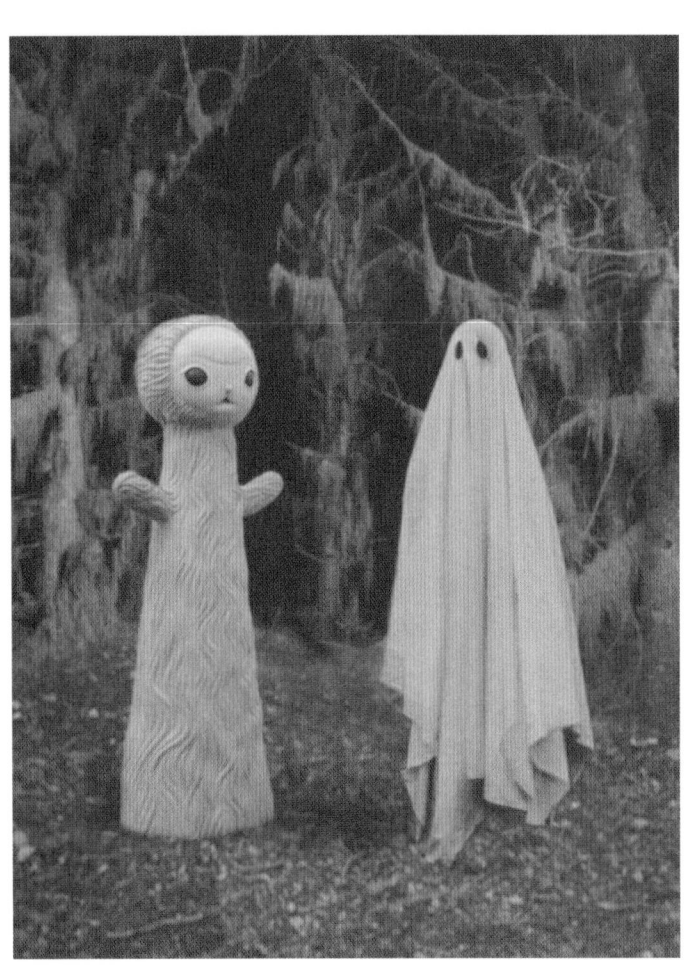
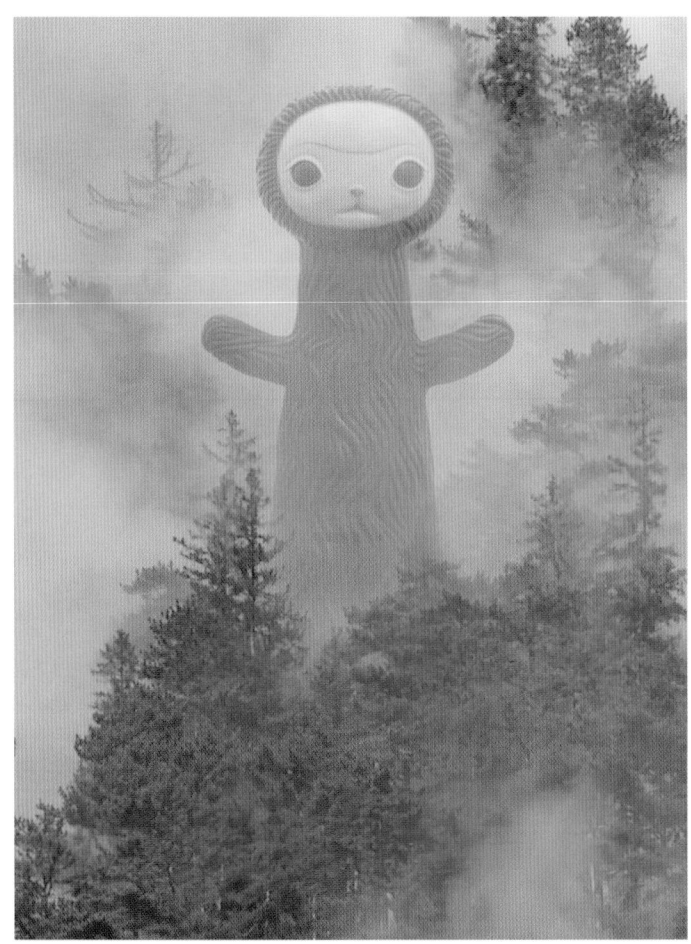

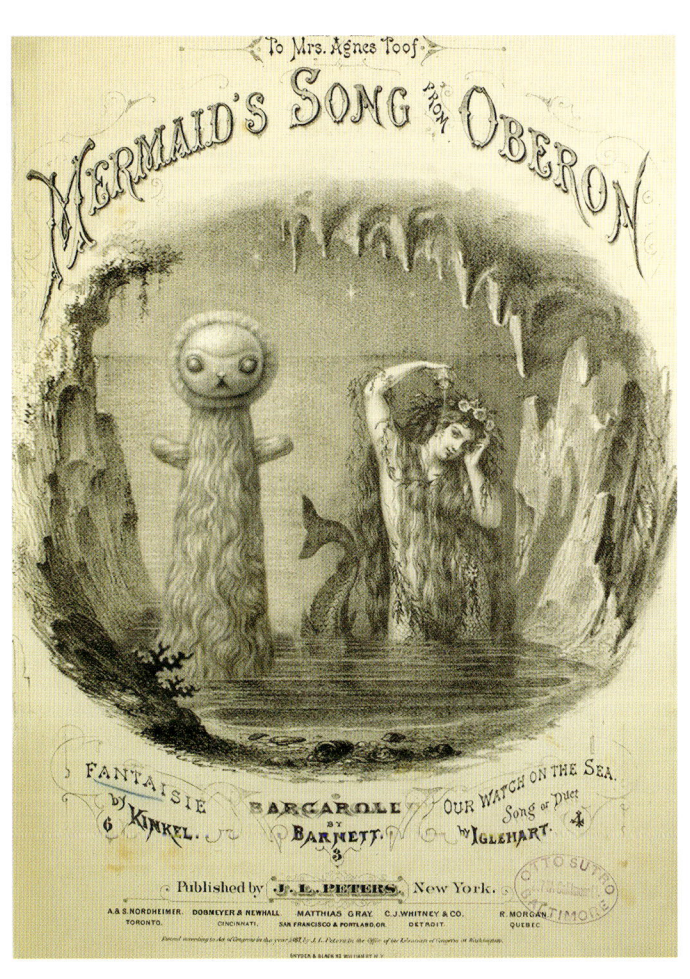
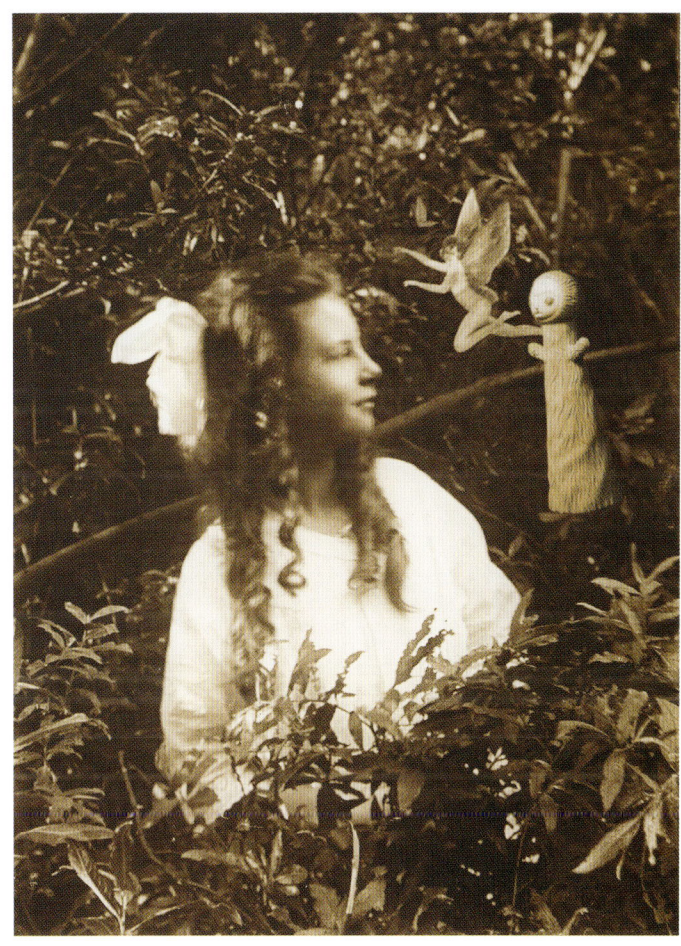

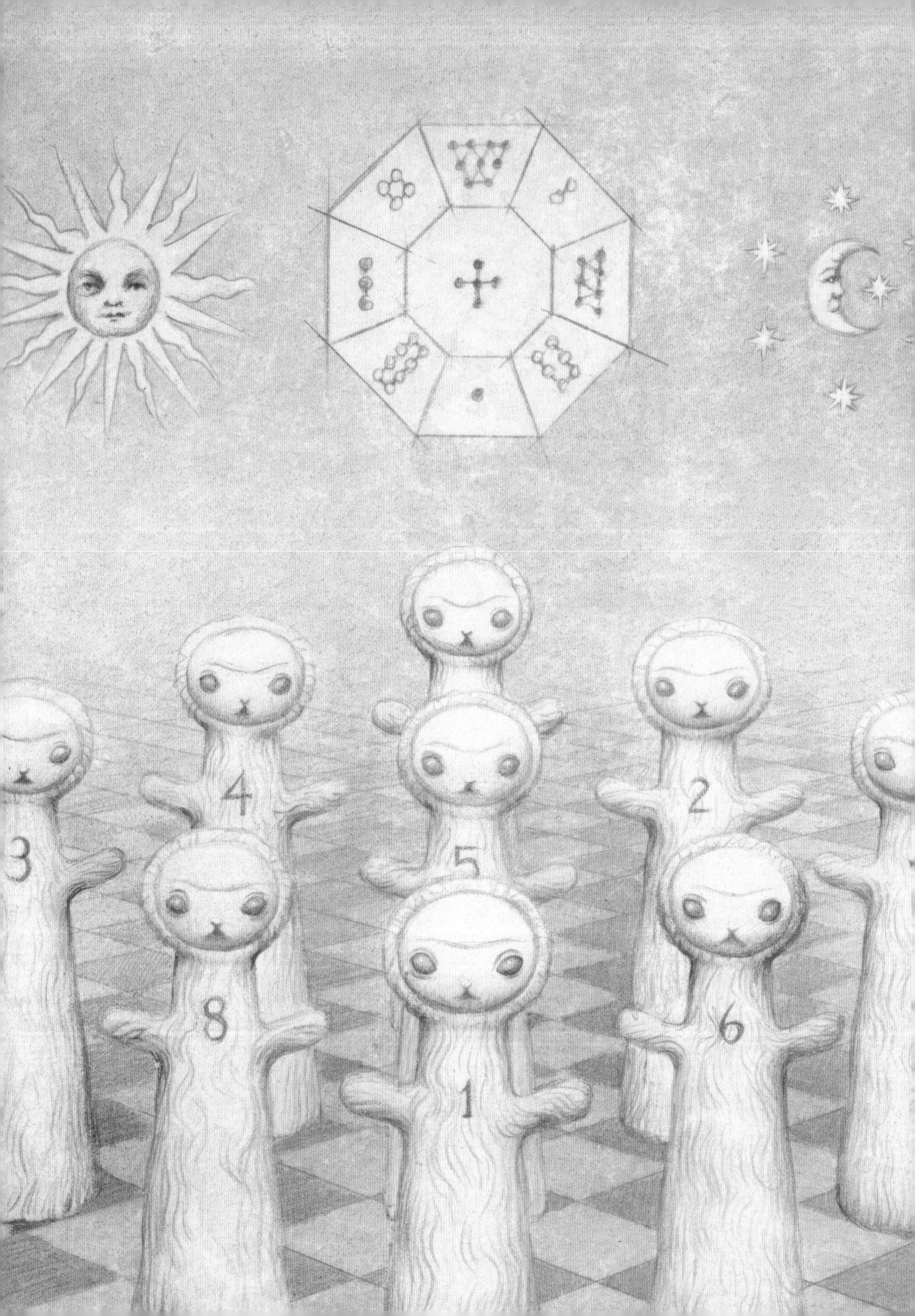

YAKALINA 9

PERROTIN, Tokyo, April 2022

SCULPTURES

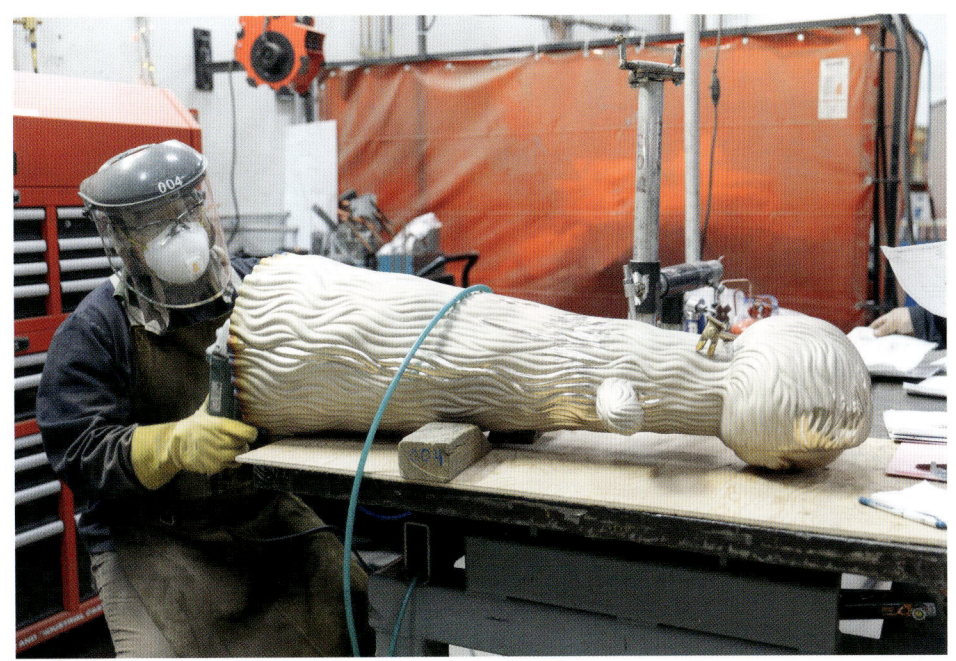

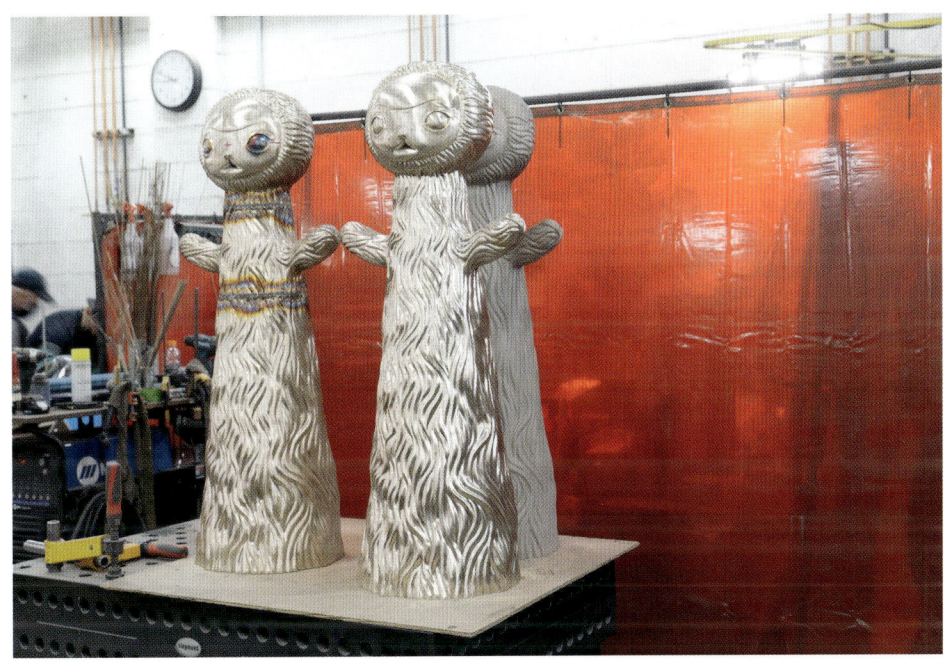

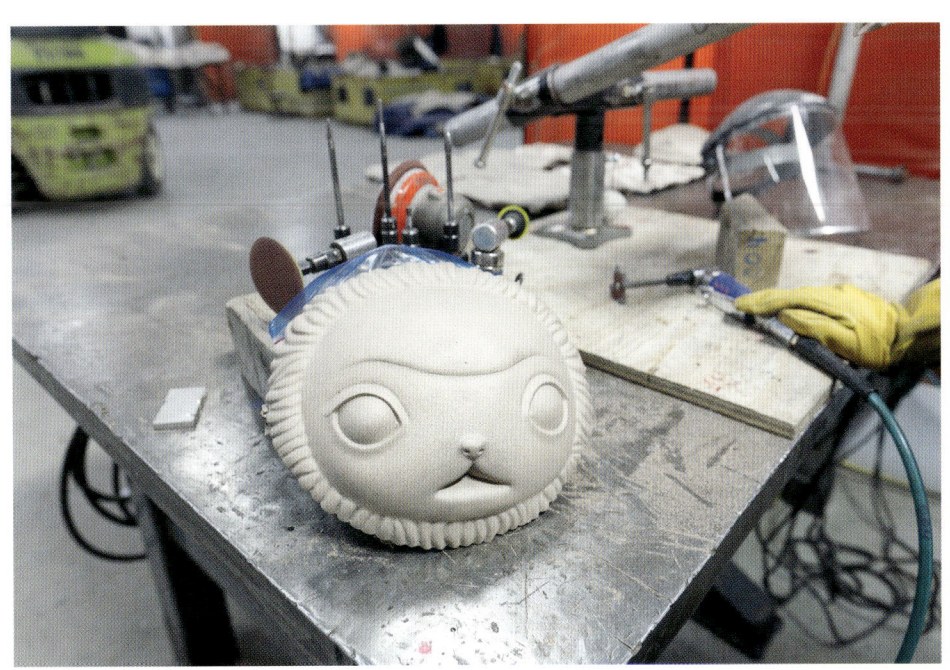

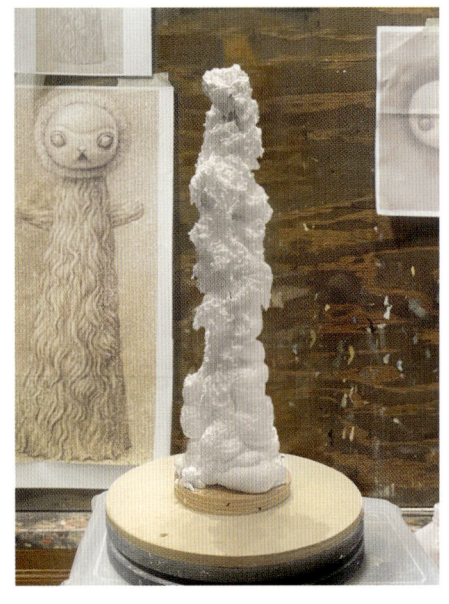
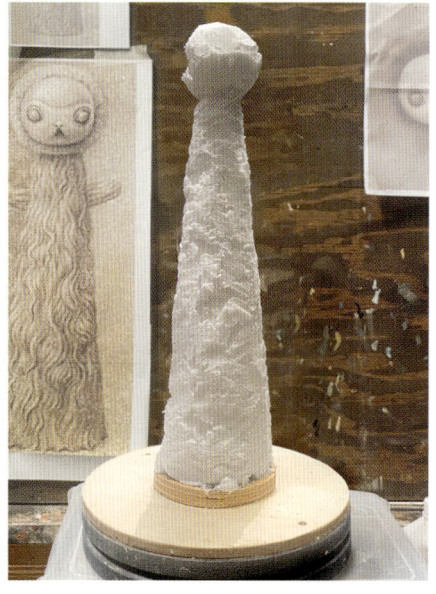
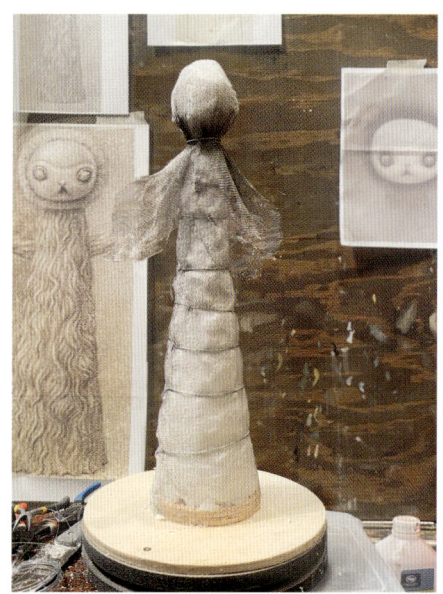
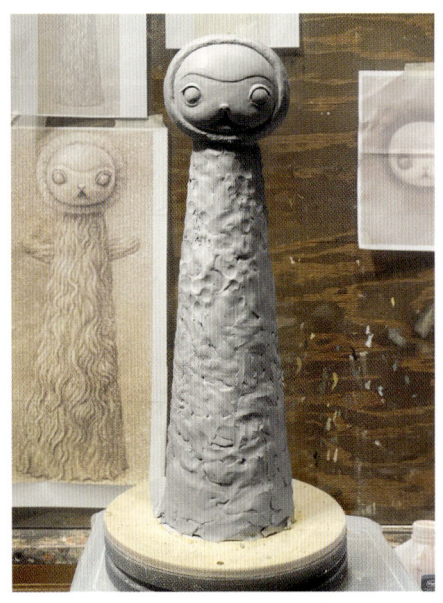
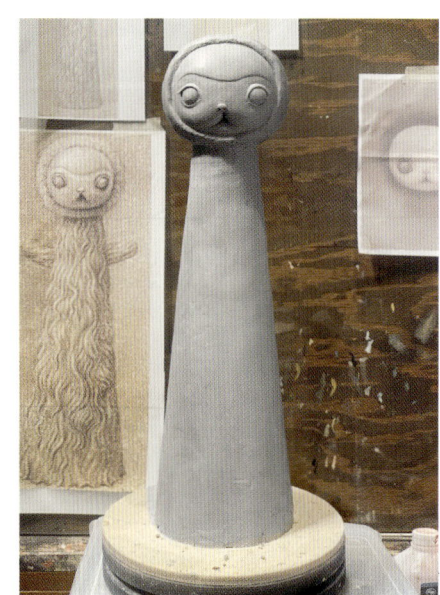
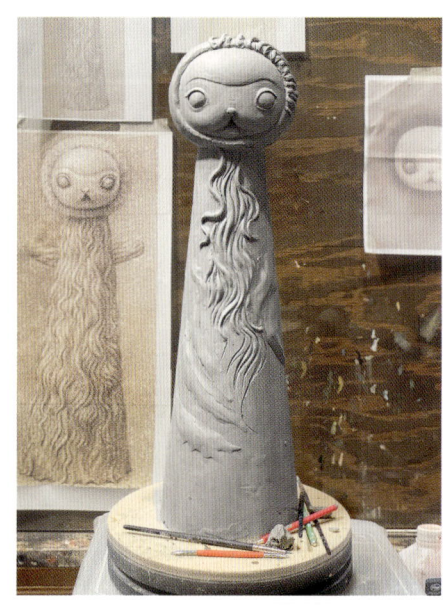
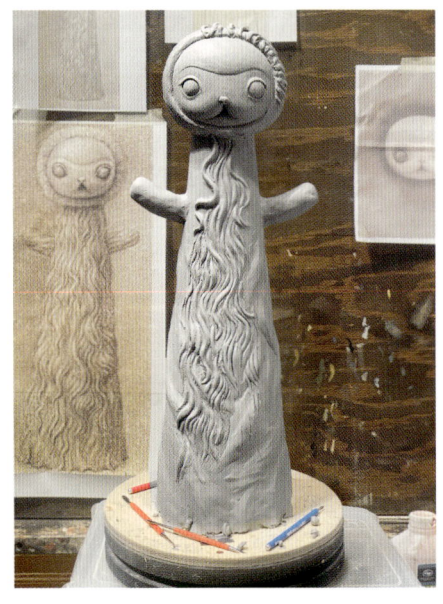
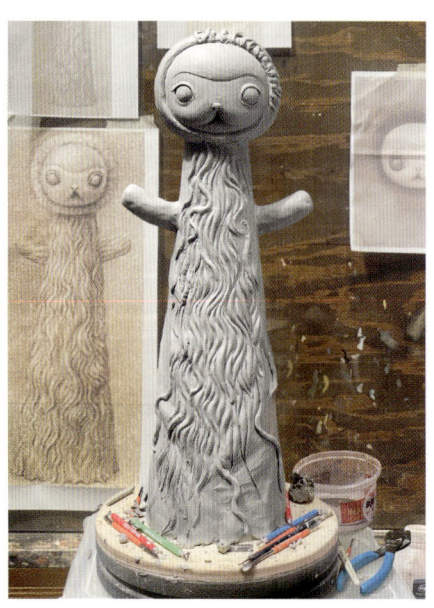
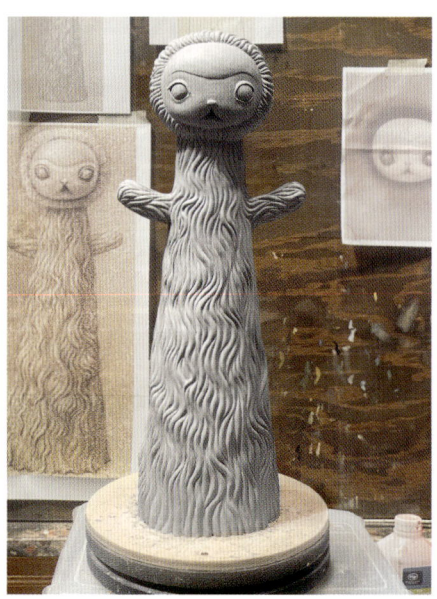

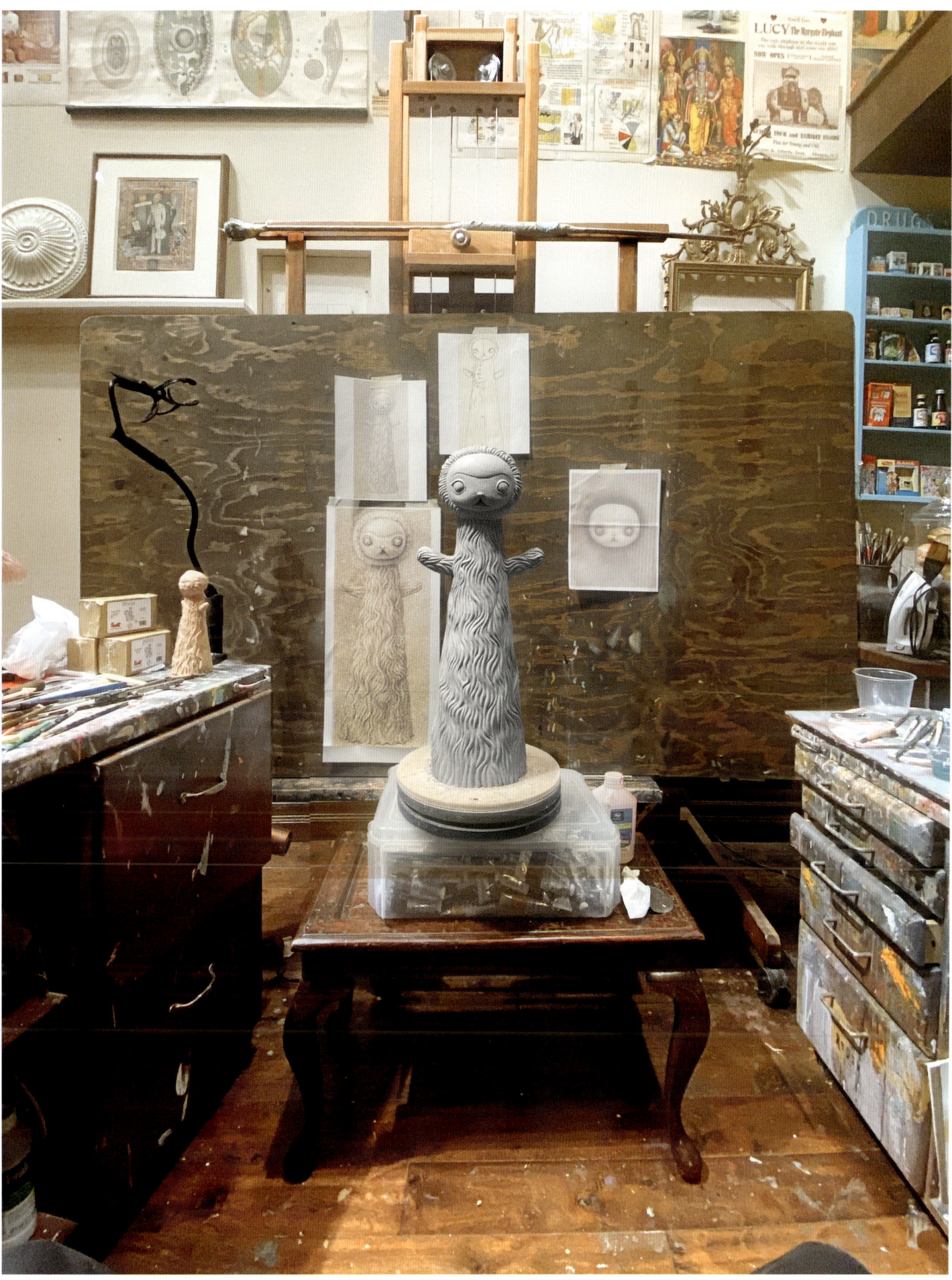

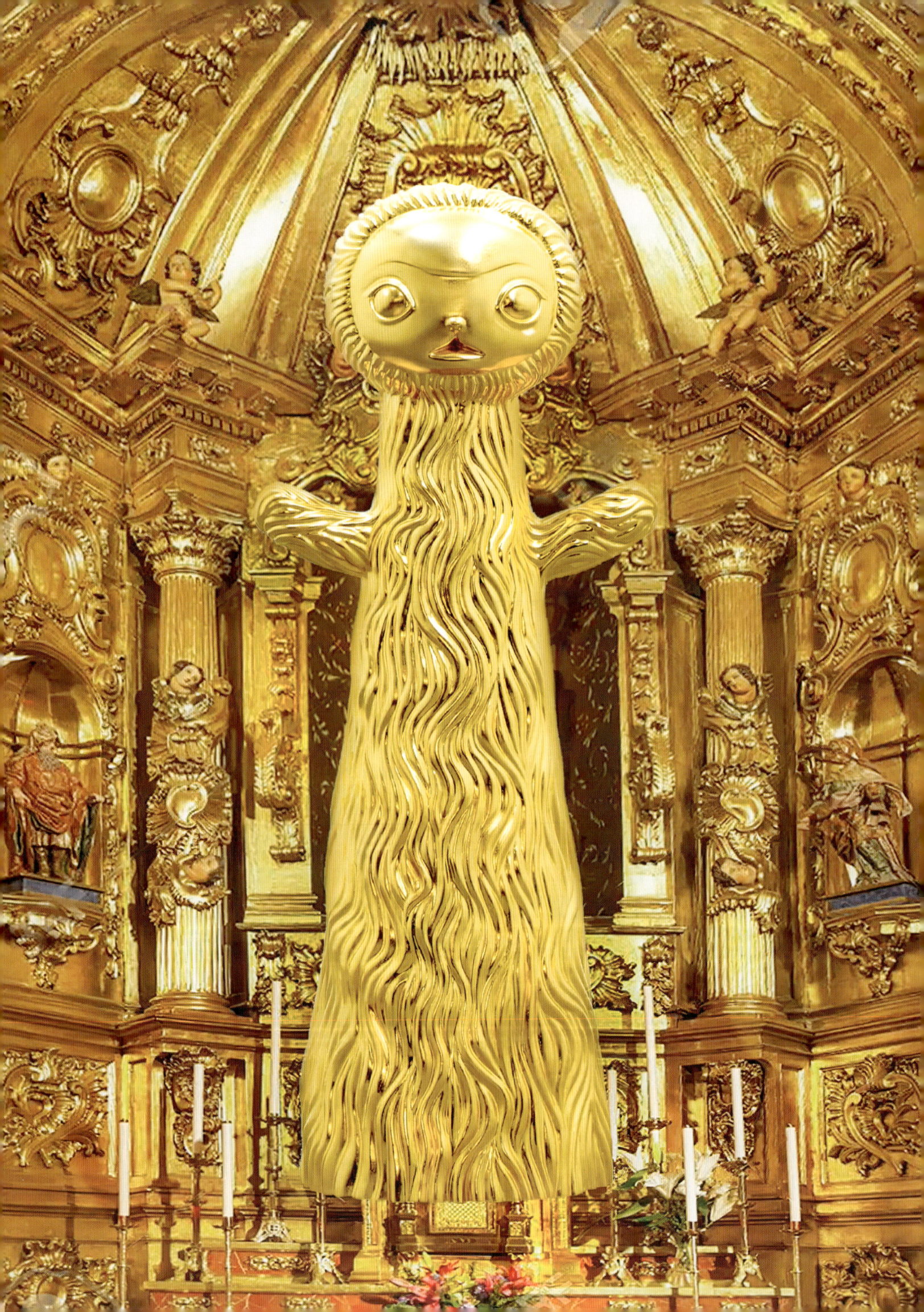

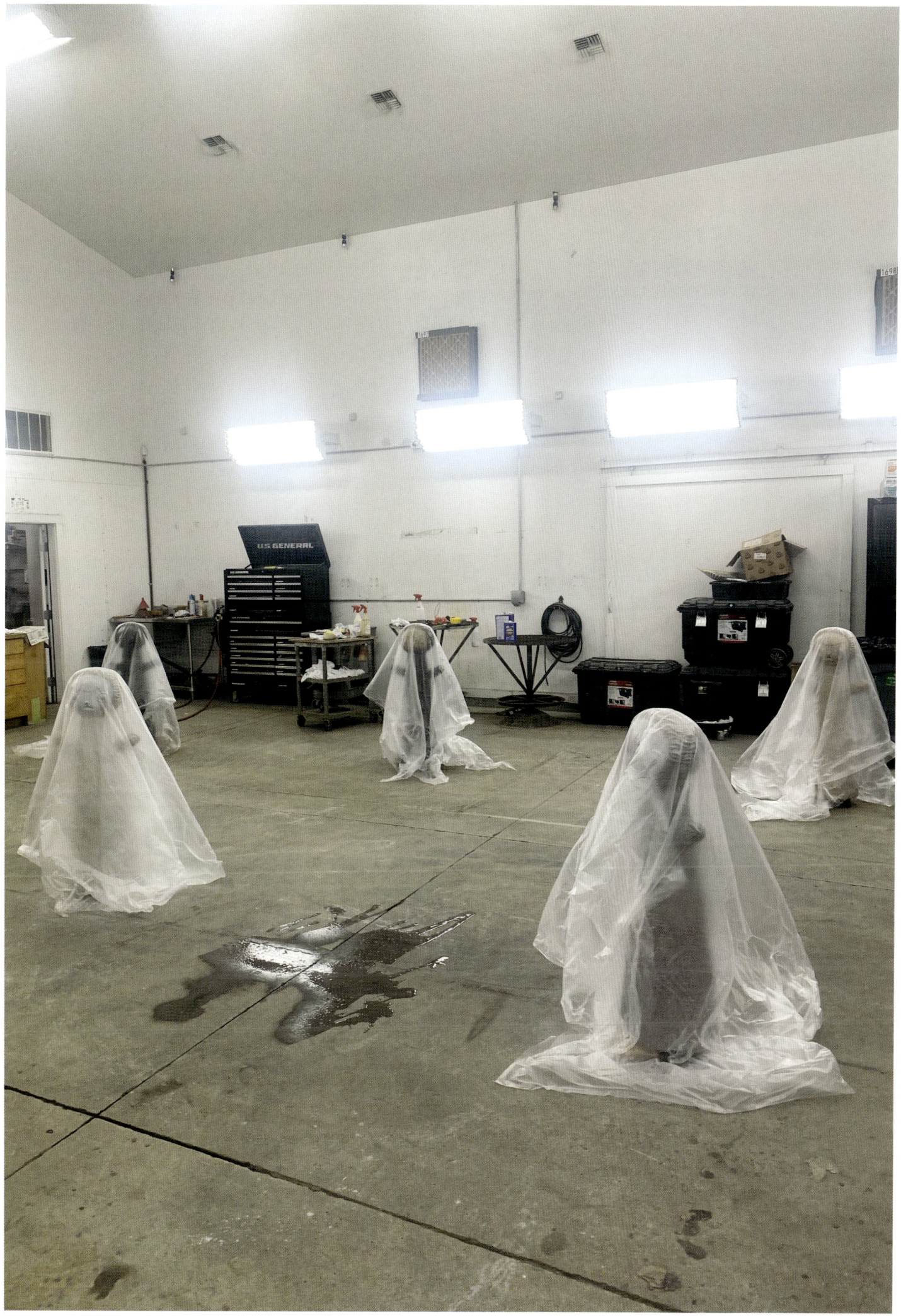

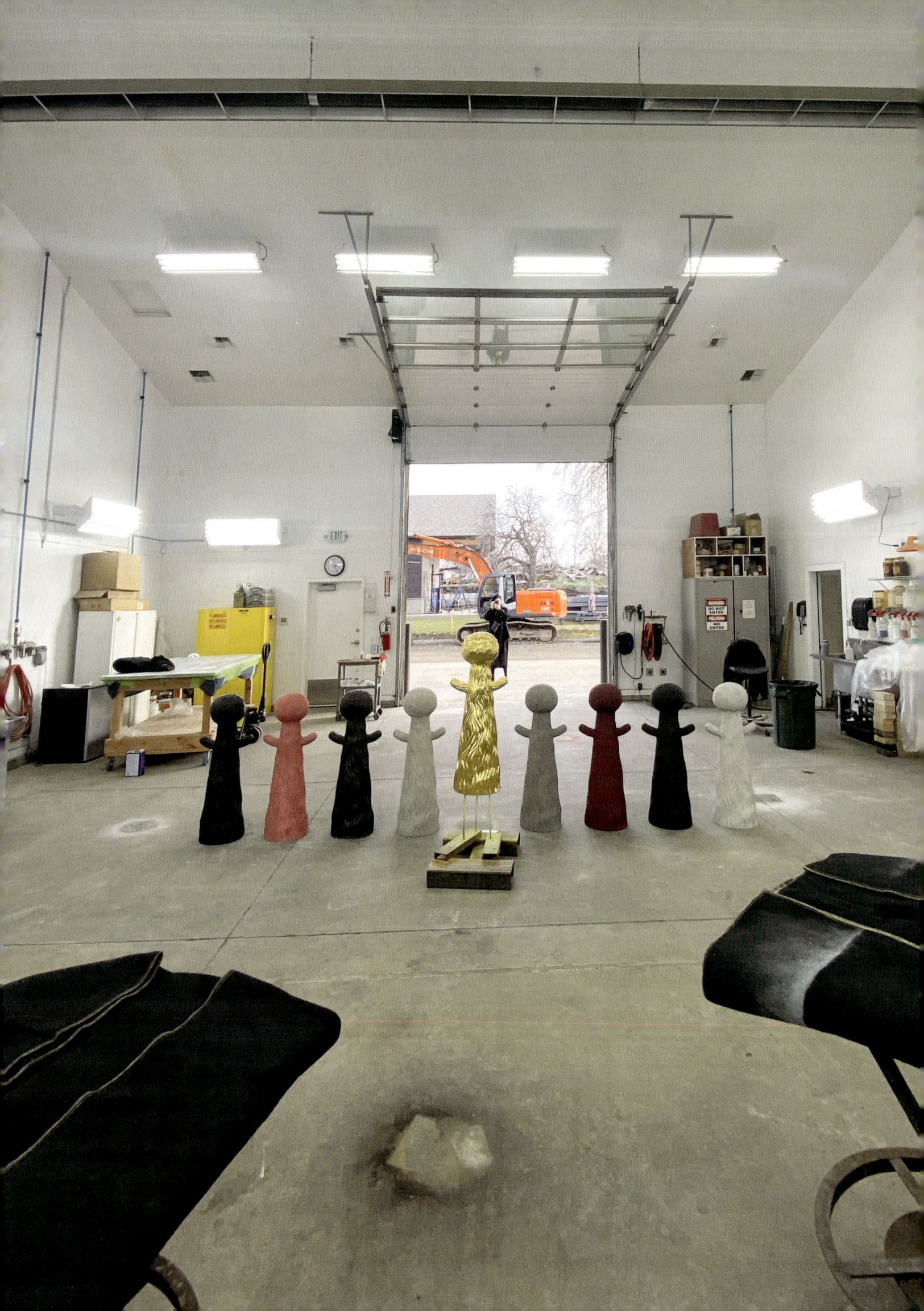

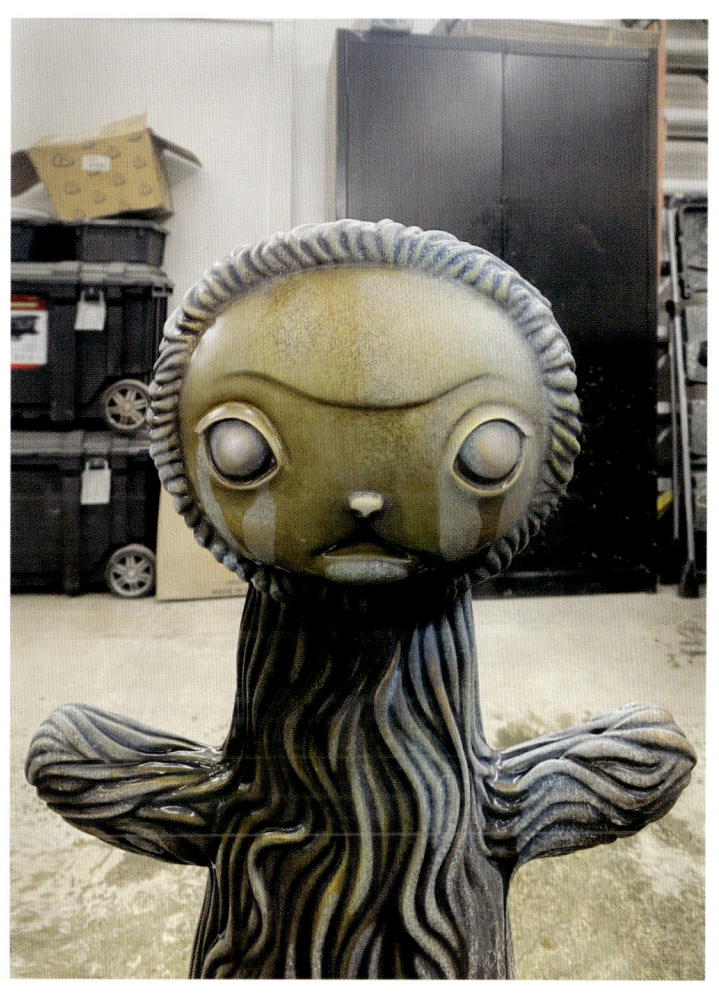

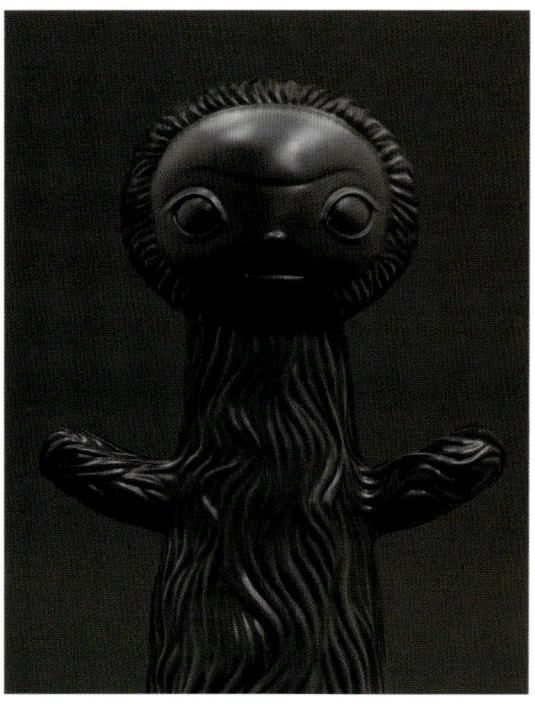

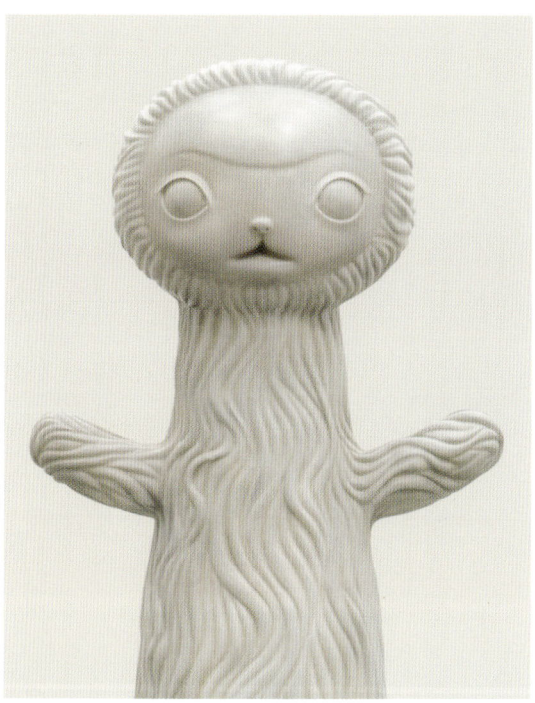

Yakalina number nine is Black. Black is the color of the subconscious. Once there was nothing in the universe at all. A lot is still there between the stars. Black knows more about dark matter than anyone.

Yakalina number eight is Bianca. Bianca swims in the sky and finds transcendence in celestial lights. For some, the brightness can be very overwhelming.

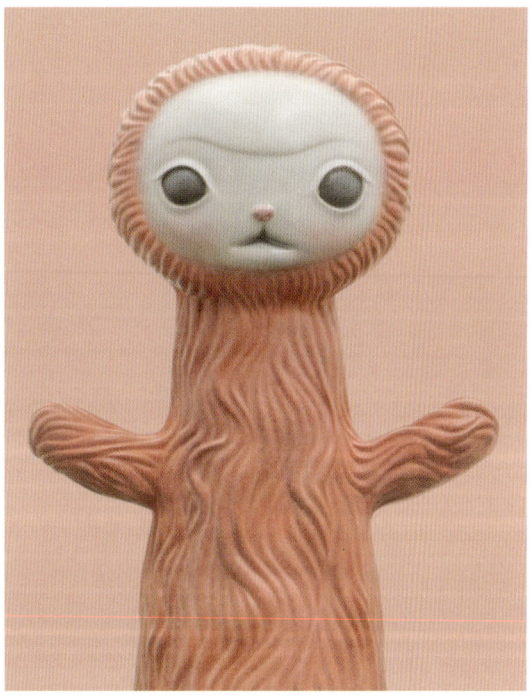

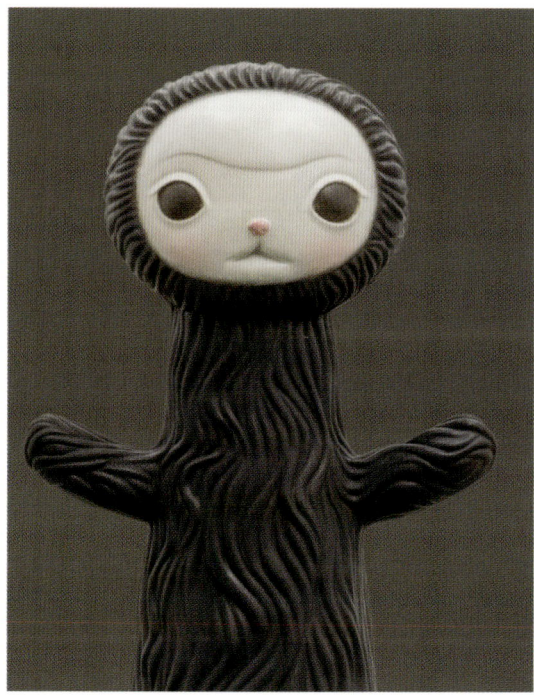

Yakalina number seven is Blush. Soft and silky, Blush is not serious. She forgets things all the time. Sometimes, very early in the morning, you can see her above the trees, but only for a moment.

Yakalina number six is Bistre. Bistre is the color of coal. She smells like the woods after a fire. She watches moss grow on fallen branches and notices the way the husks of insects dissolve on the forest floor.

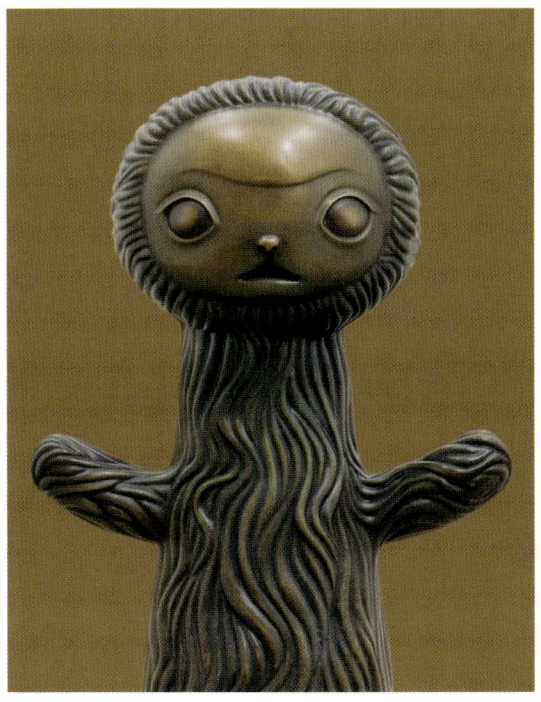

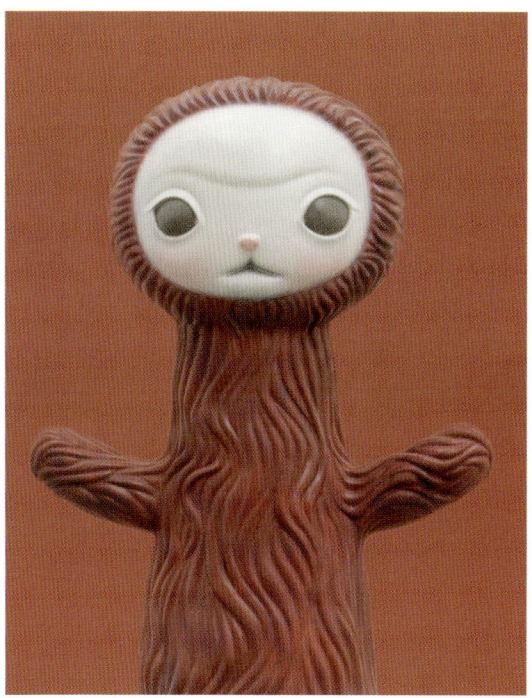

Yakalina number five is Bronze. Bronze remembers the heat of forges in the hands of many farmers. Time has taught Bronze about beauty and transformation. But she has also seen many wars and conflicts and thinks of them sadly.

Yakalina number four is Blood. Blood is very serious because she remembers more than any of the other Yakalina. She holds many old rituals dear to her heart, which beats very slowly. Most people have forgotten about these ceremonies, but Blood has not.

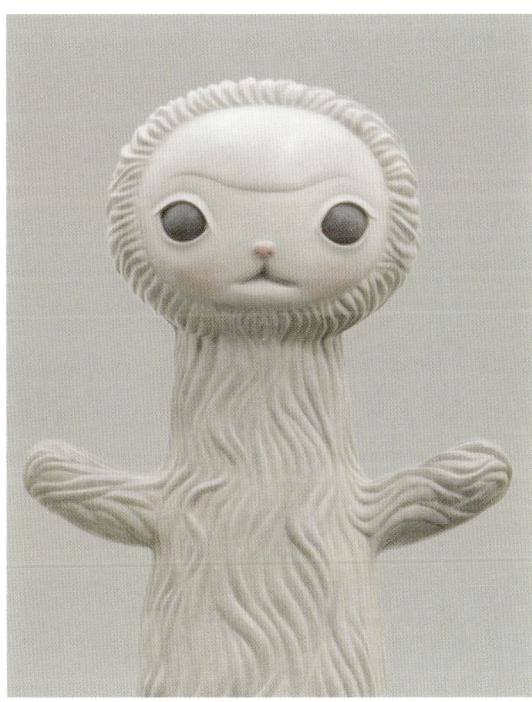

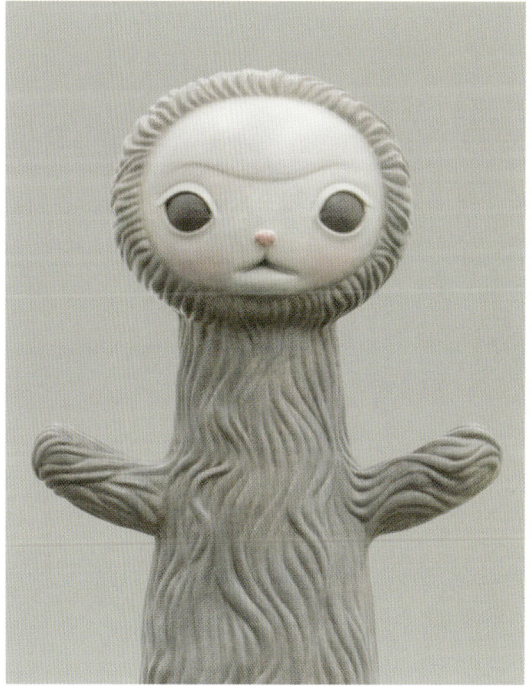

Yakalina number three is Buff. The sun bleached Buff, just like it bleaches shells and bones. Buff is very quiet. She doesn't even whisper.

Yakalina number two is Bombay. Bombay is pale like the moon, the thin smoke that rises from incense, and the thick mist that drapes a cold beach.

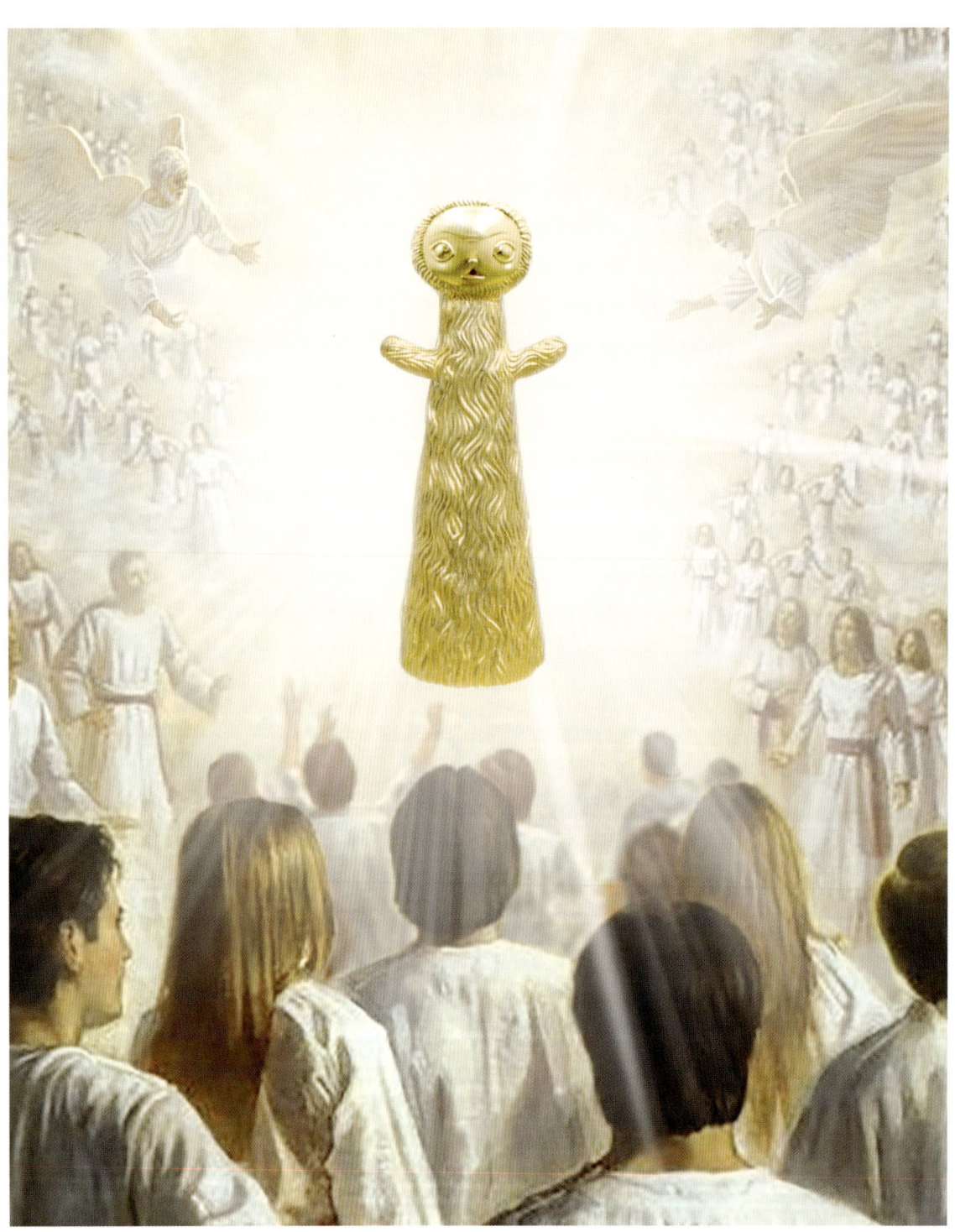

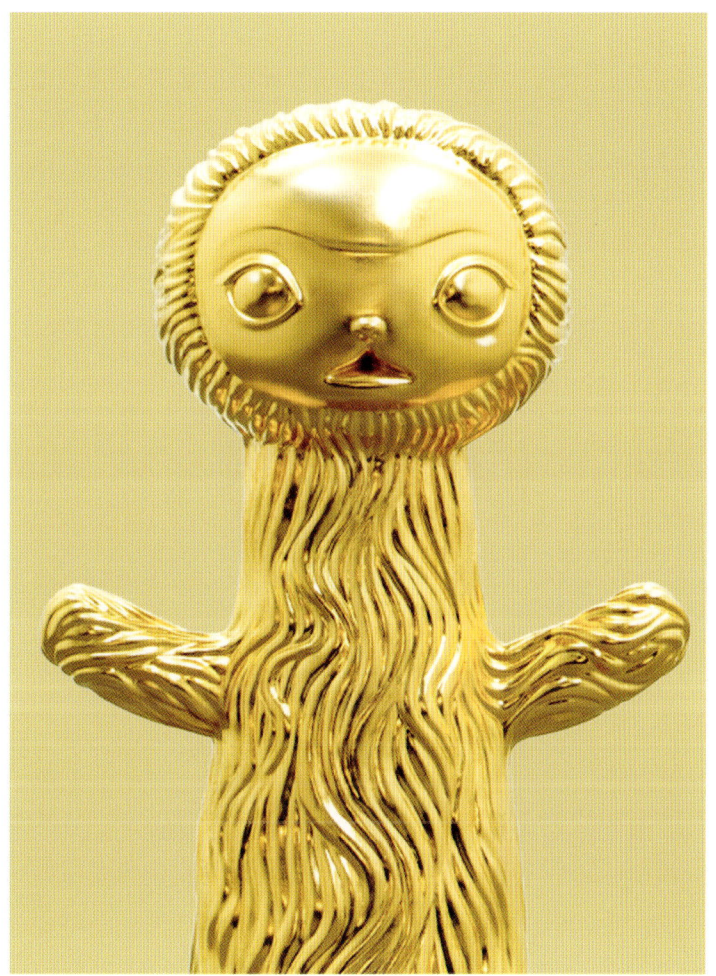

Yakalina number one is Brilliant. Gold is a natural substance infused with supernatural brilliance. The seventy-ninth element has been used to create spiritual objects throughout our human history. Brilliant has powerful magical qualities and is a bridge to the spiritual world. Gold is the sun and the daylight.

DRAWINGS

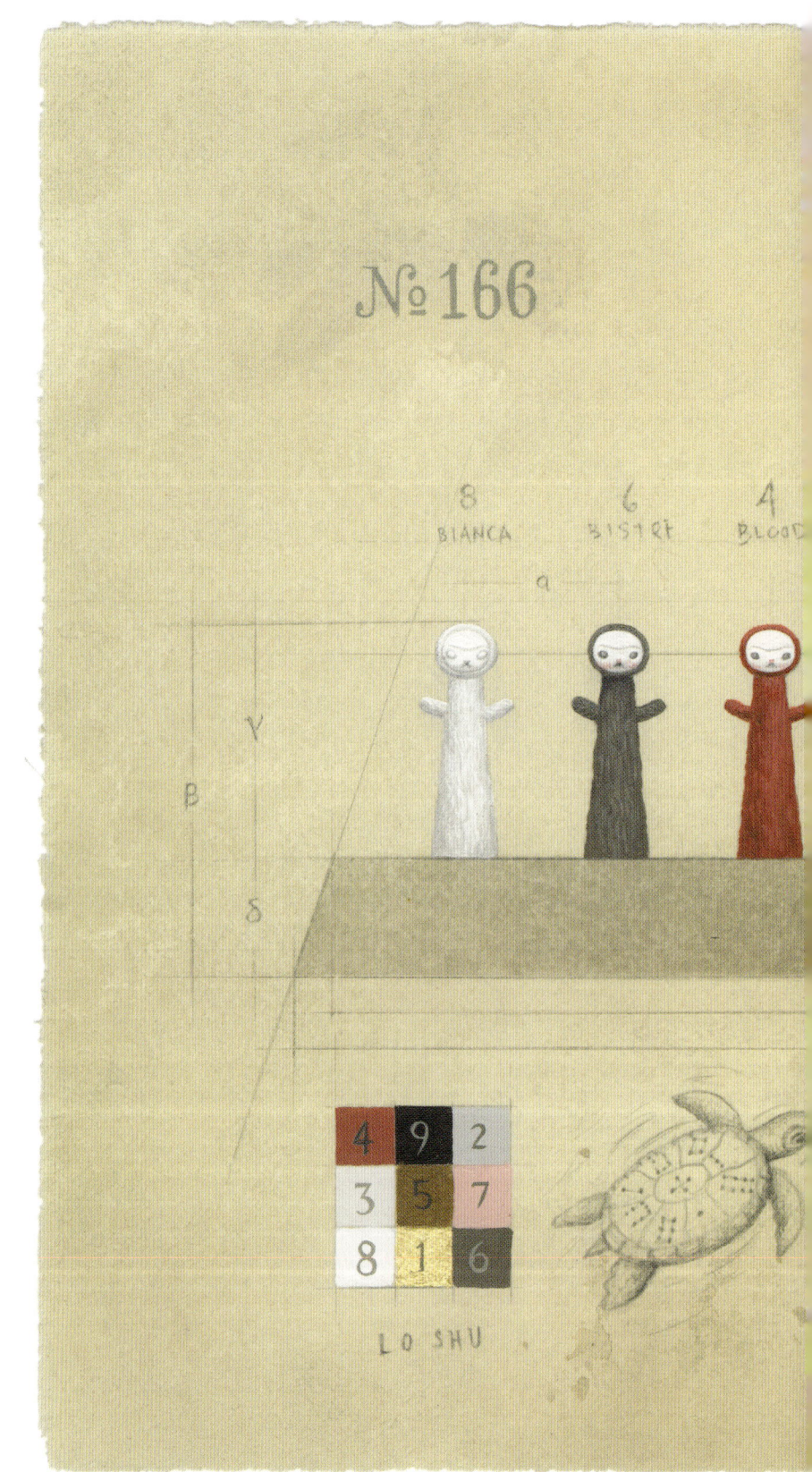

YAKALINA ARRAY

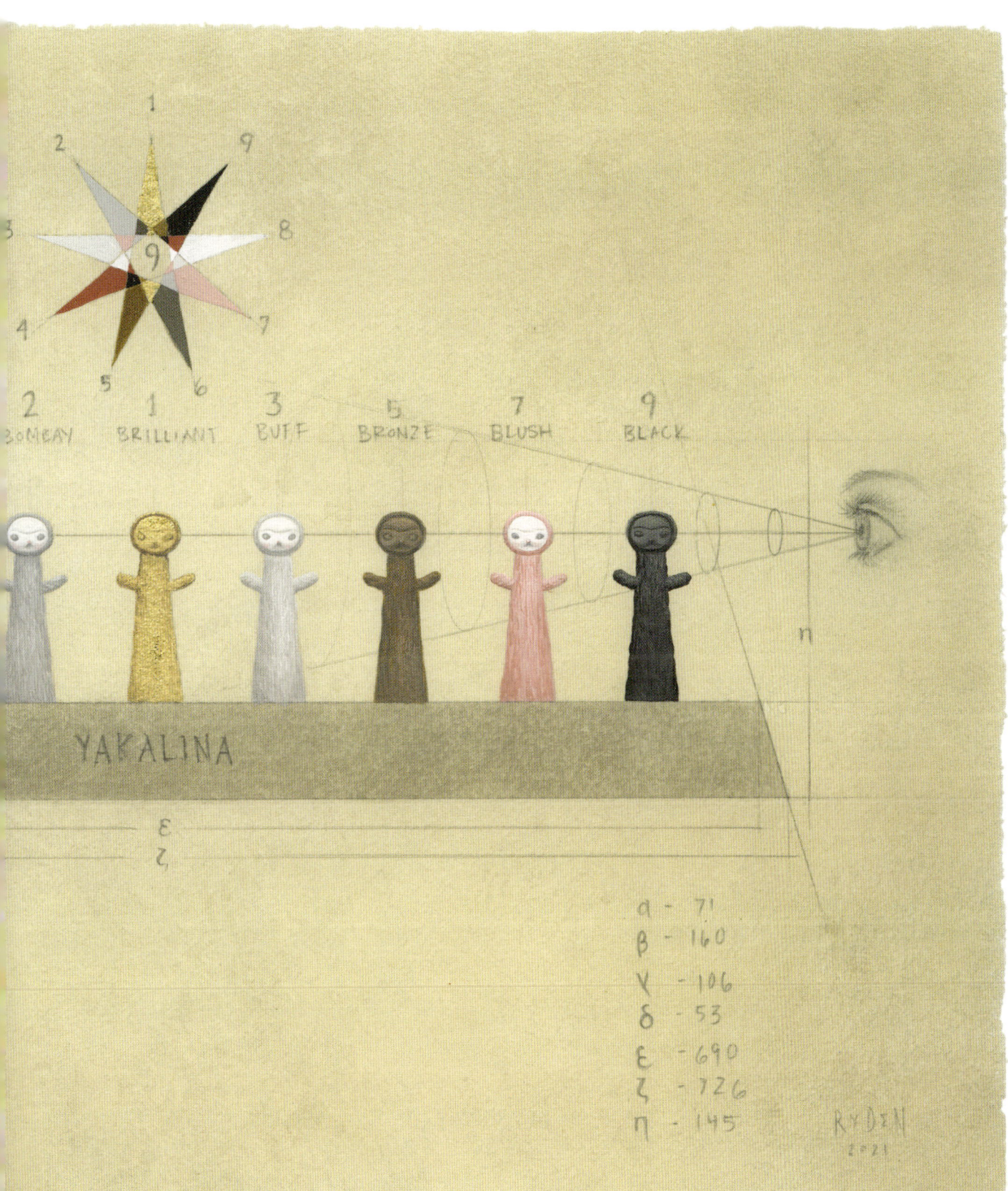

YAKALINA

α - 71
β - 160
γ - 106
δ - 53
ε - 690
ζ - 726
η - 145

RYDEN
2021

YAKALINA PORTRAIT

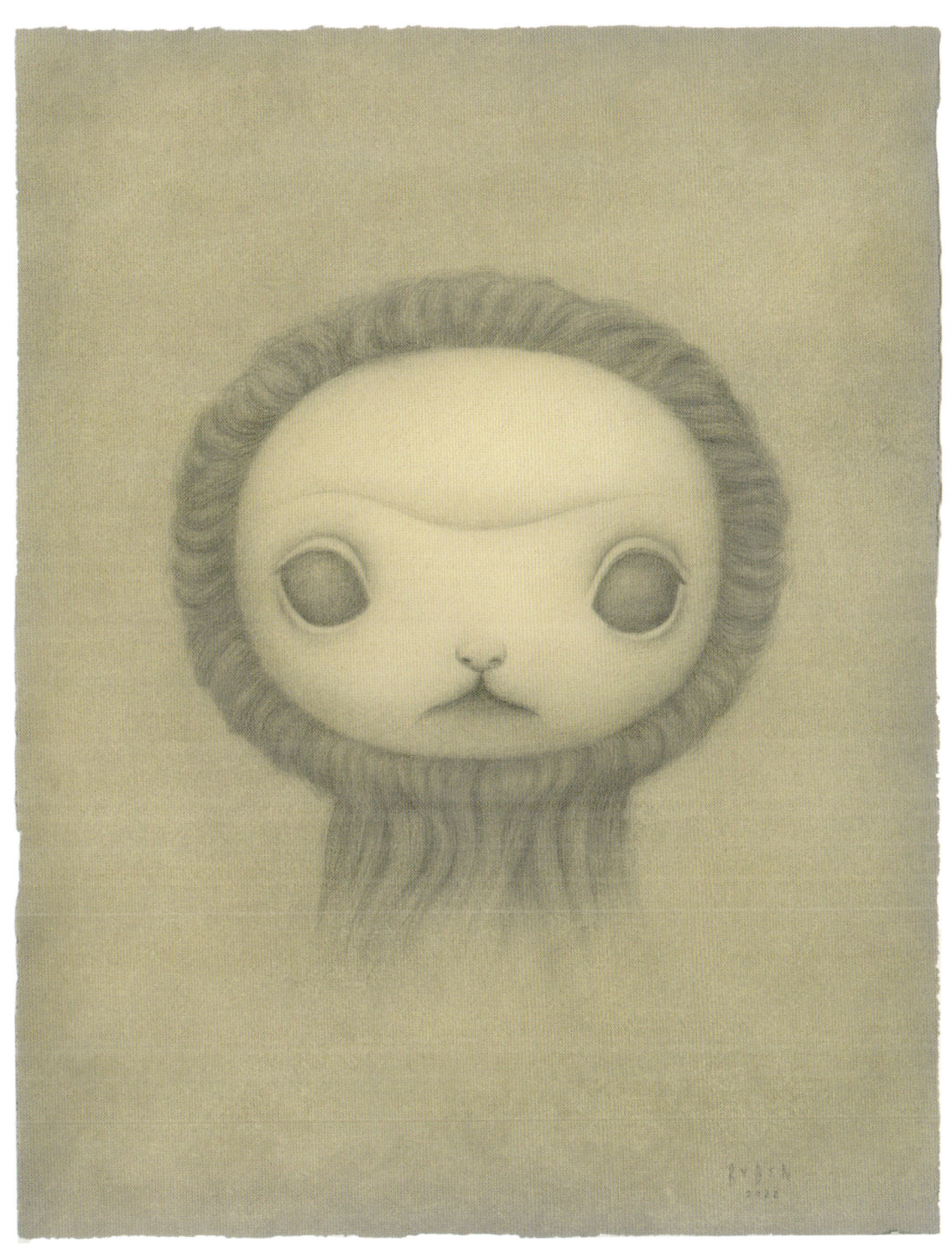

YAKALINA VISIBLE AND INVISIBLE

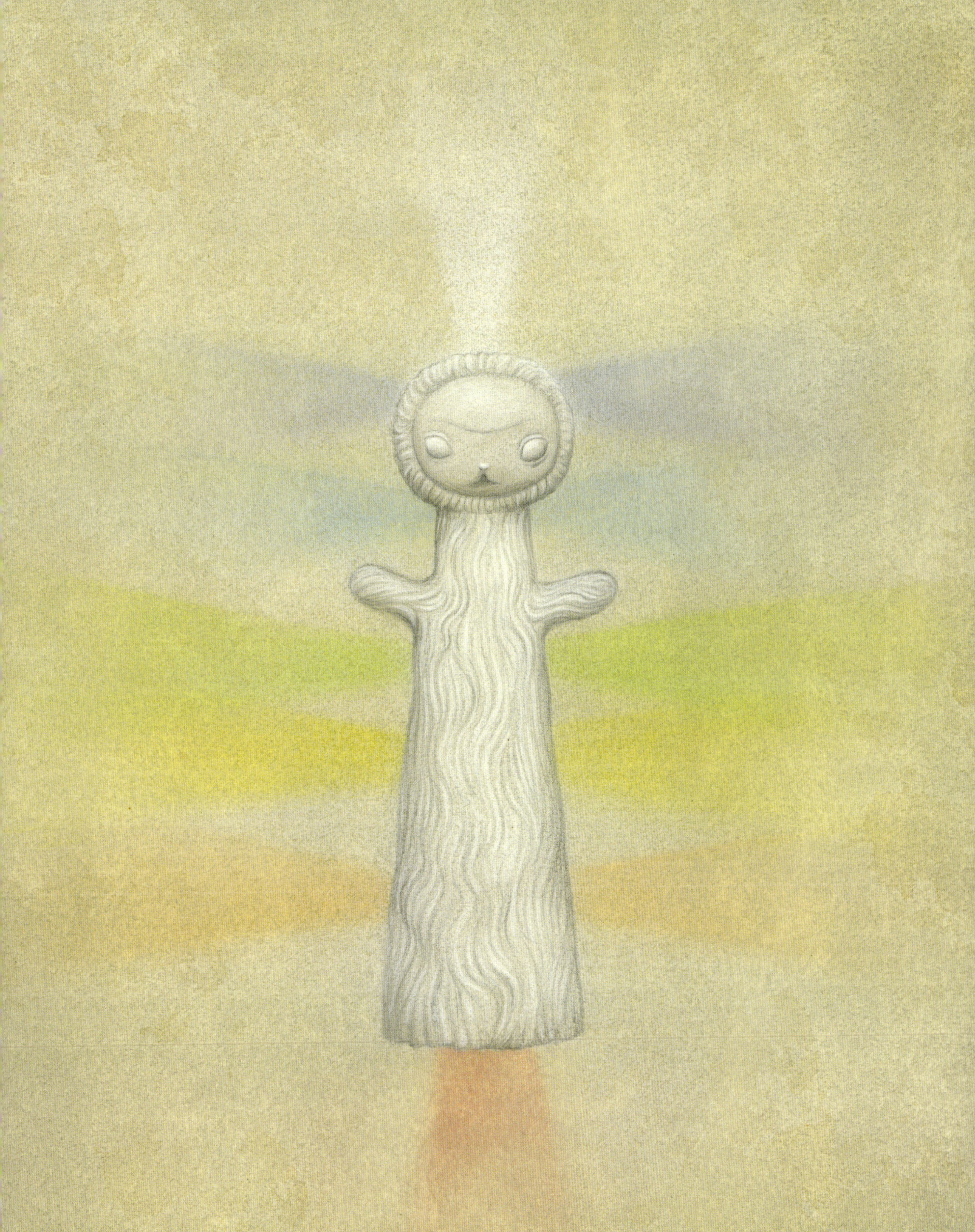

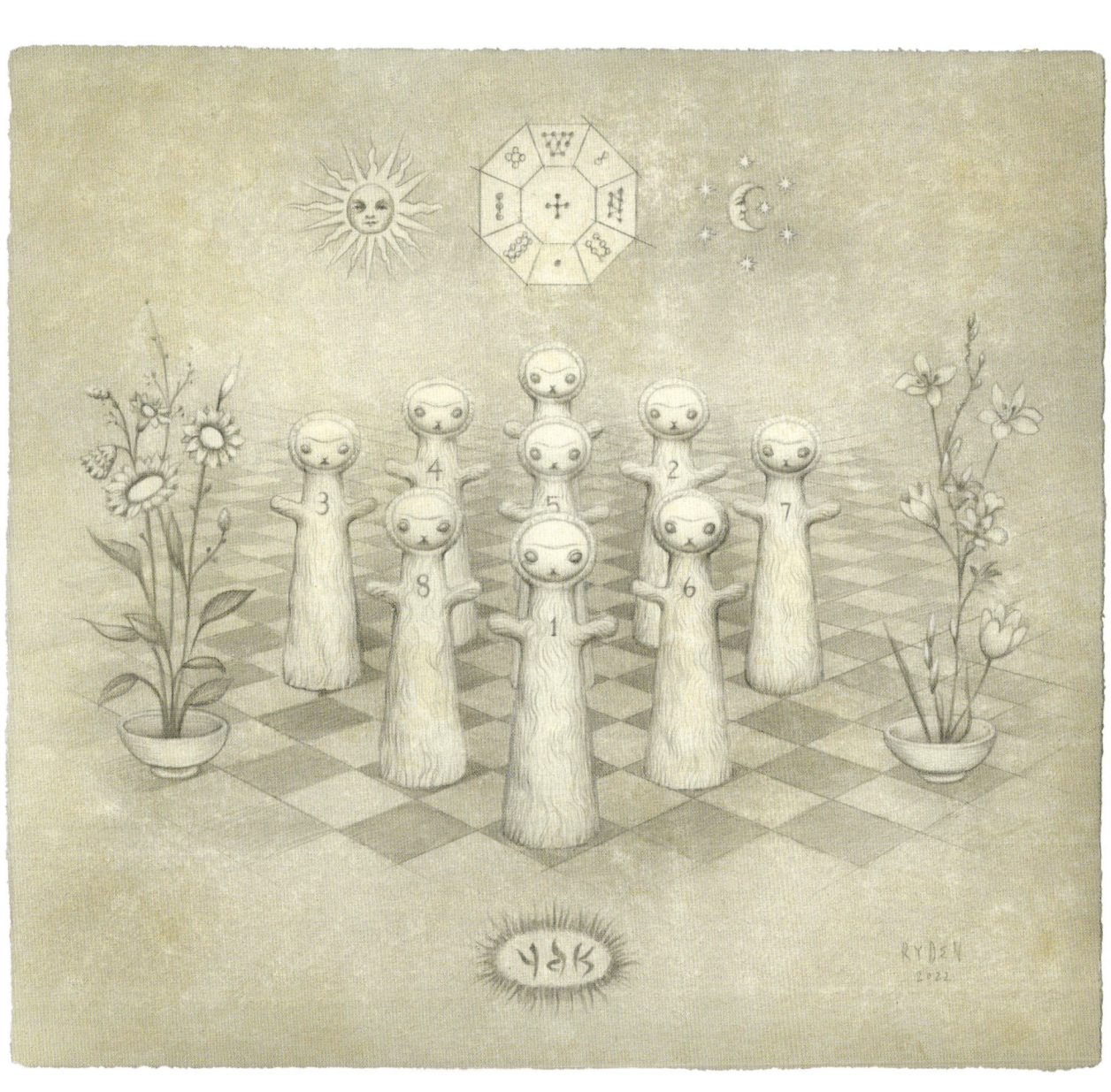

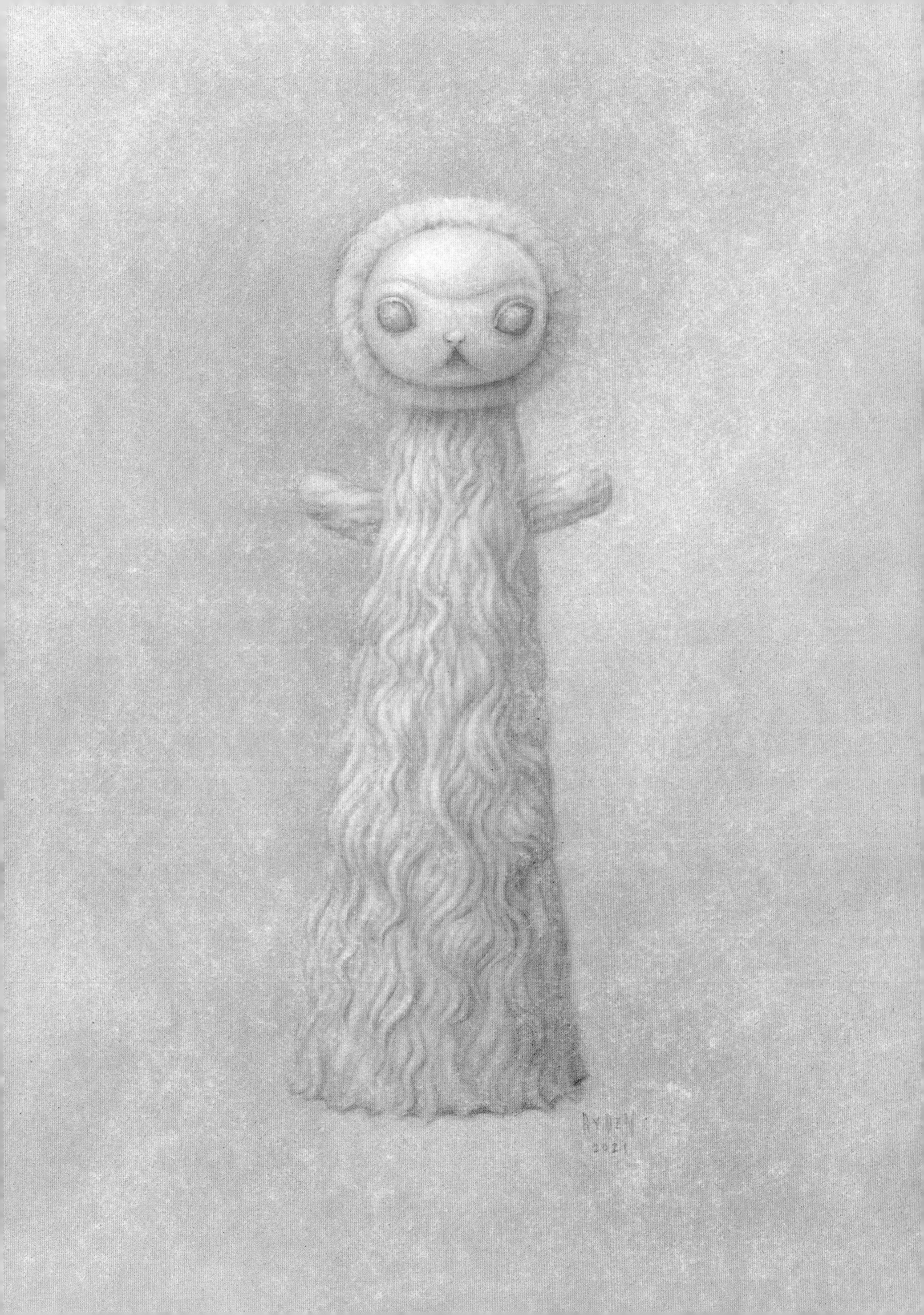

INSTALLATIONS

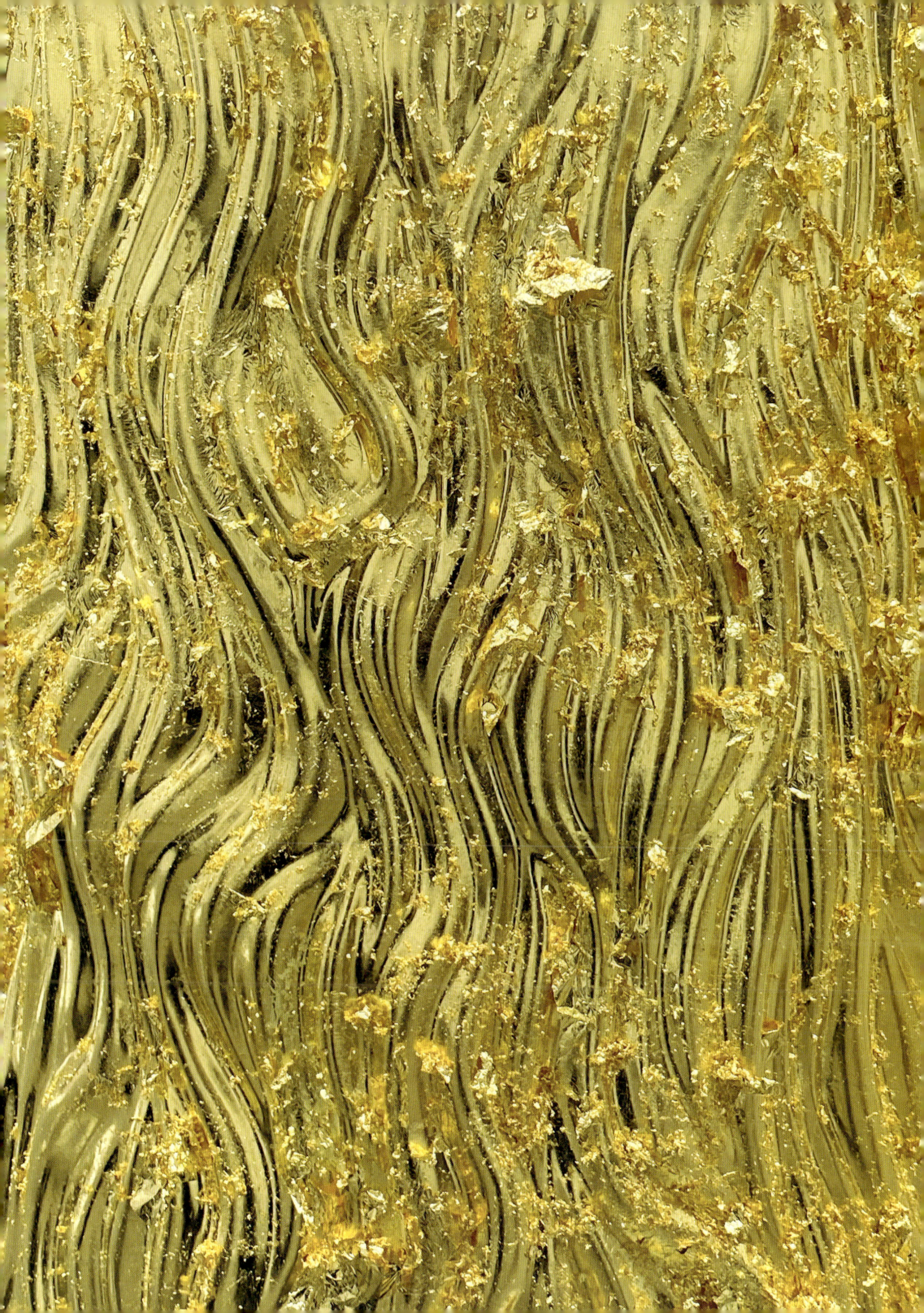

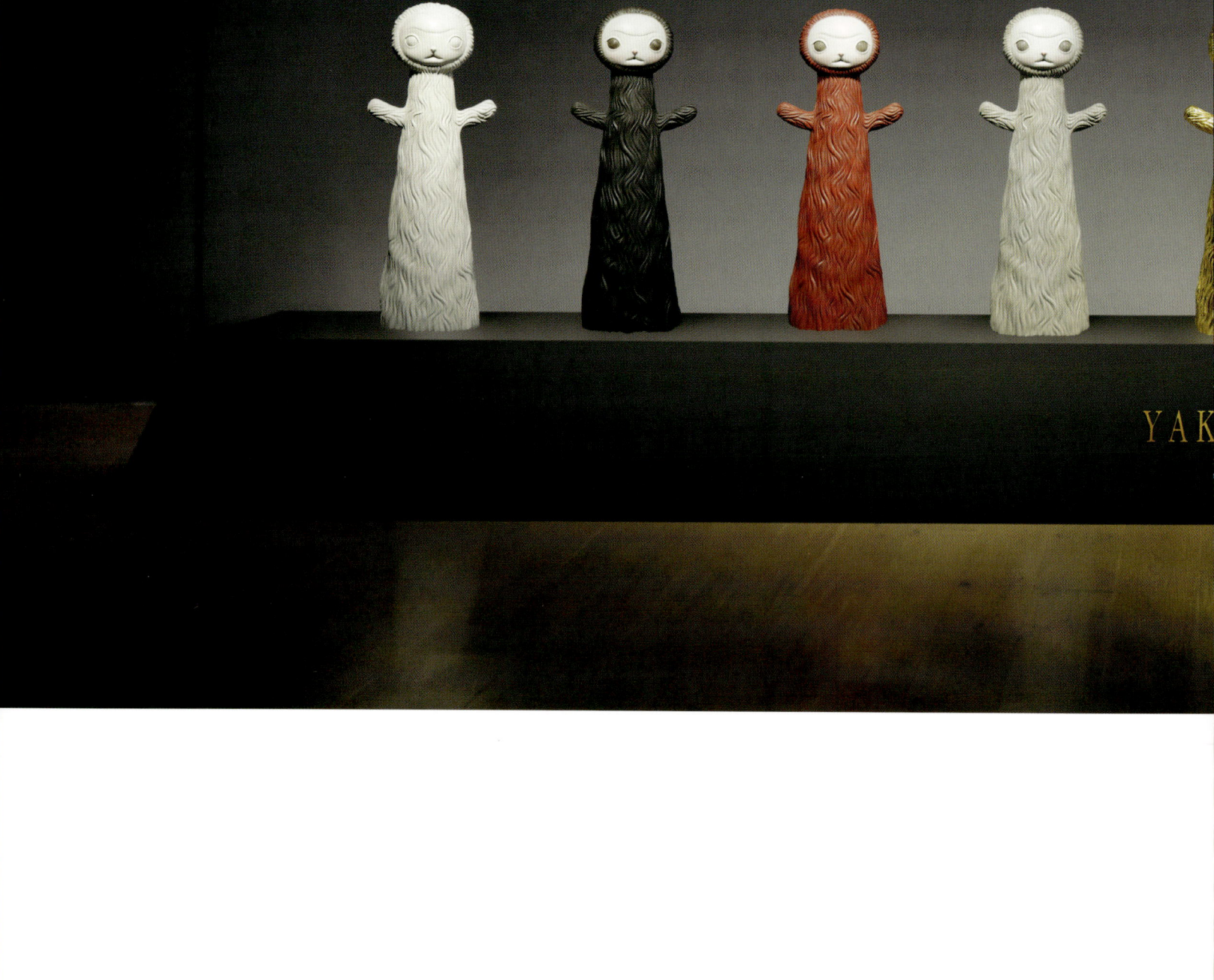

YAK

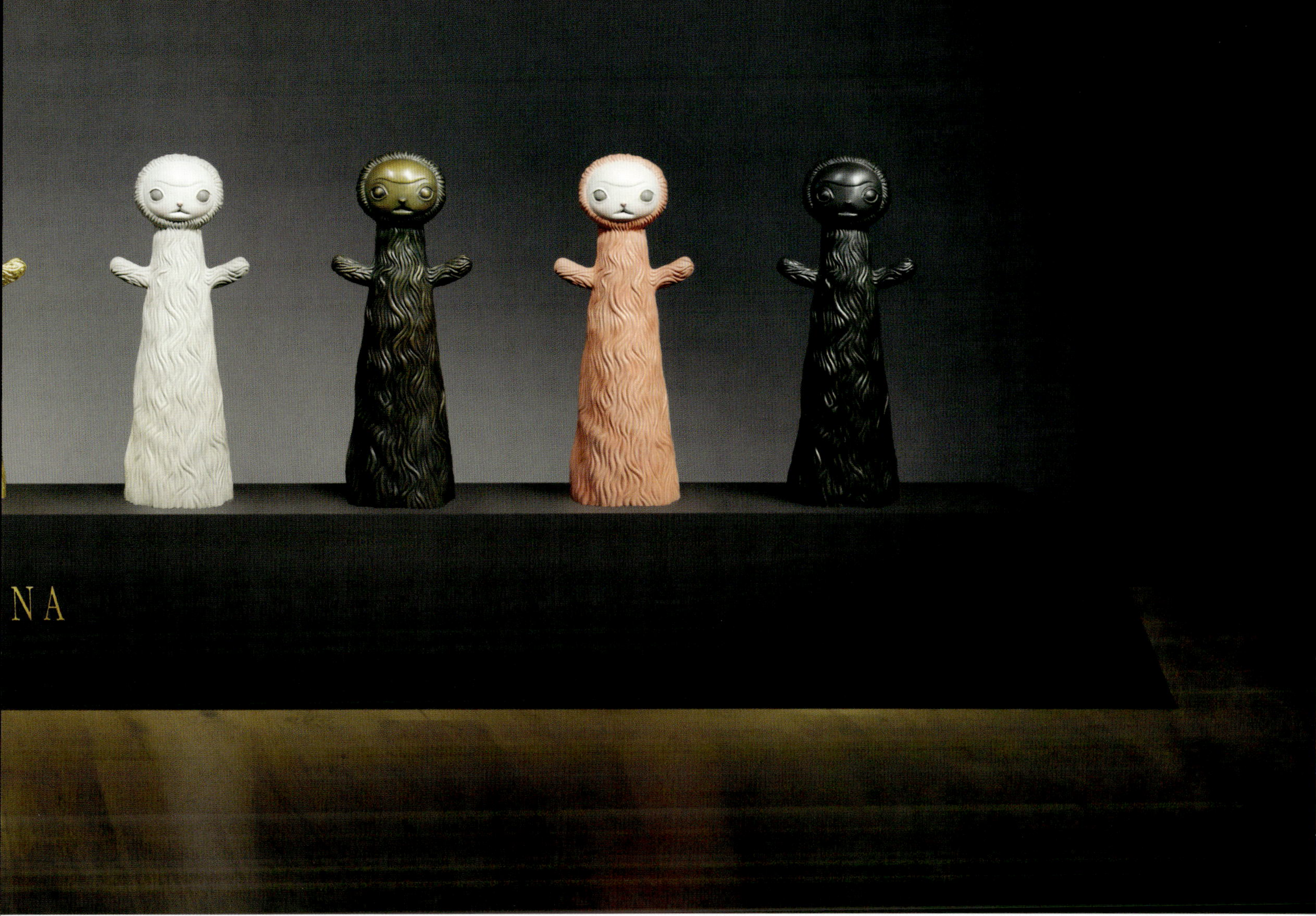

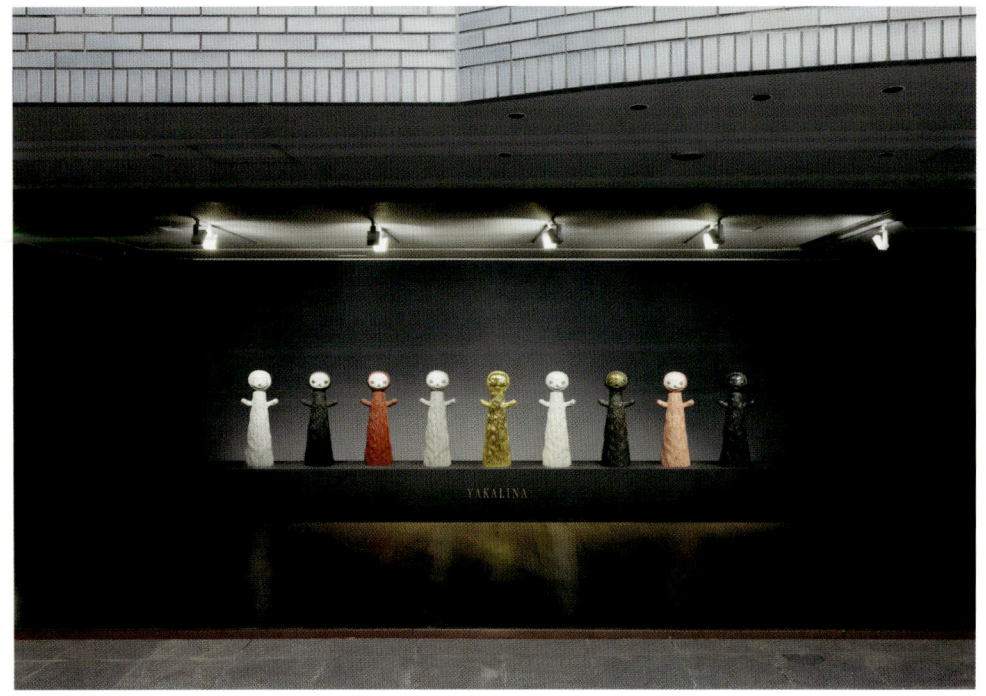

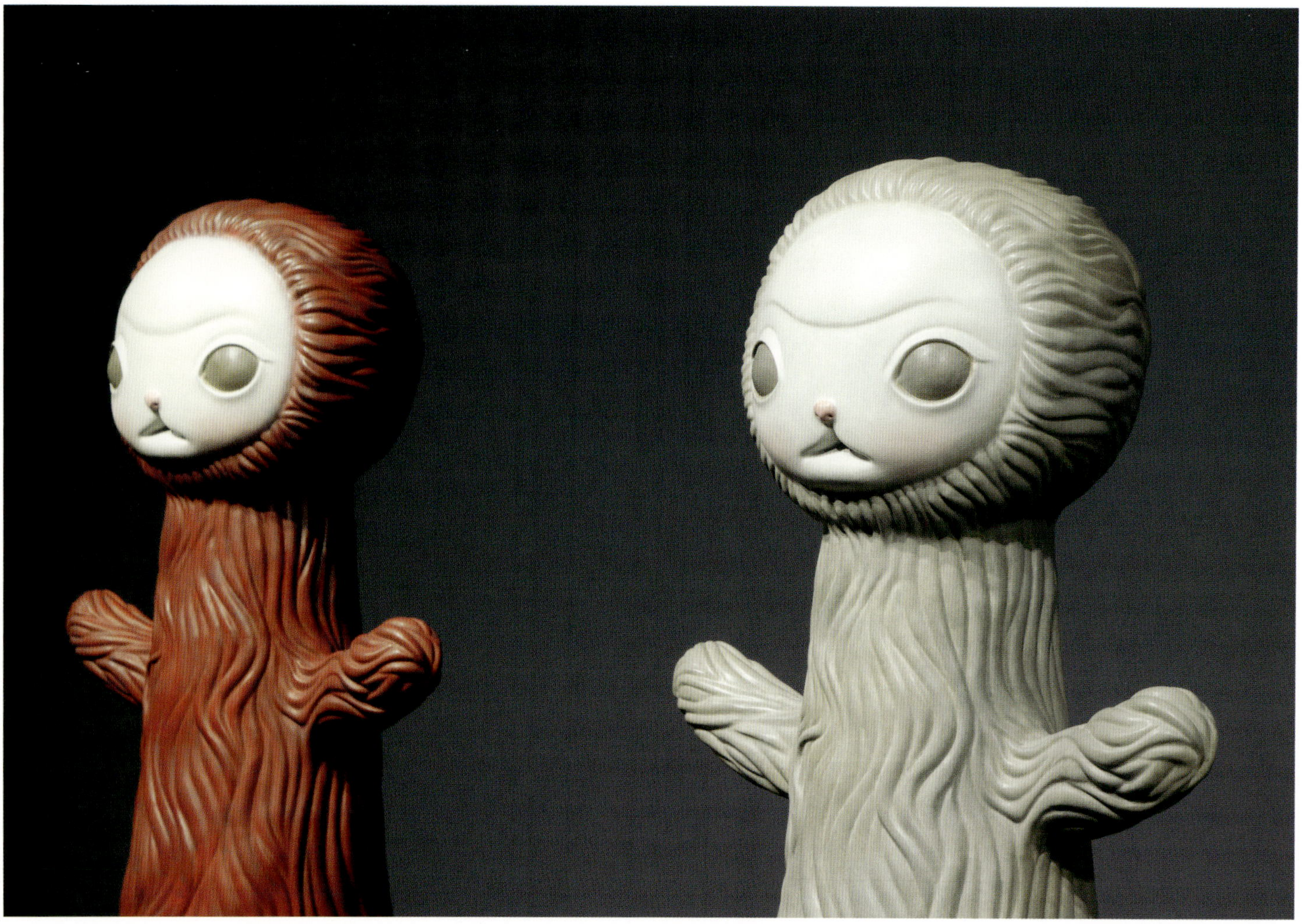

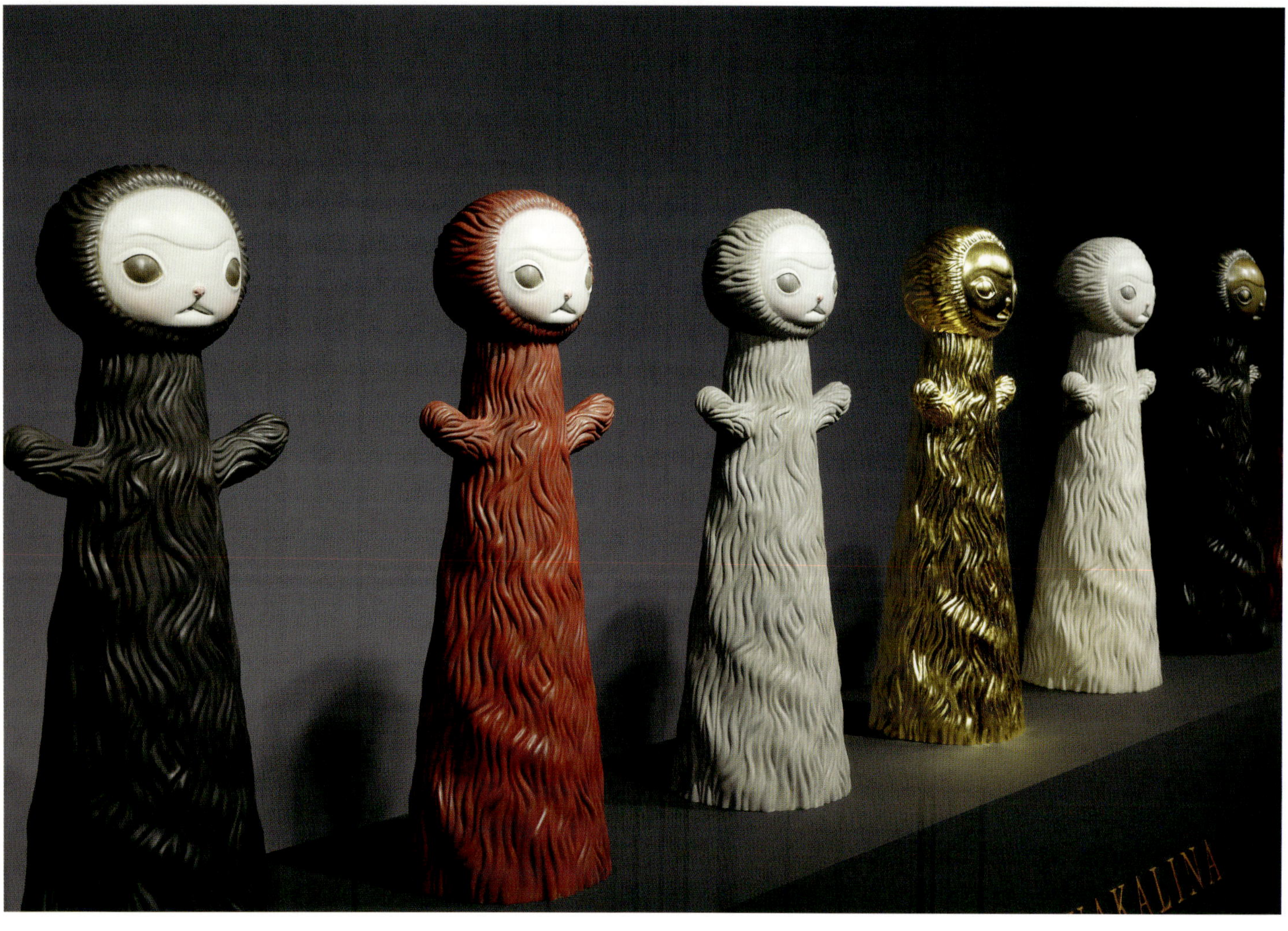

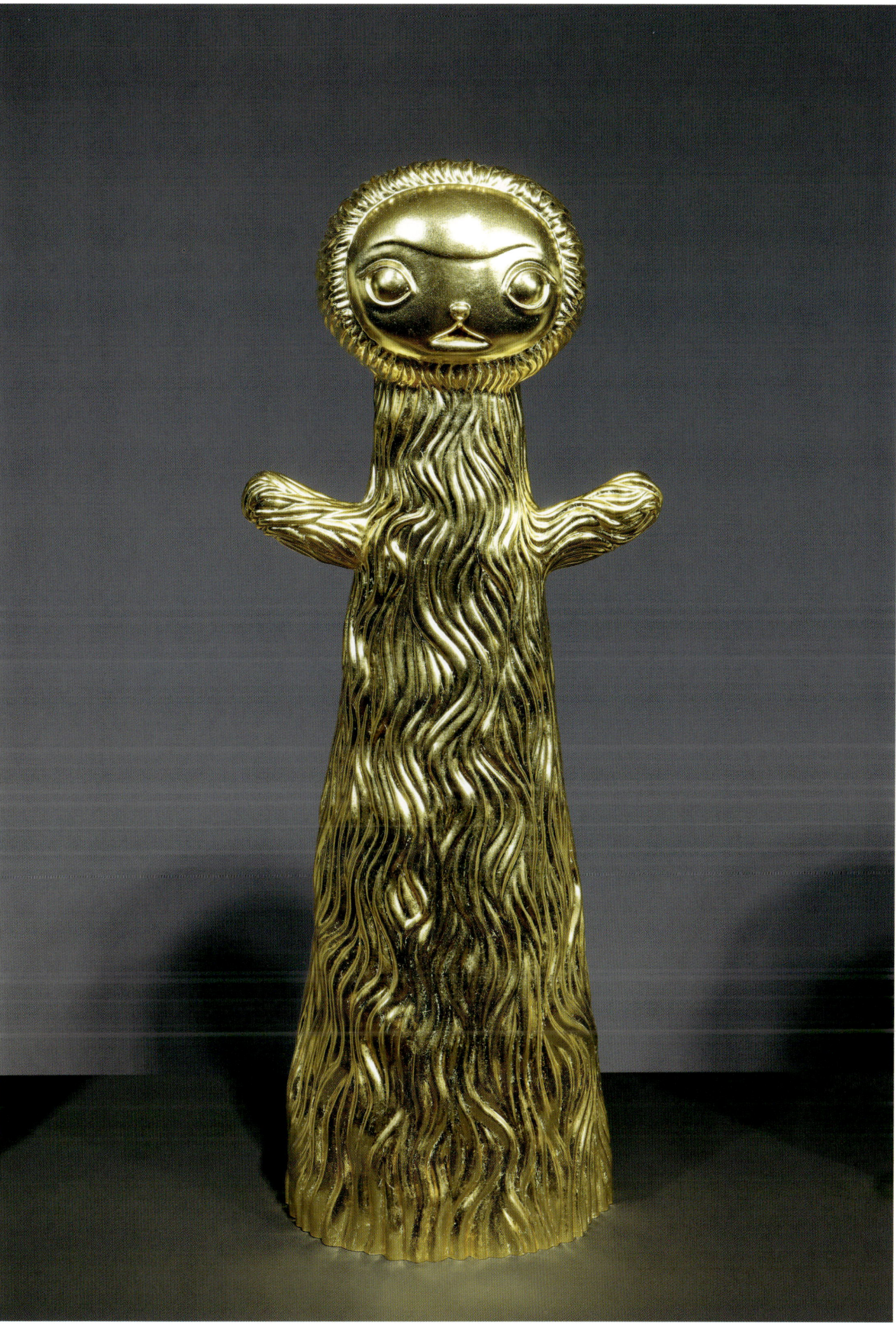

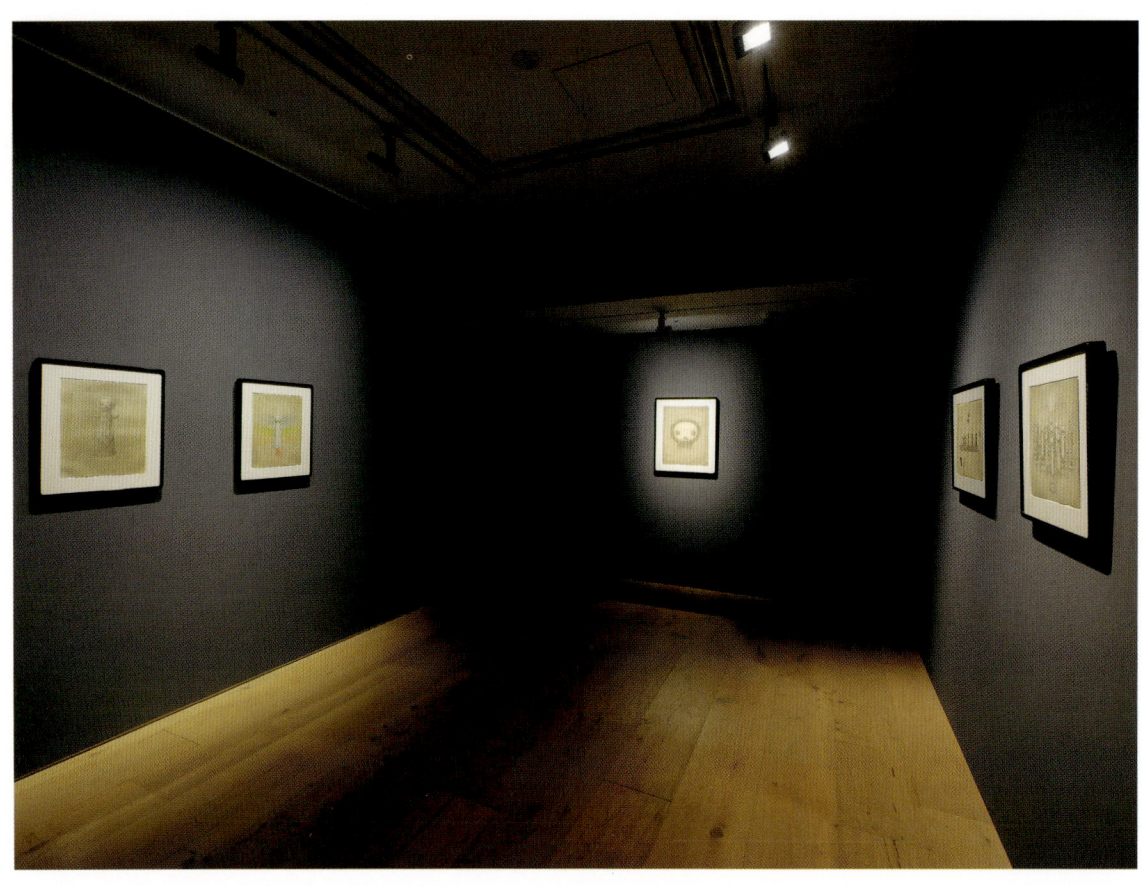

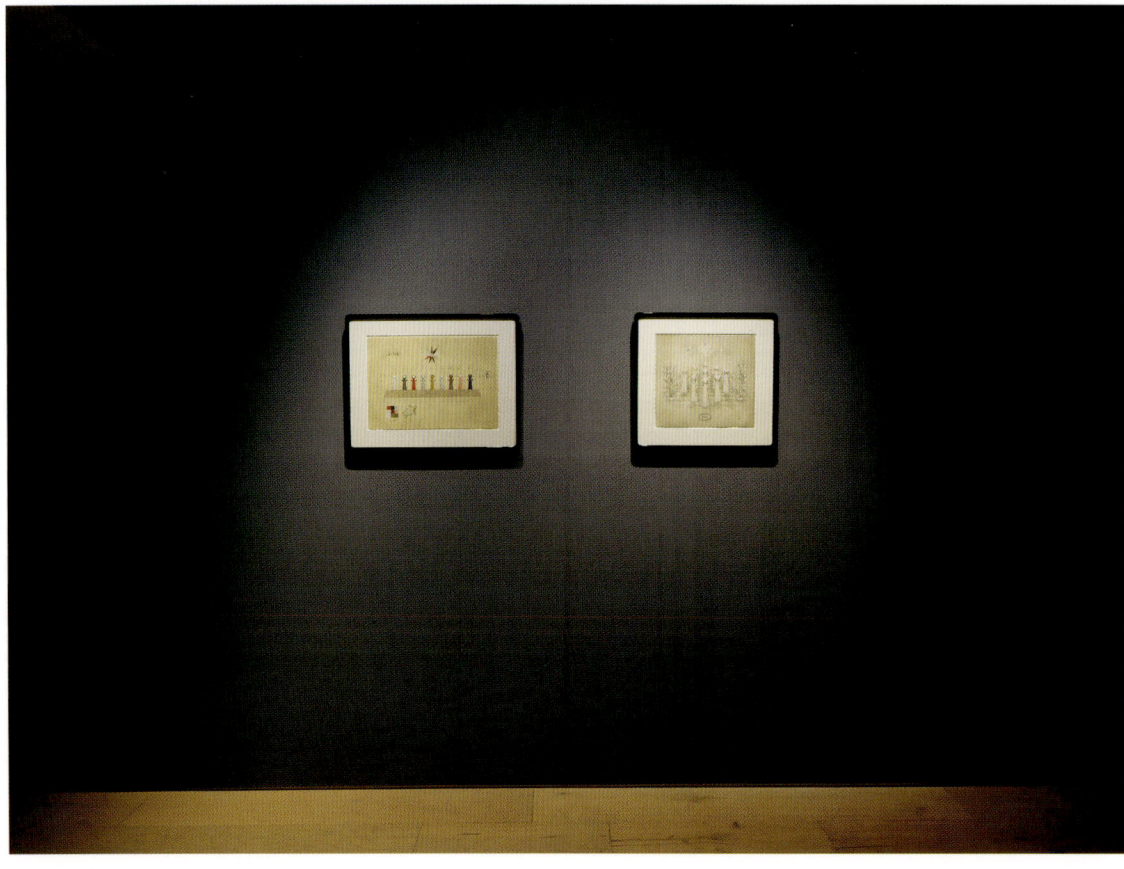

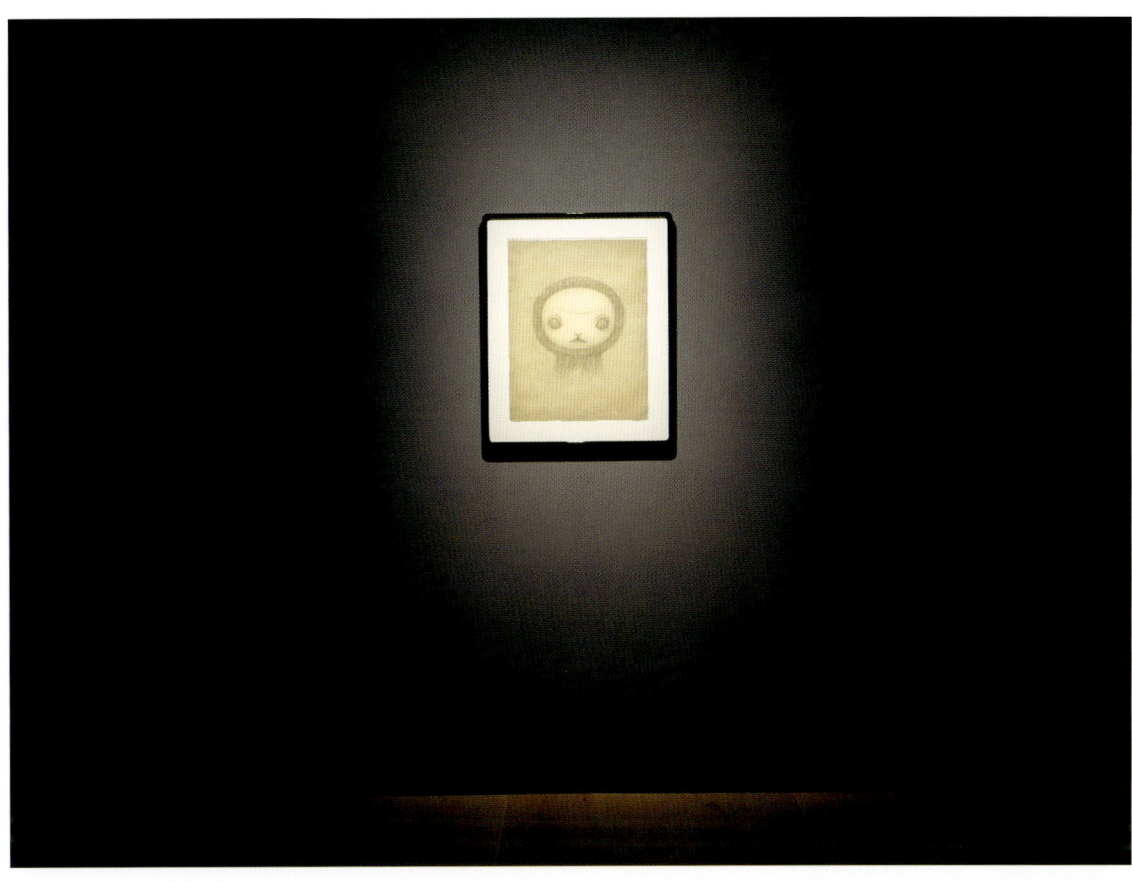

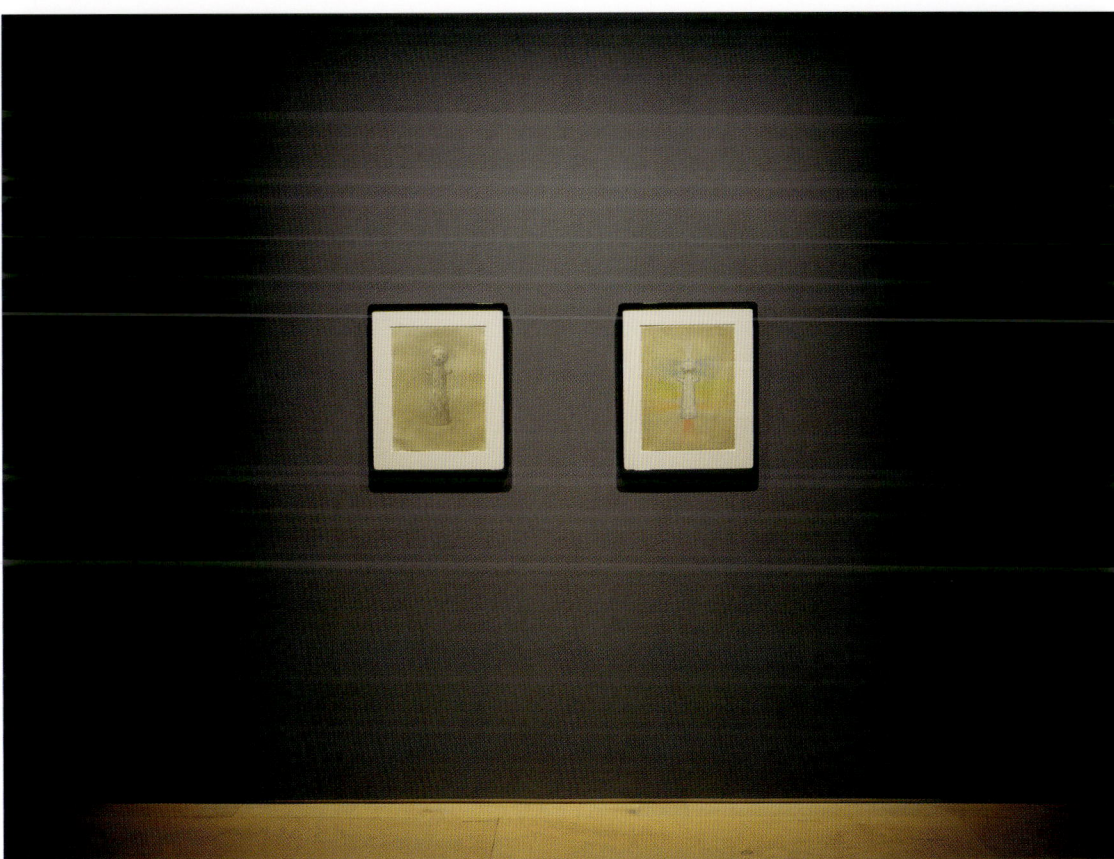

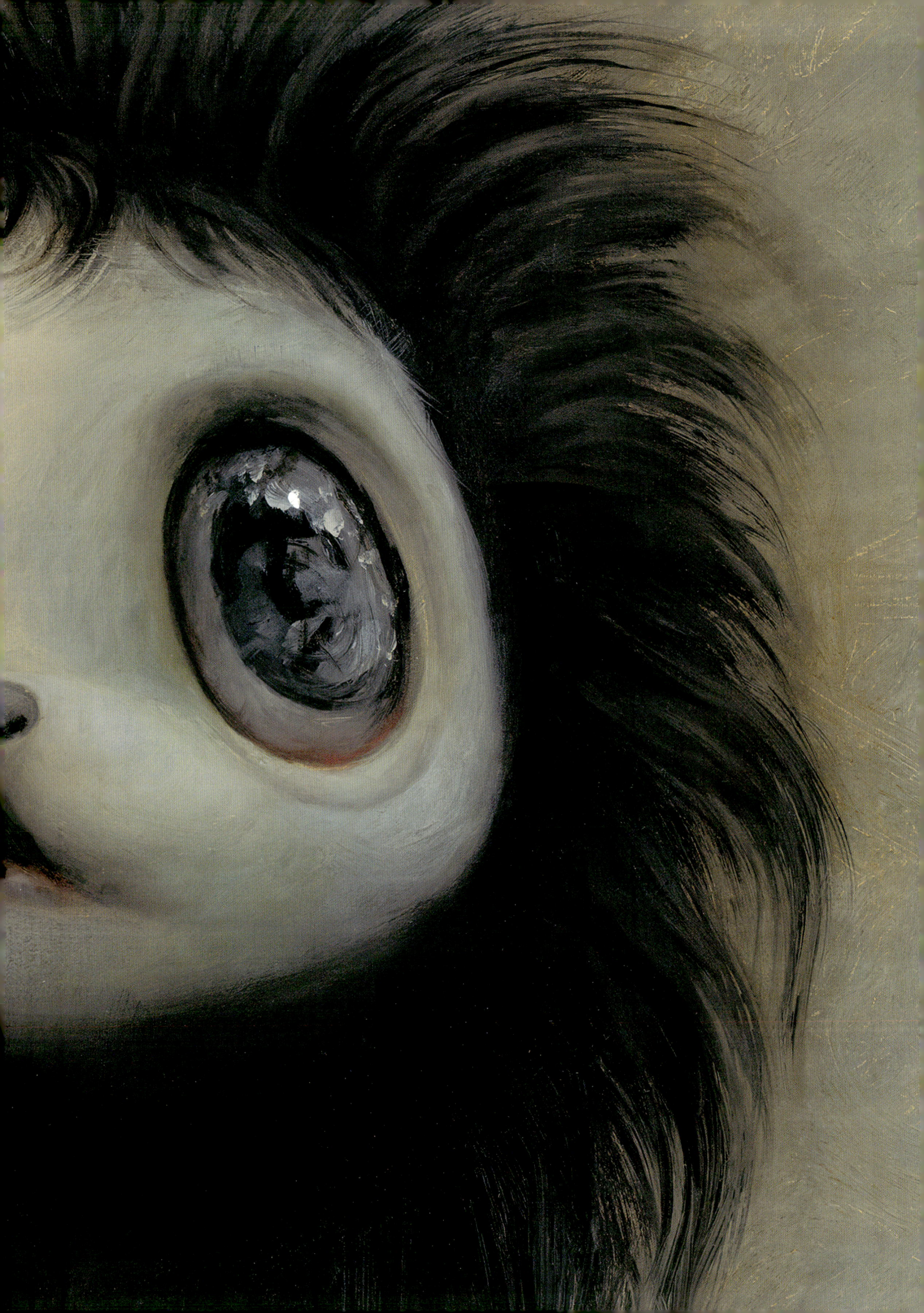

ANIMAL SECRETS

PERROTIN, Paris, June 2022

PAINTINGS

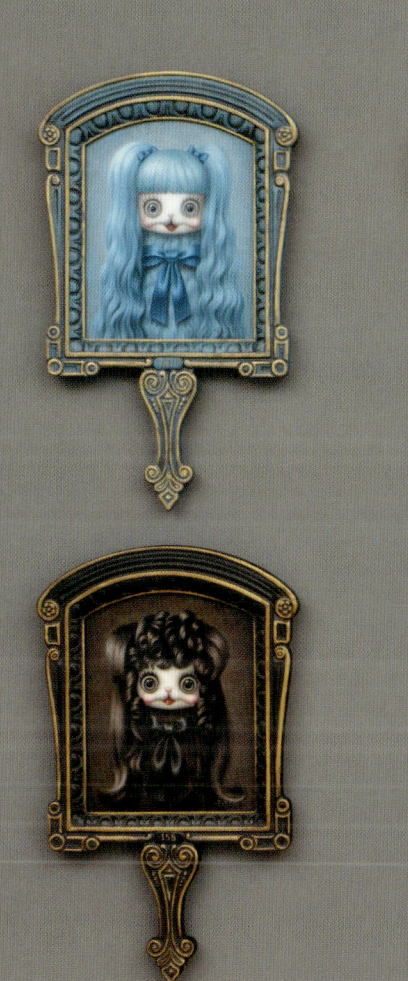
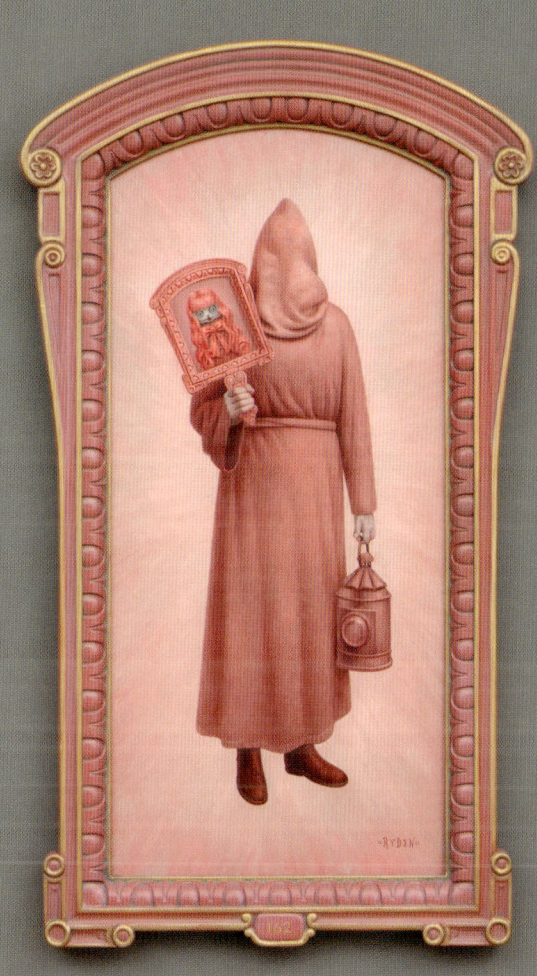
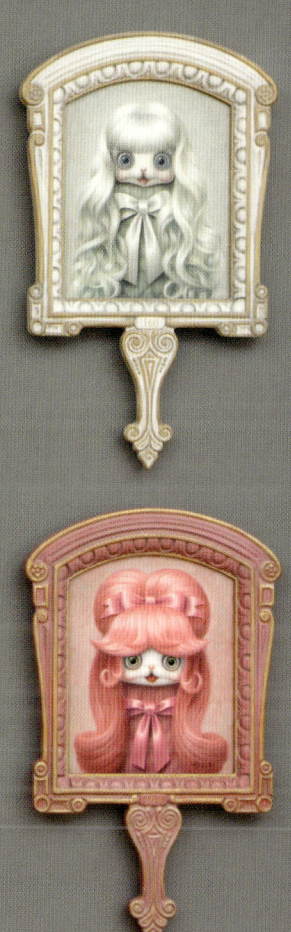

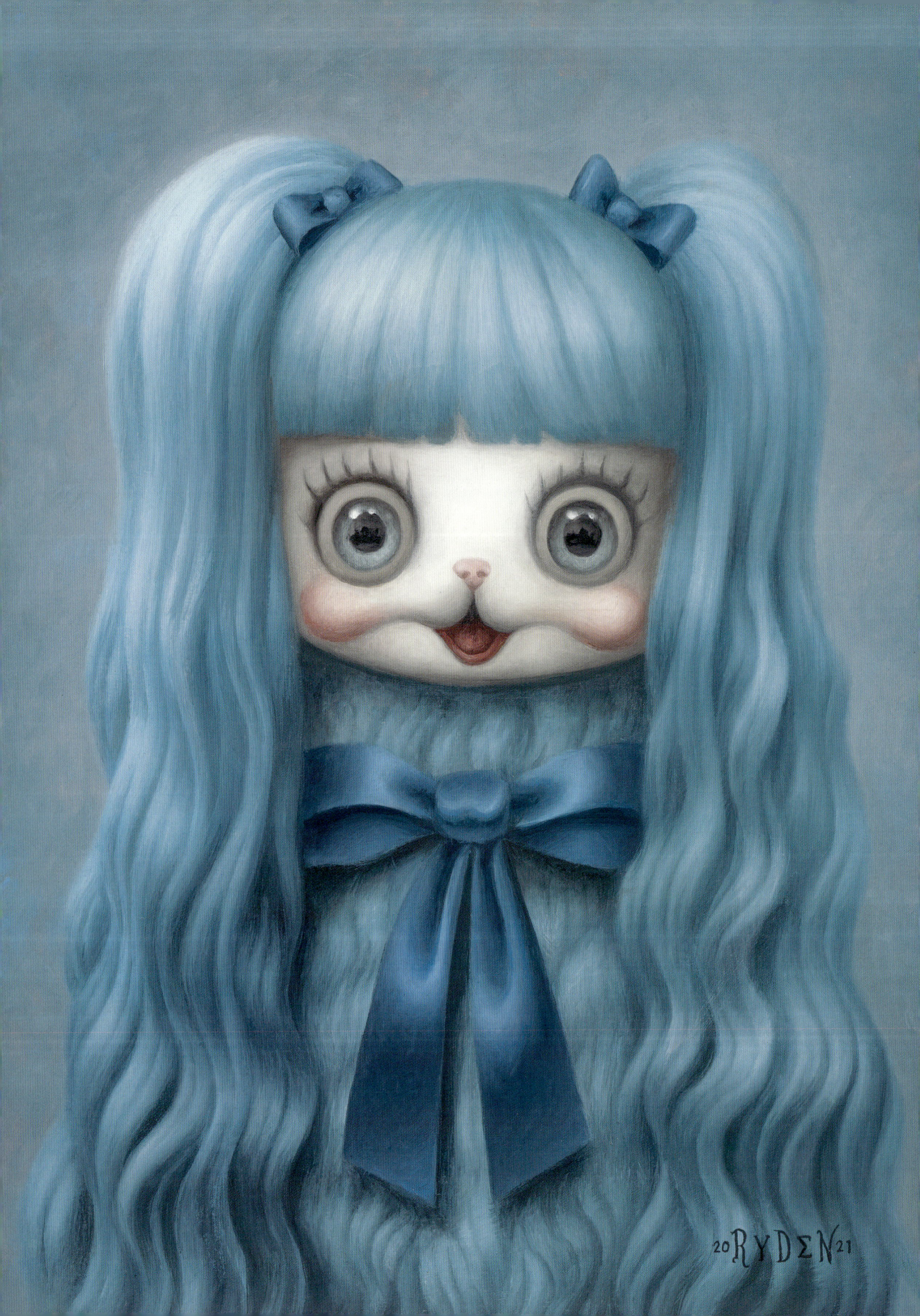

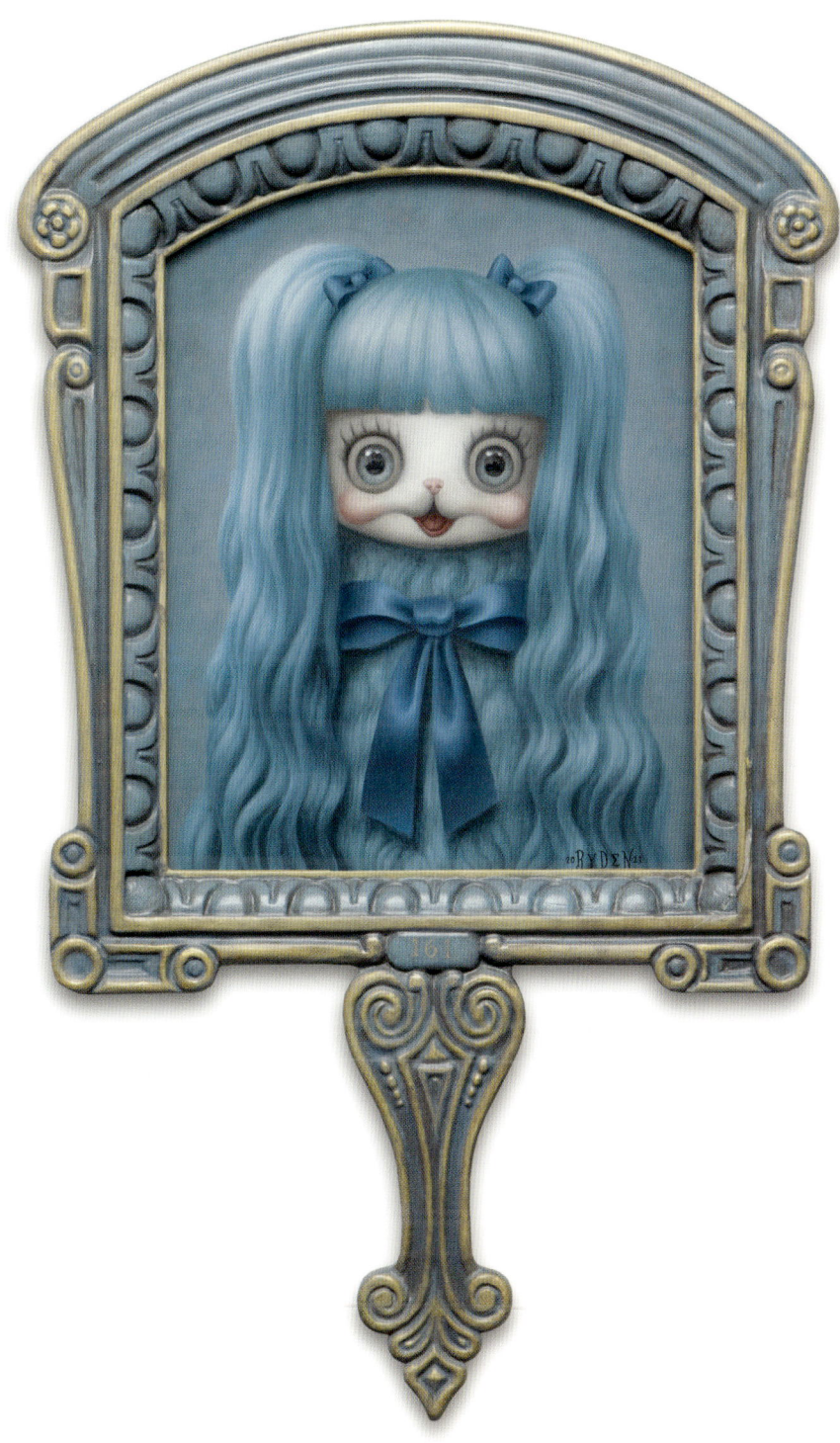

No 161
TAVOLETTA AZZURRI
(BLUE)

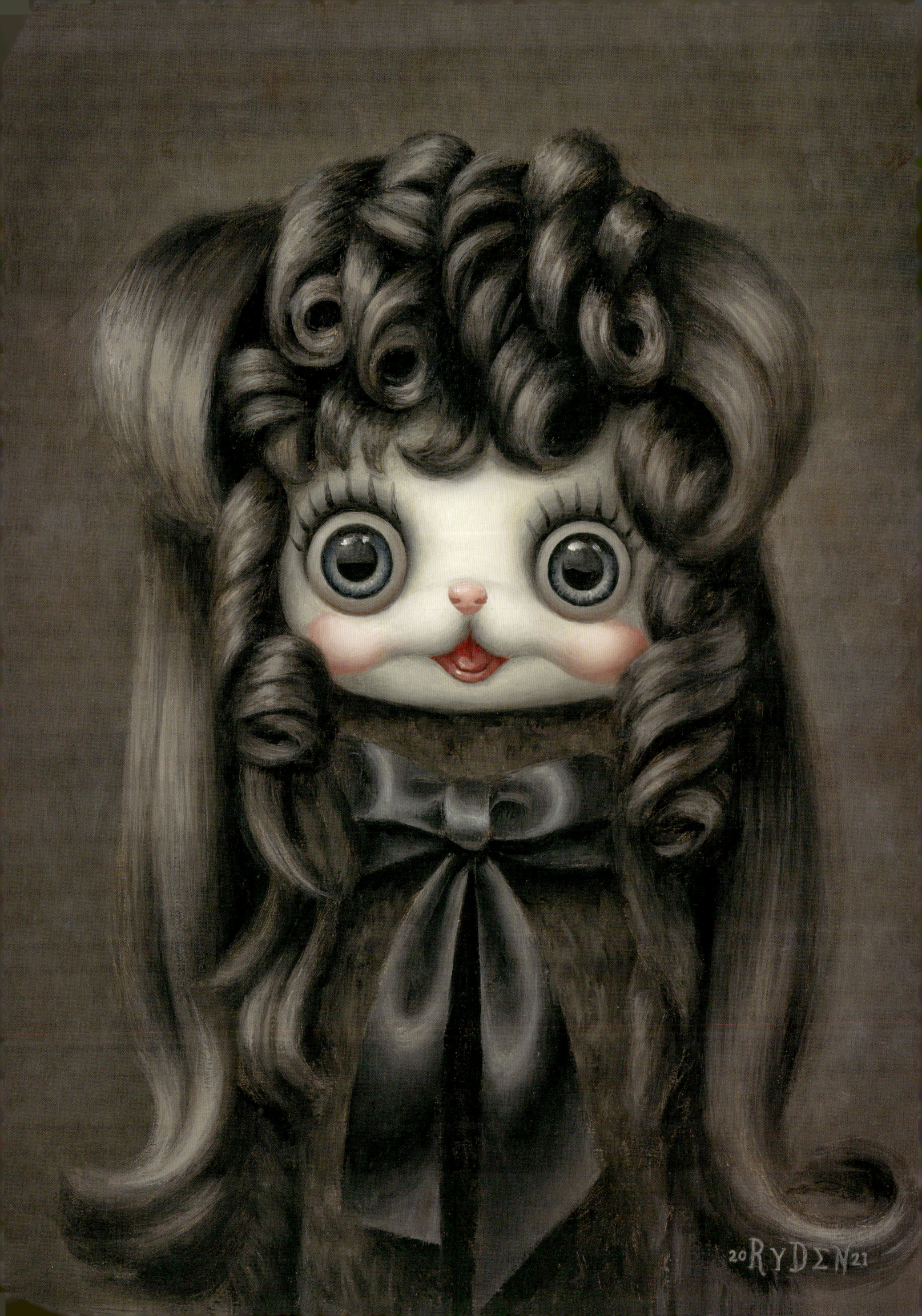

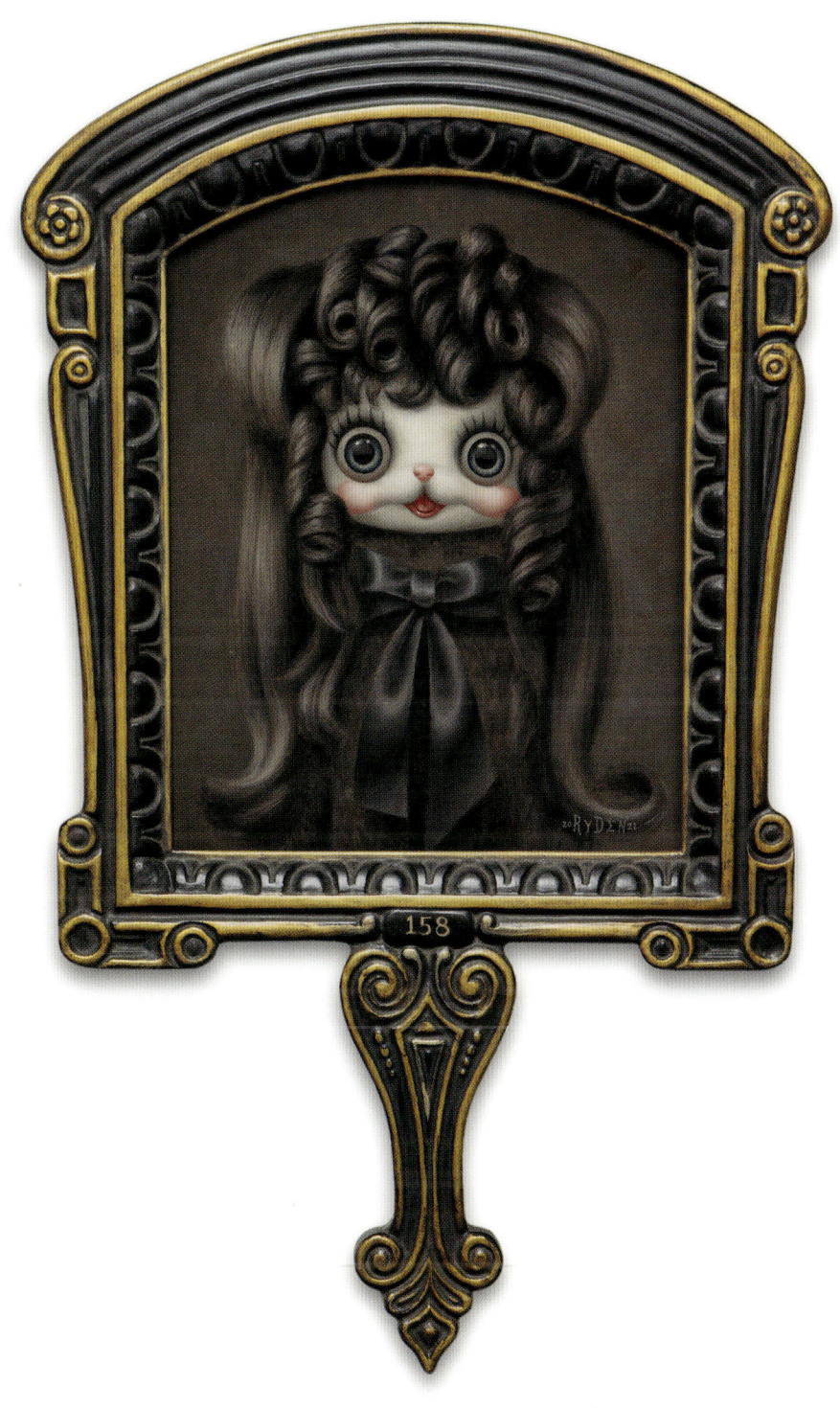

No 158
TAVOLETTA BRUNA
(BRUNETTE)

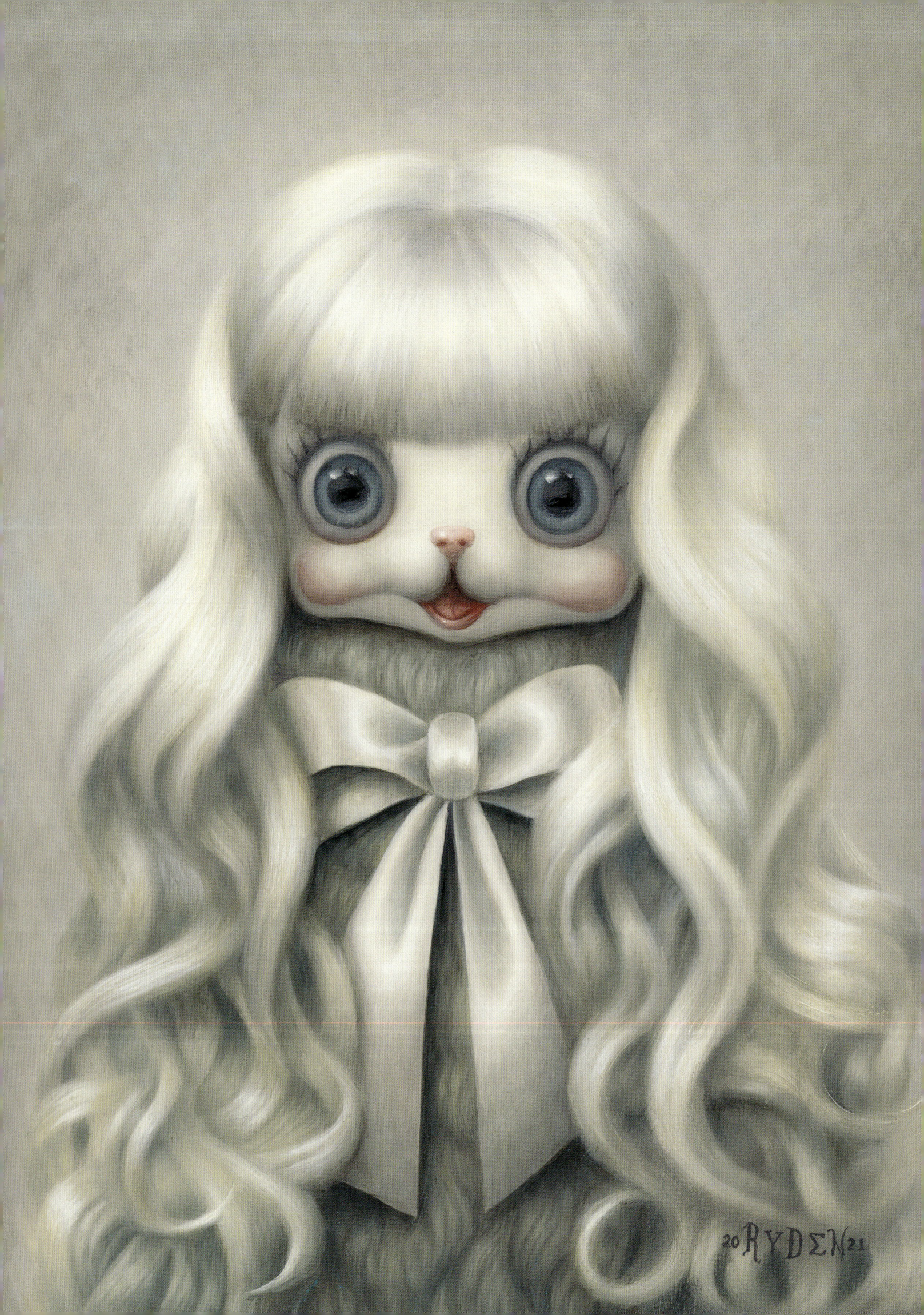

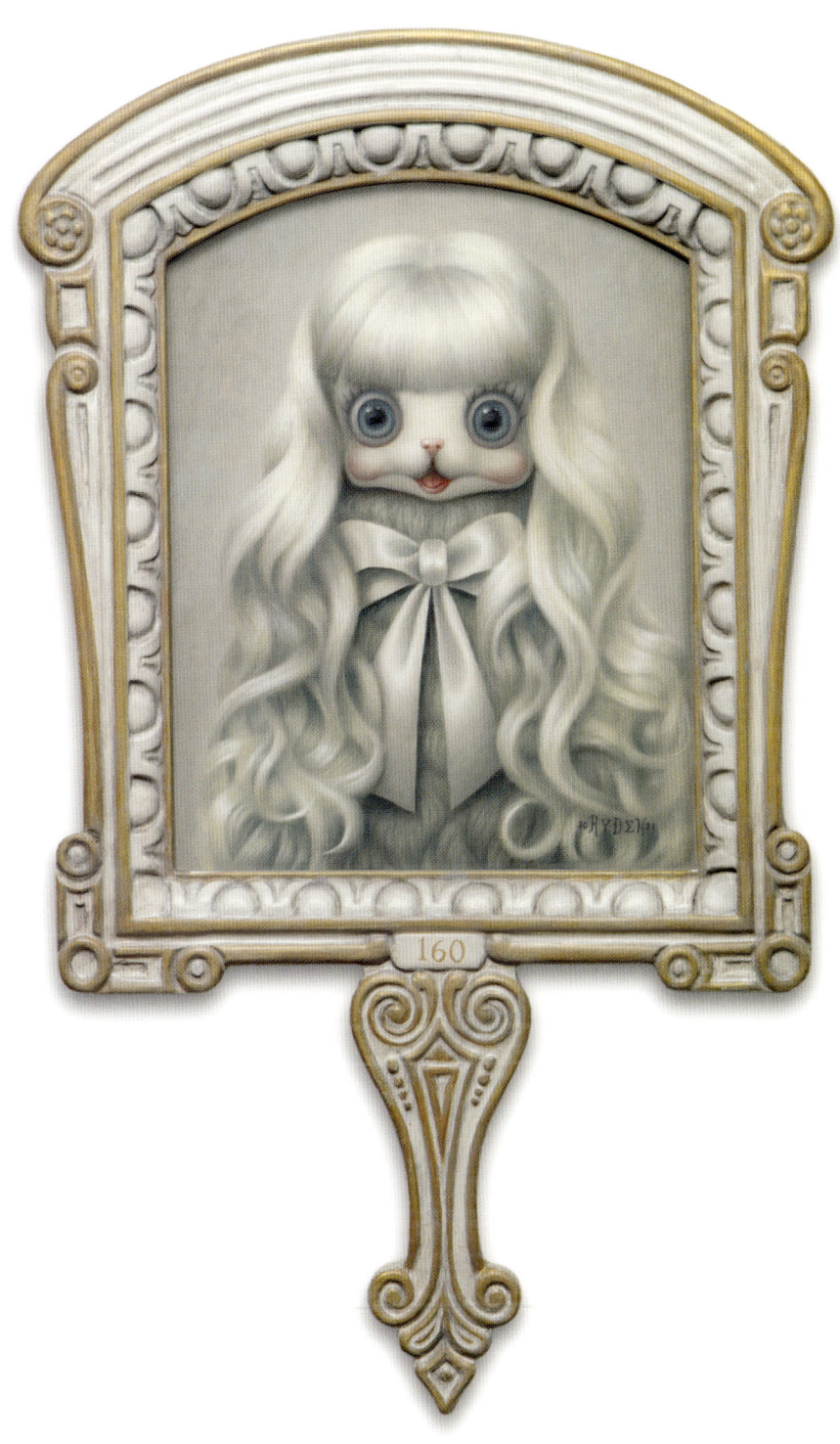

No 160
TAVOLETTA BIONDA
(BLONDE)

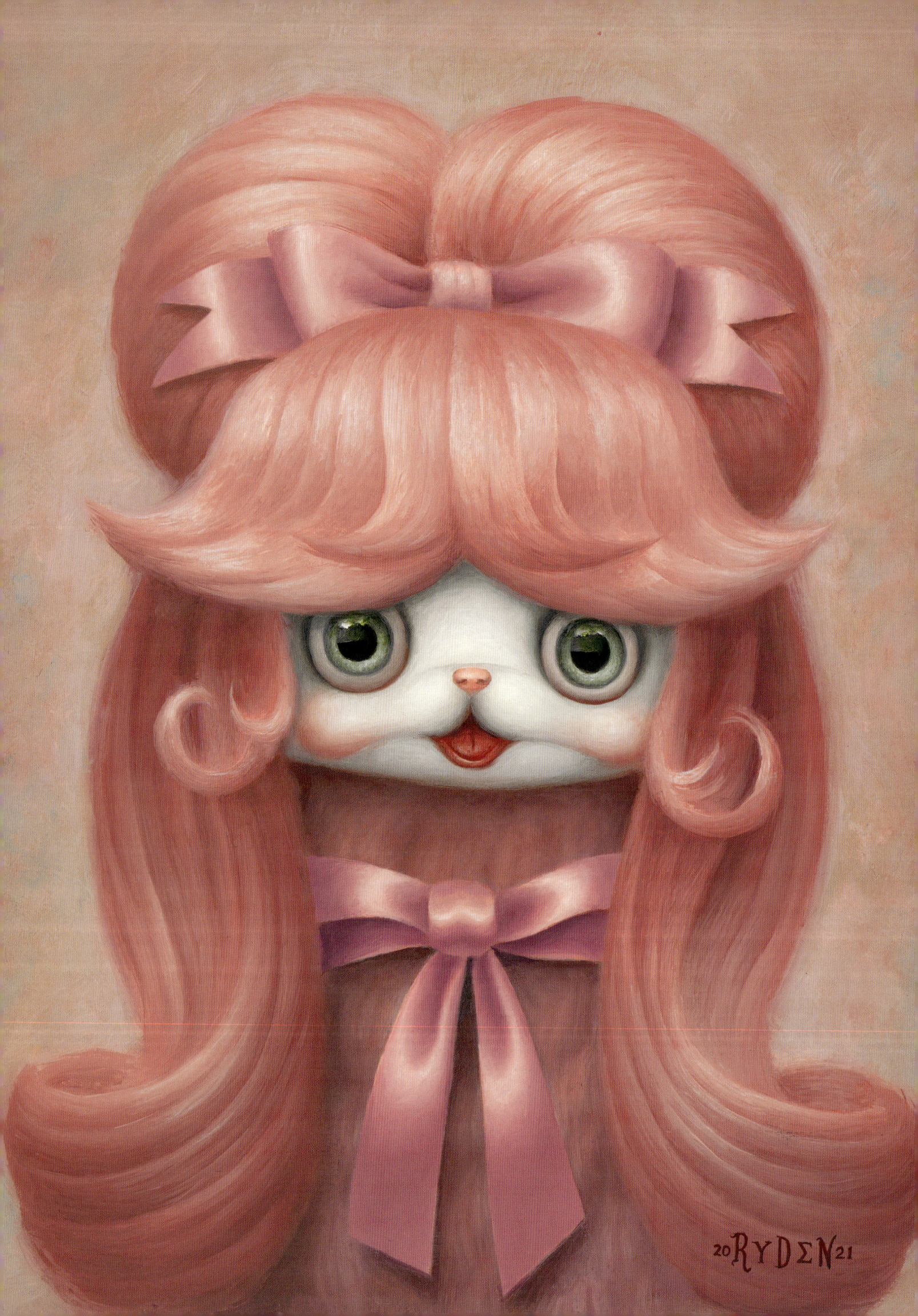

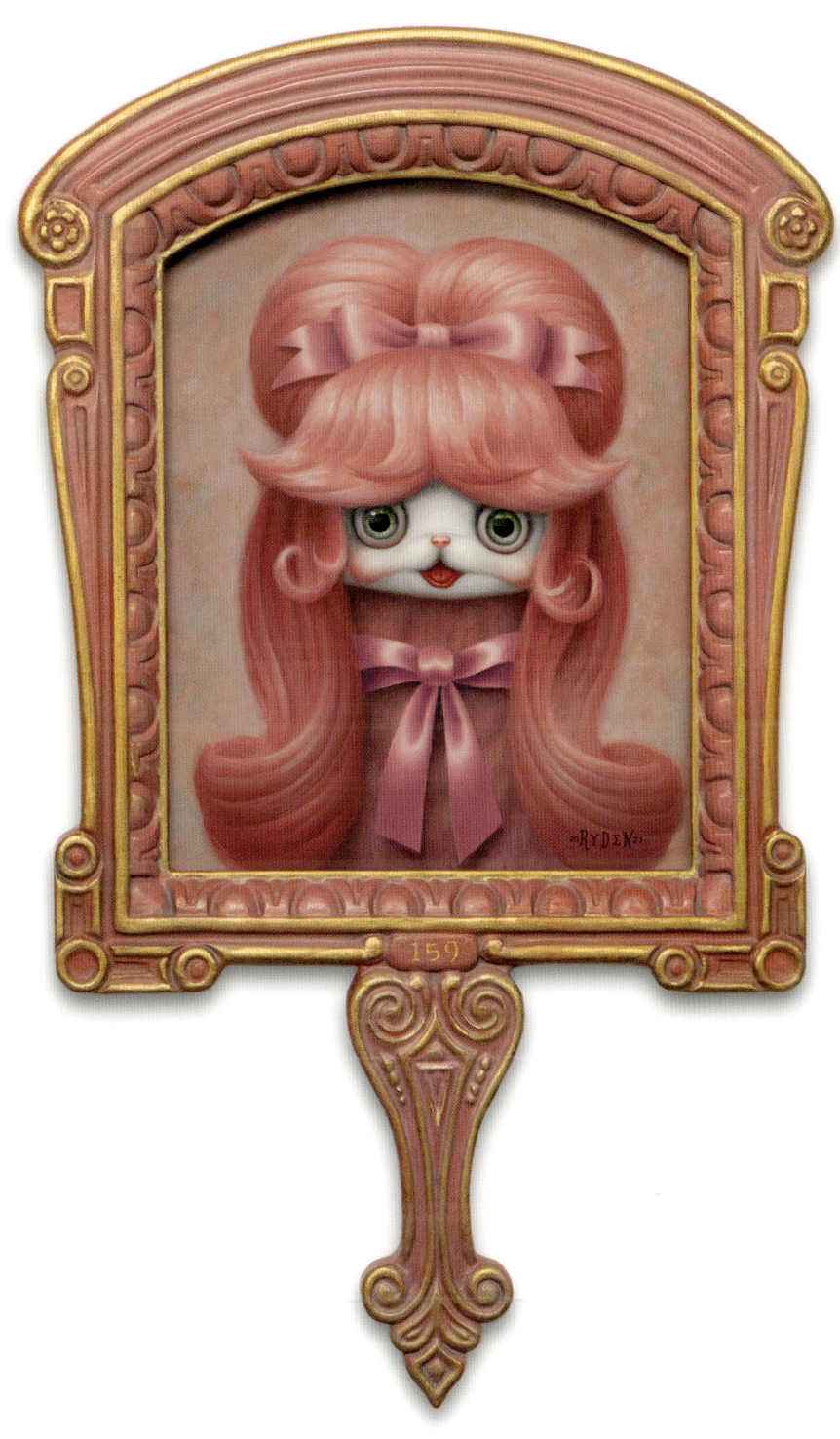

No 159
TAVOLETTA ROSA
(PINK)

No 162
FRATELLO DELLA TAVOLETTA

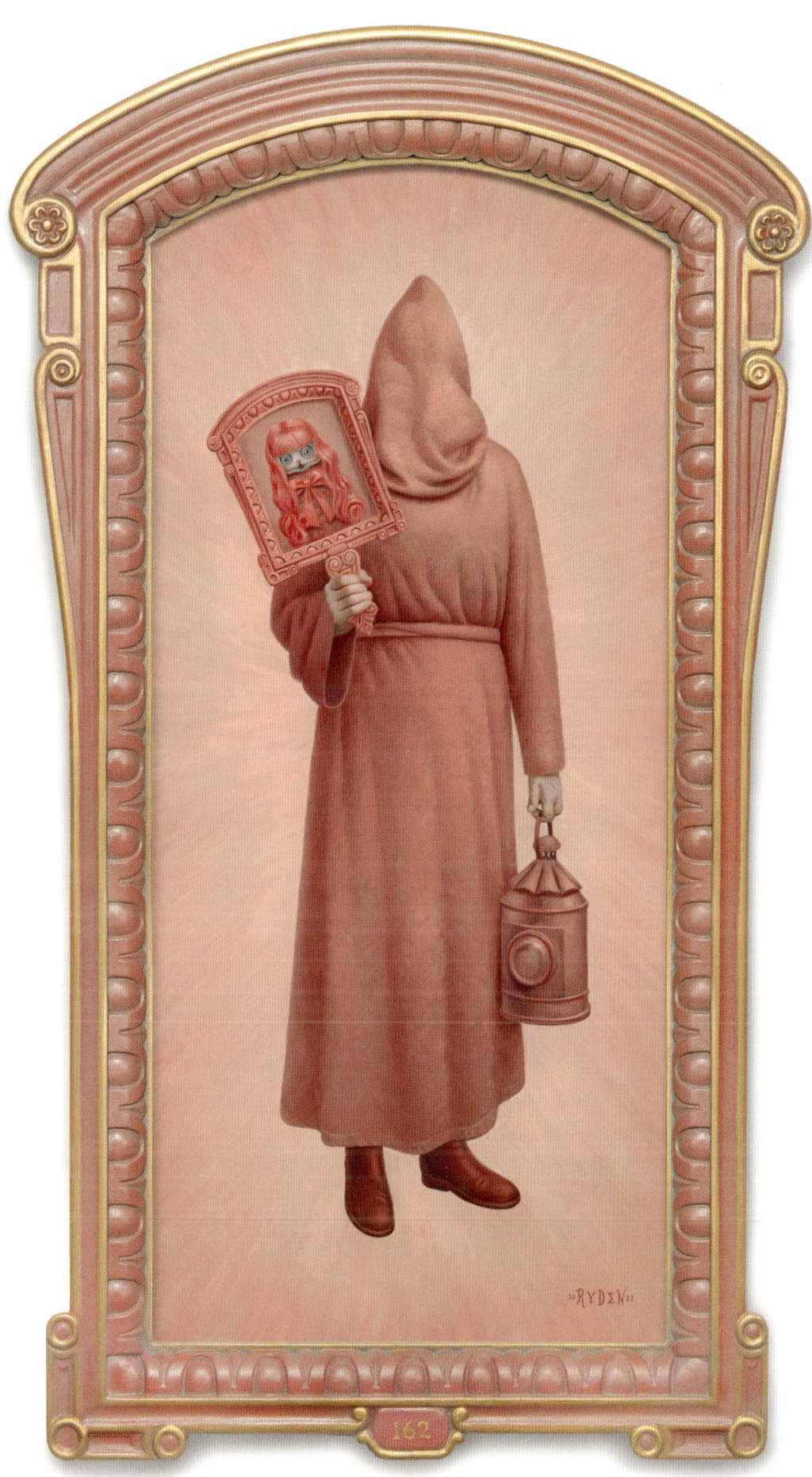

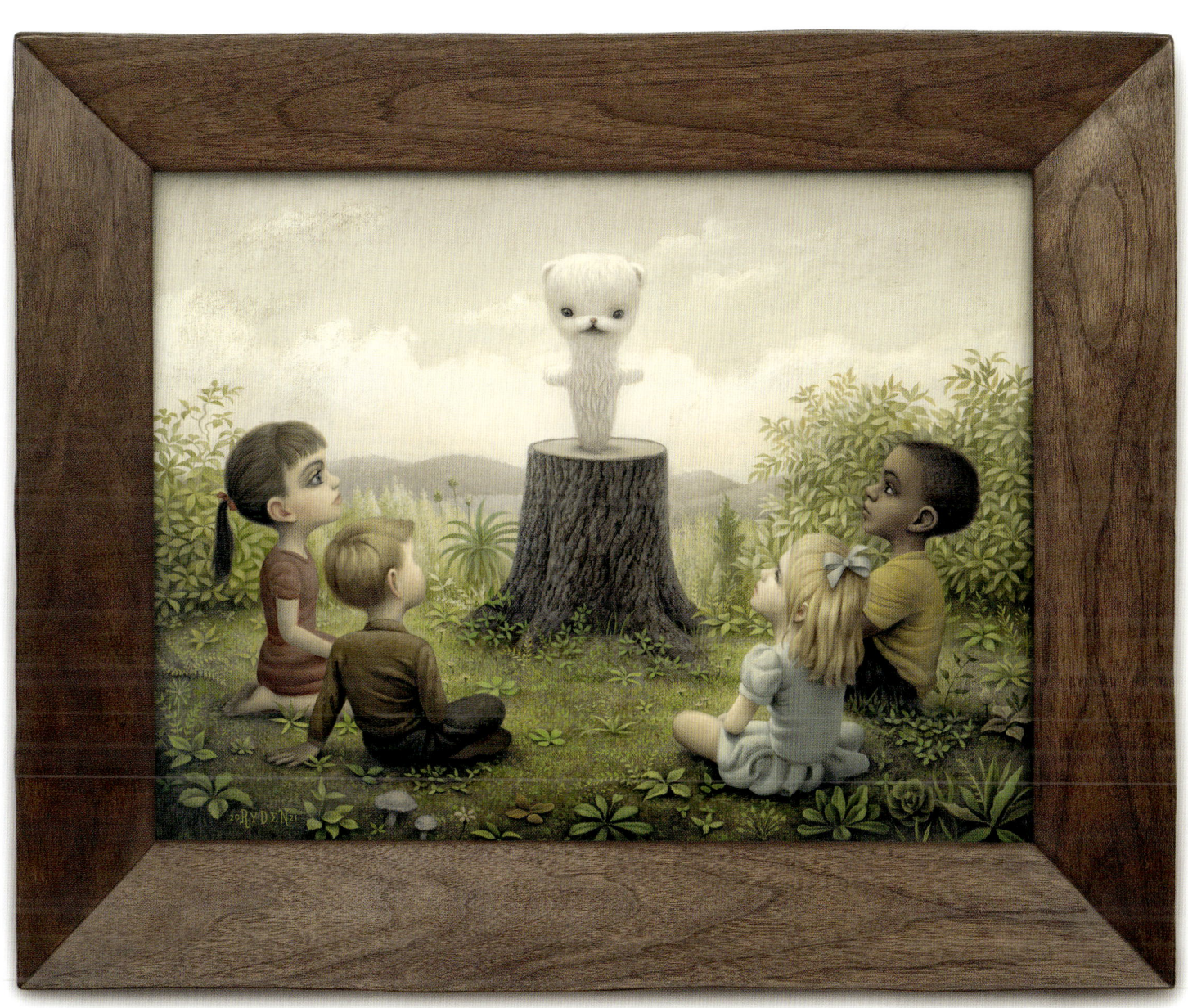

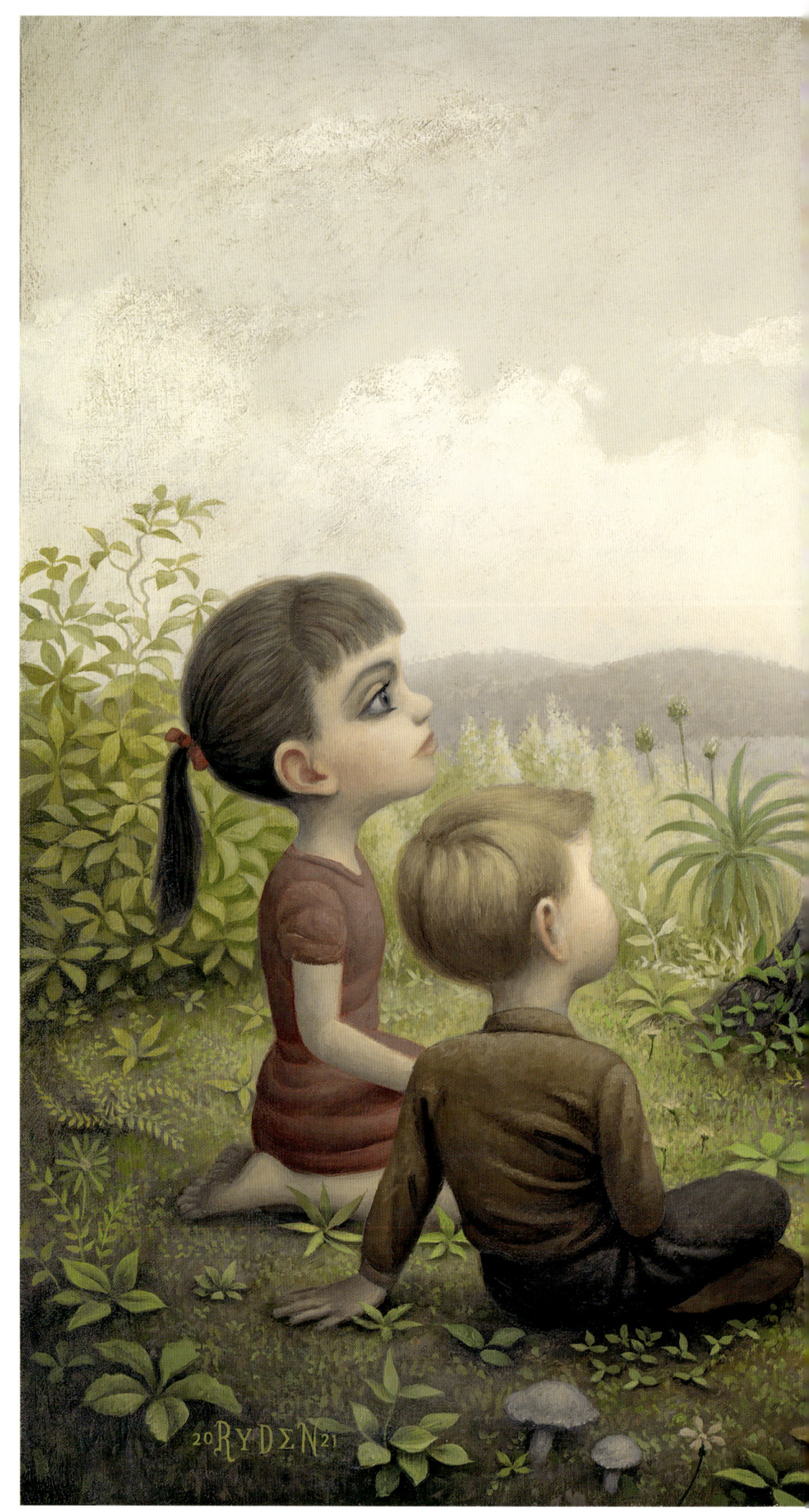

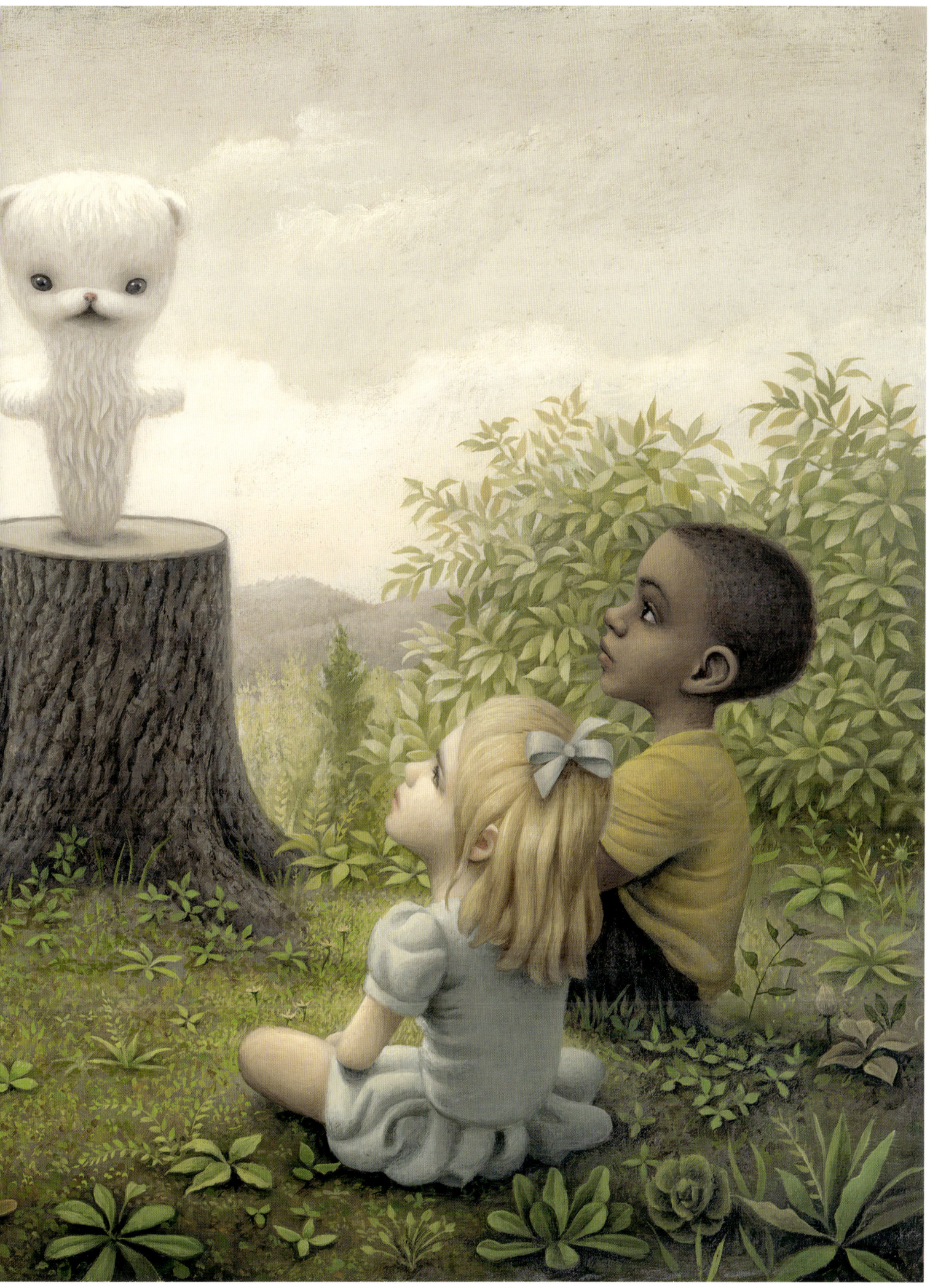

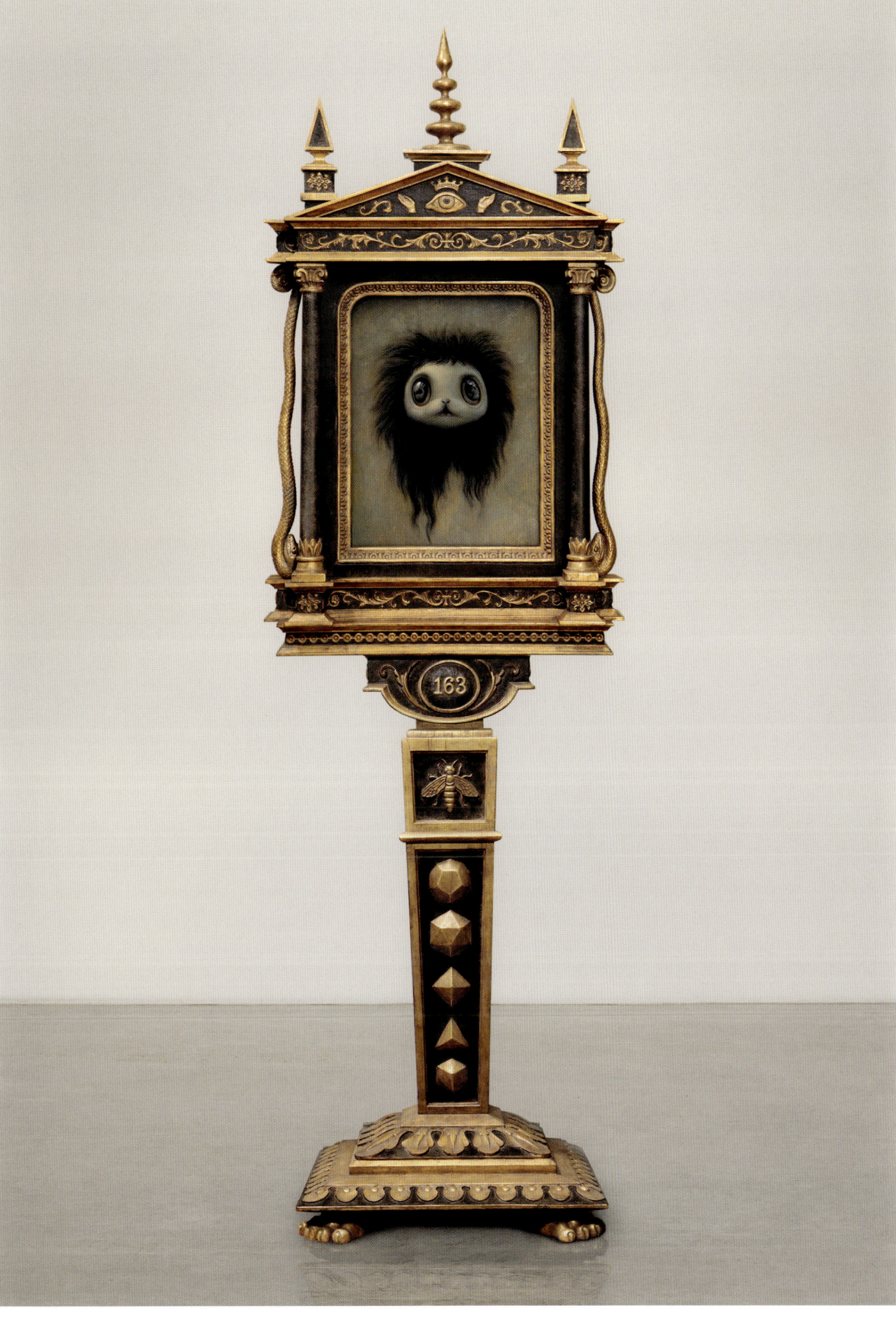

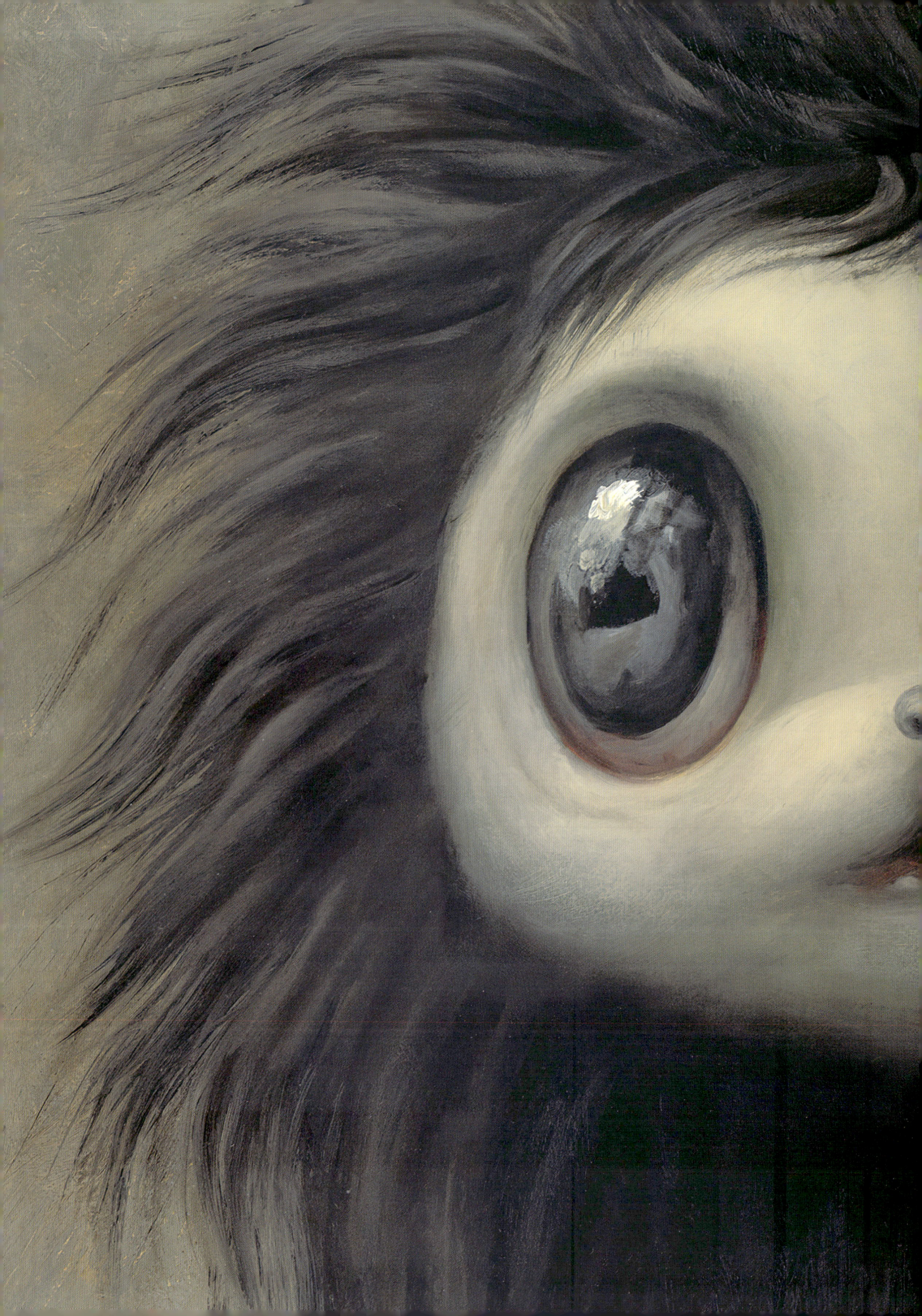

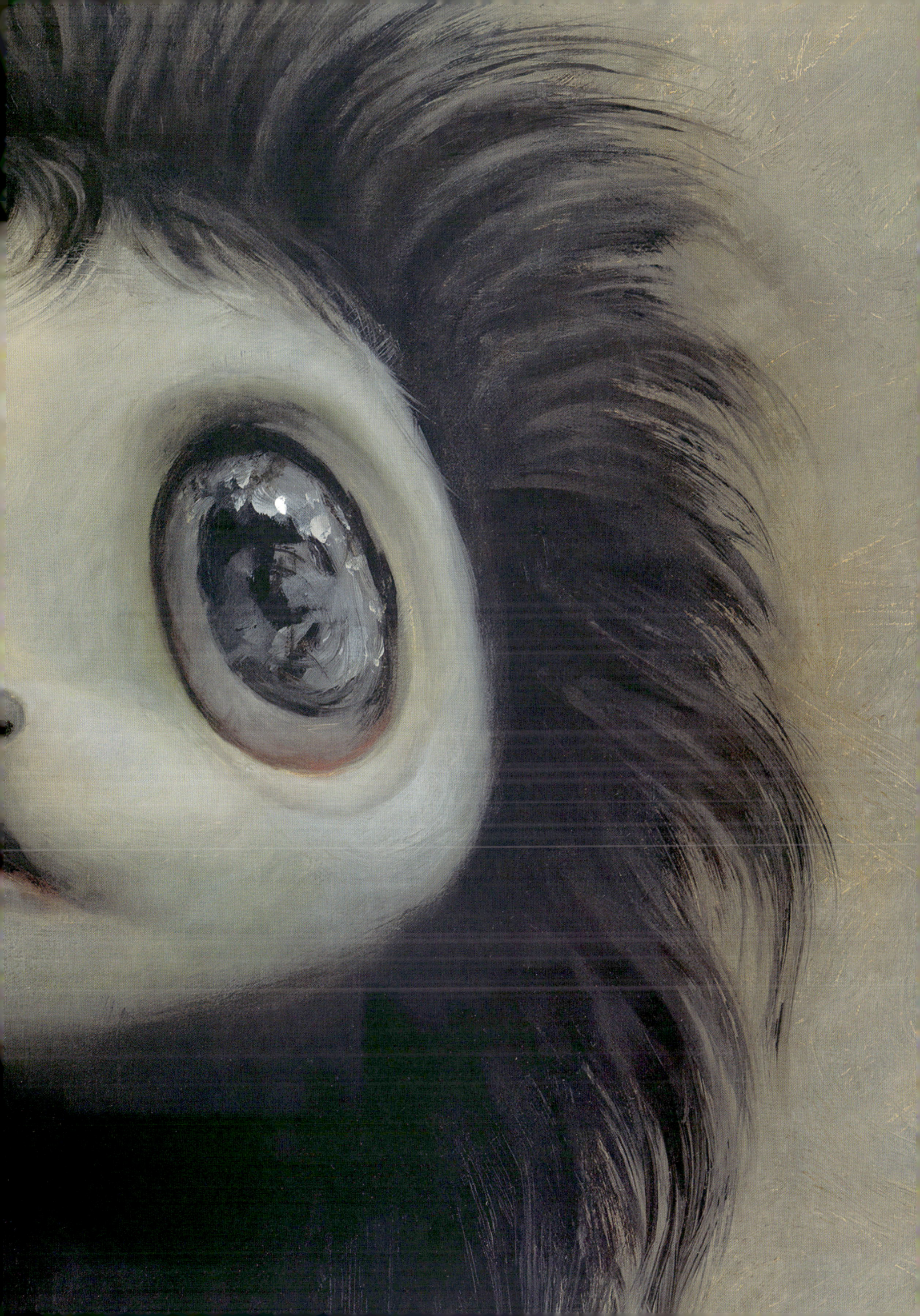

No 165
KAMI

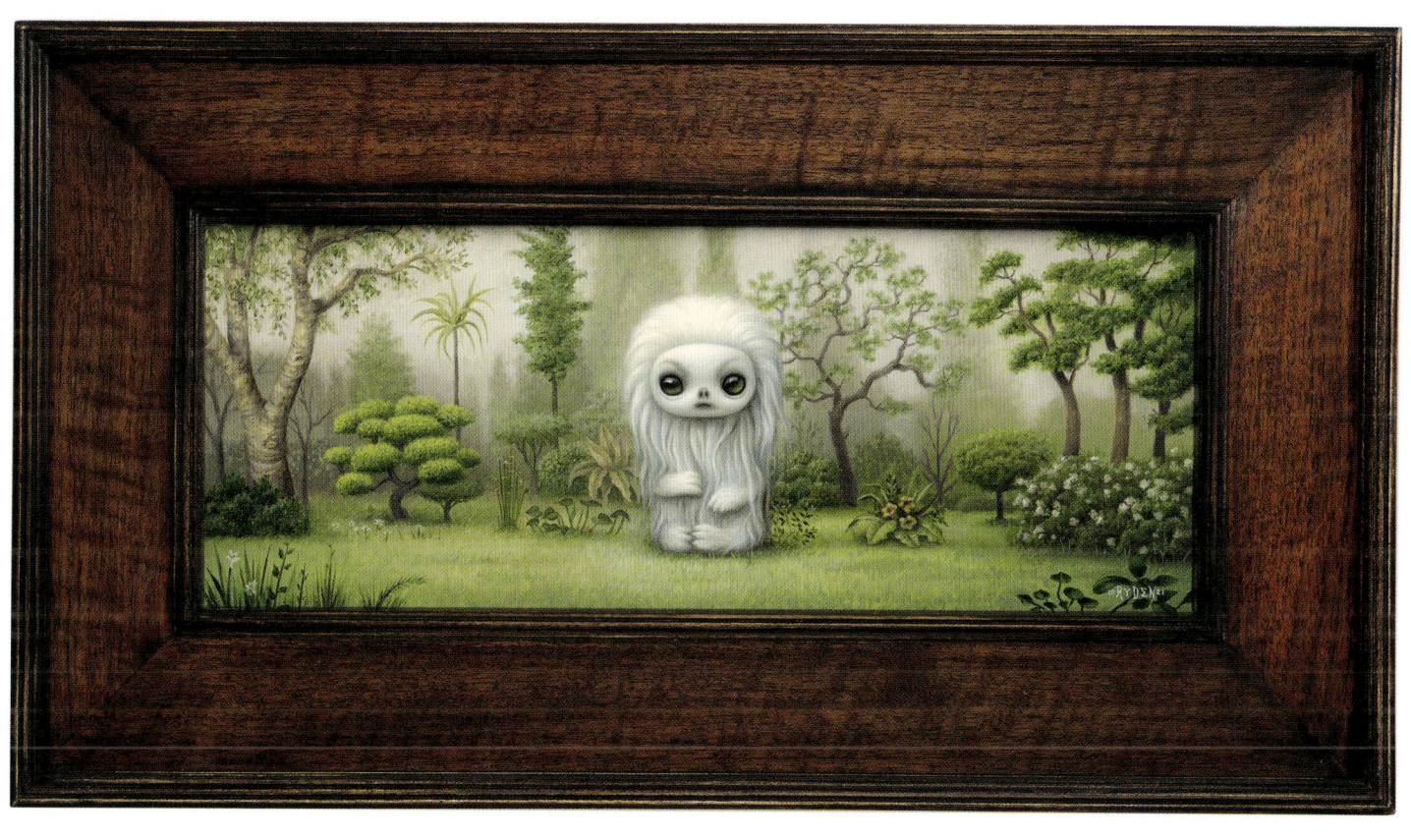

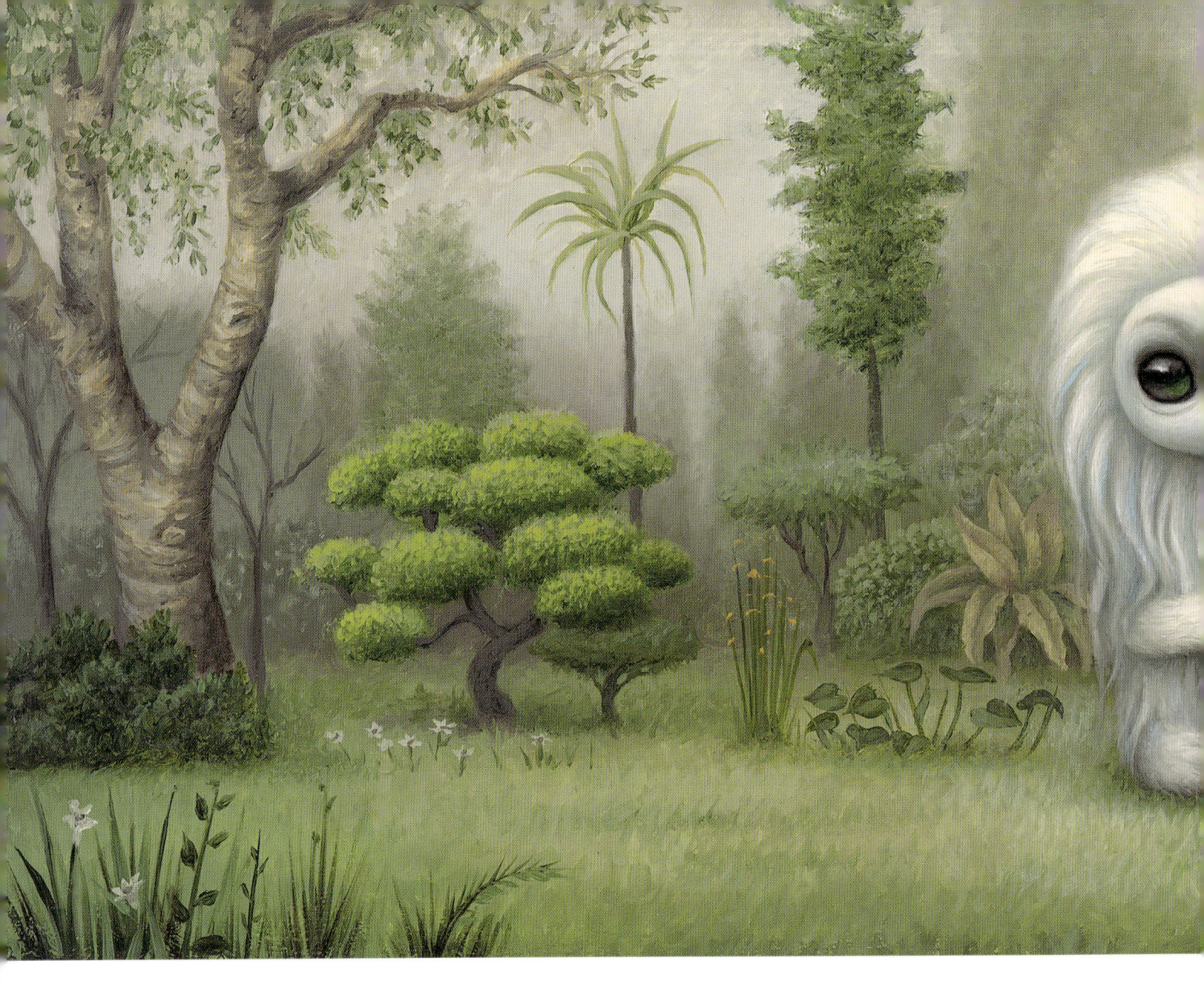

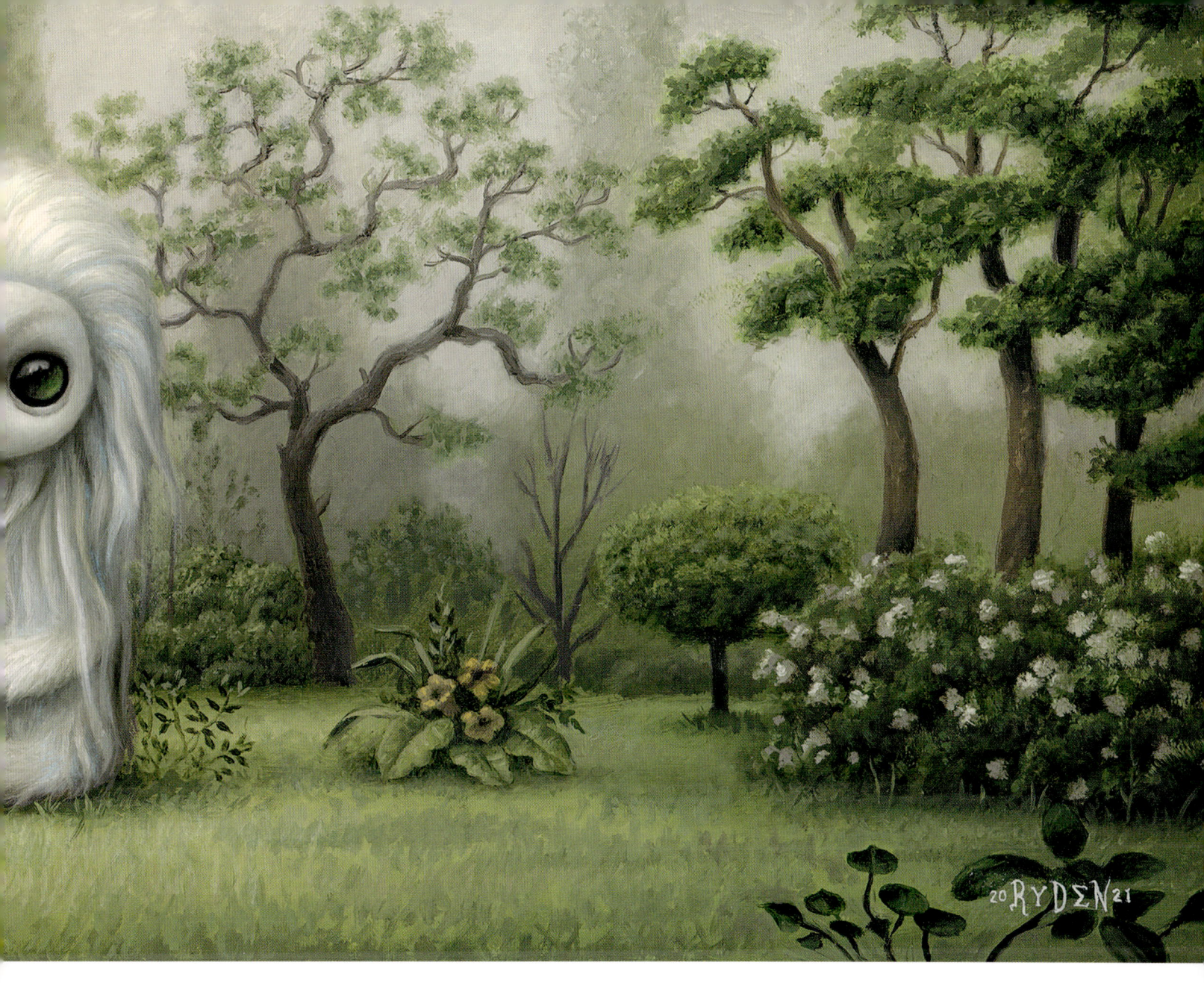

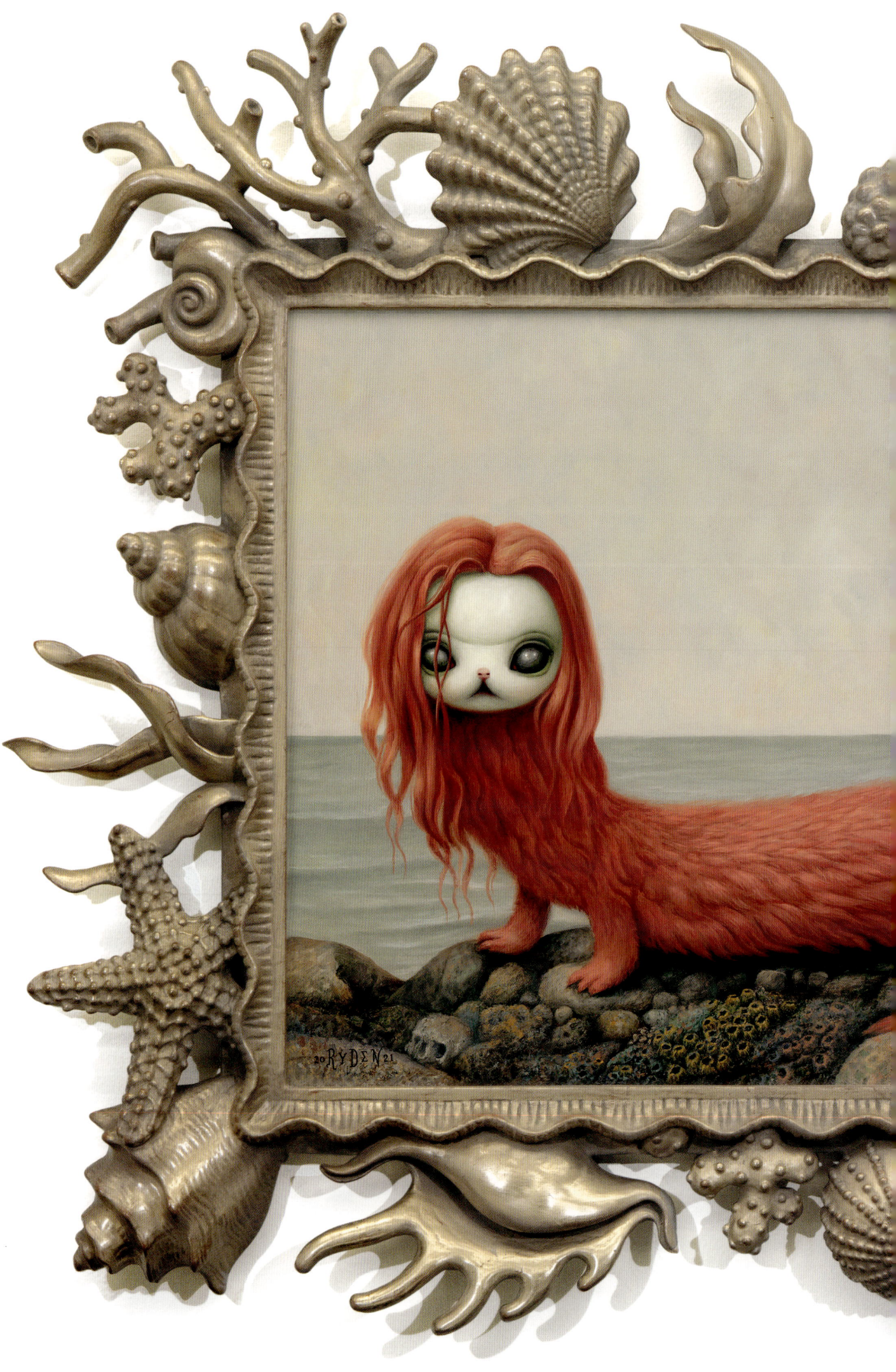

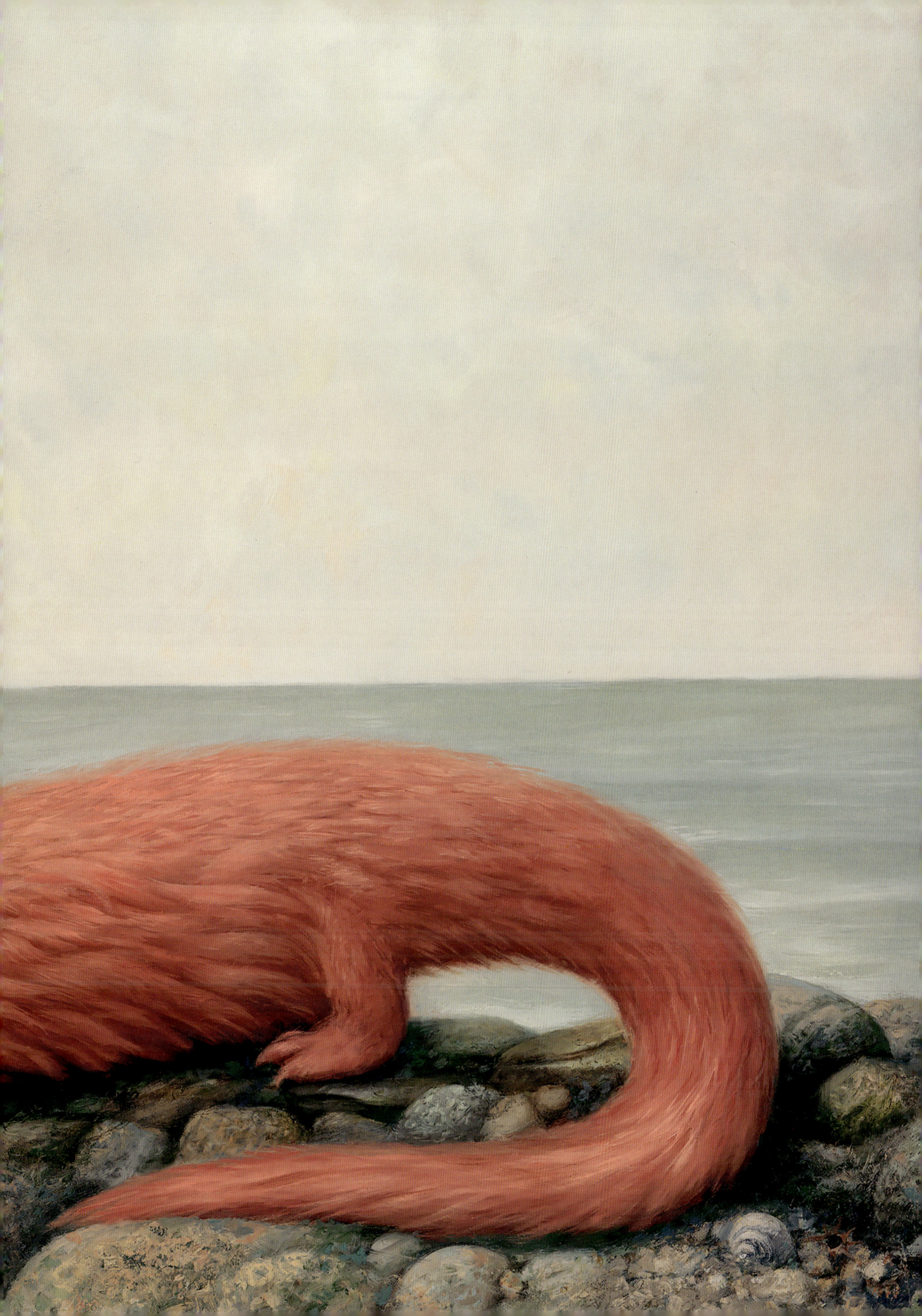

No 157
YUKI THE YOUNG YAK

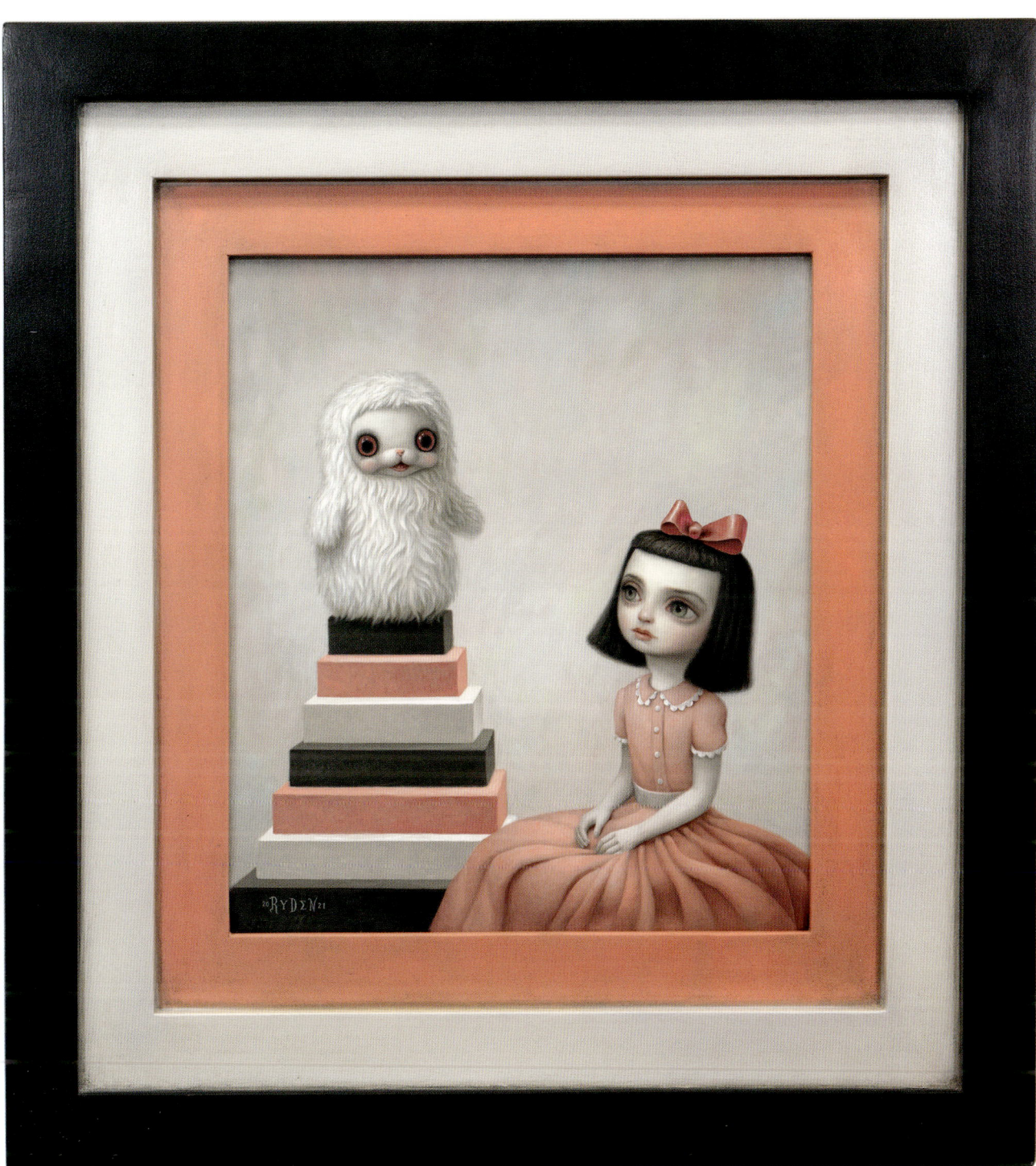

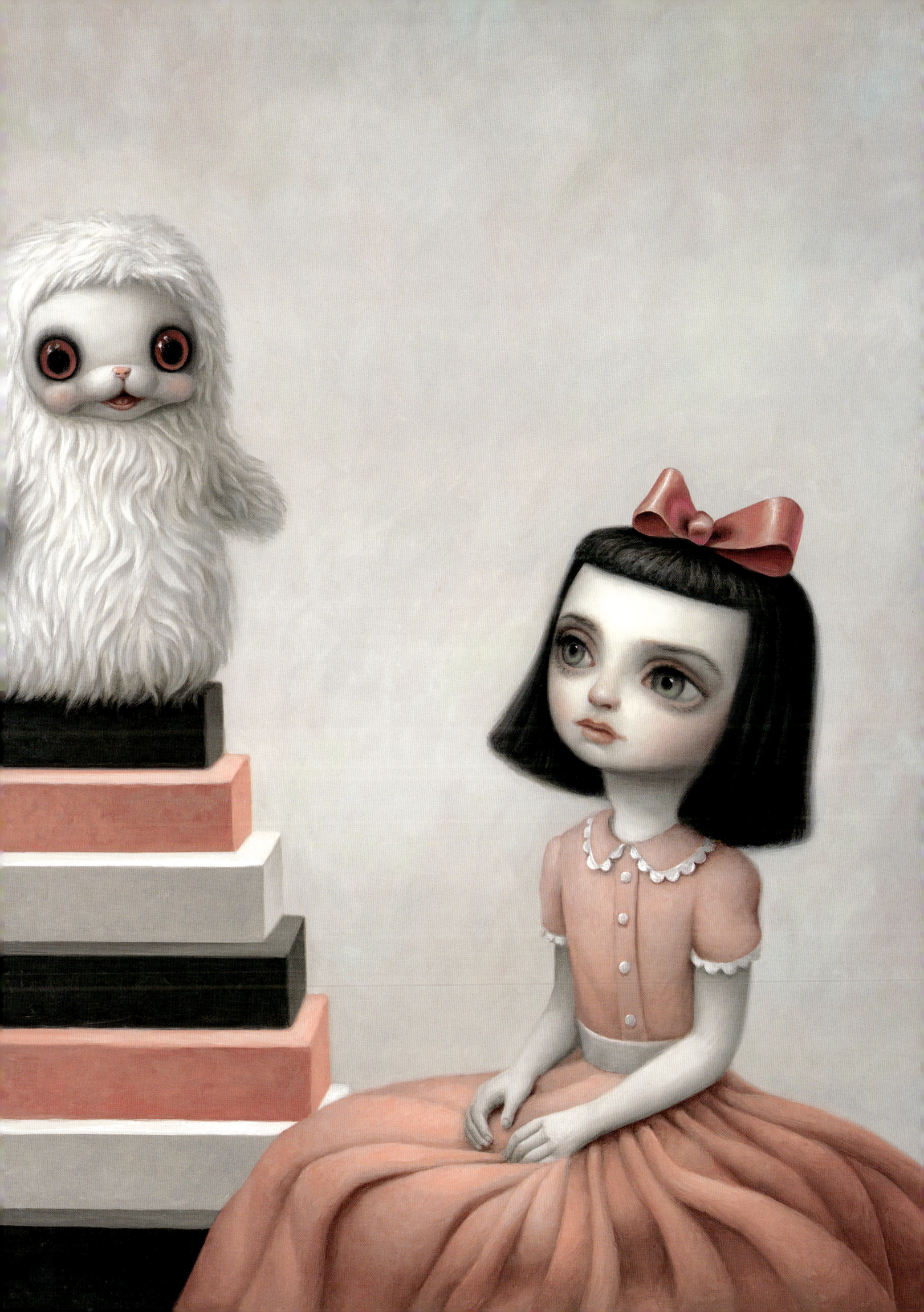

DRAWINGS

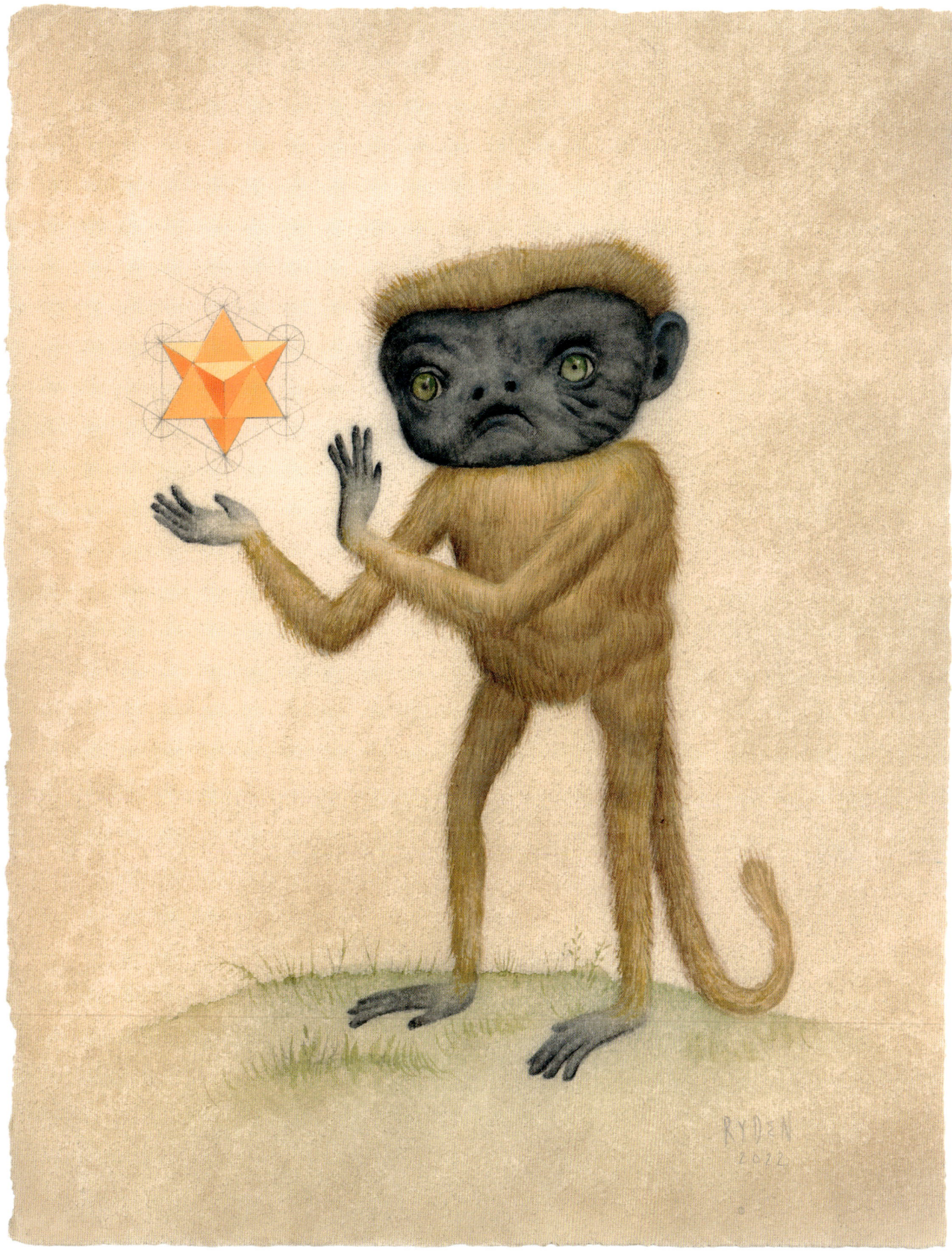

MERKABA EMERALD

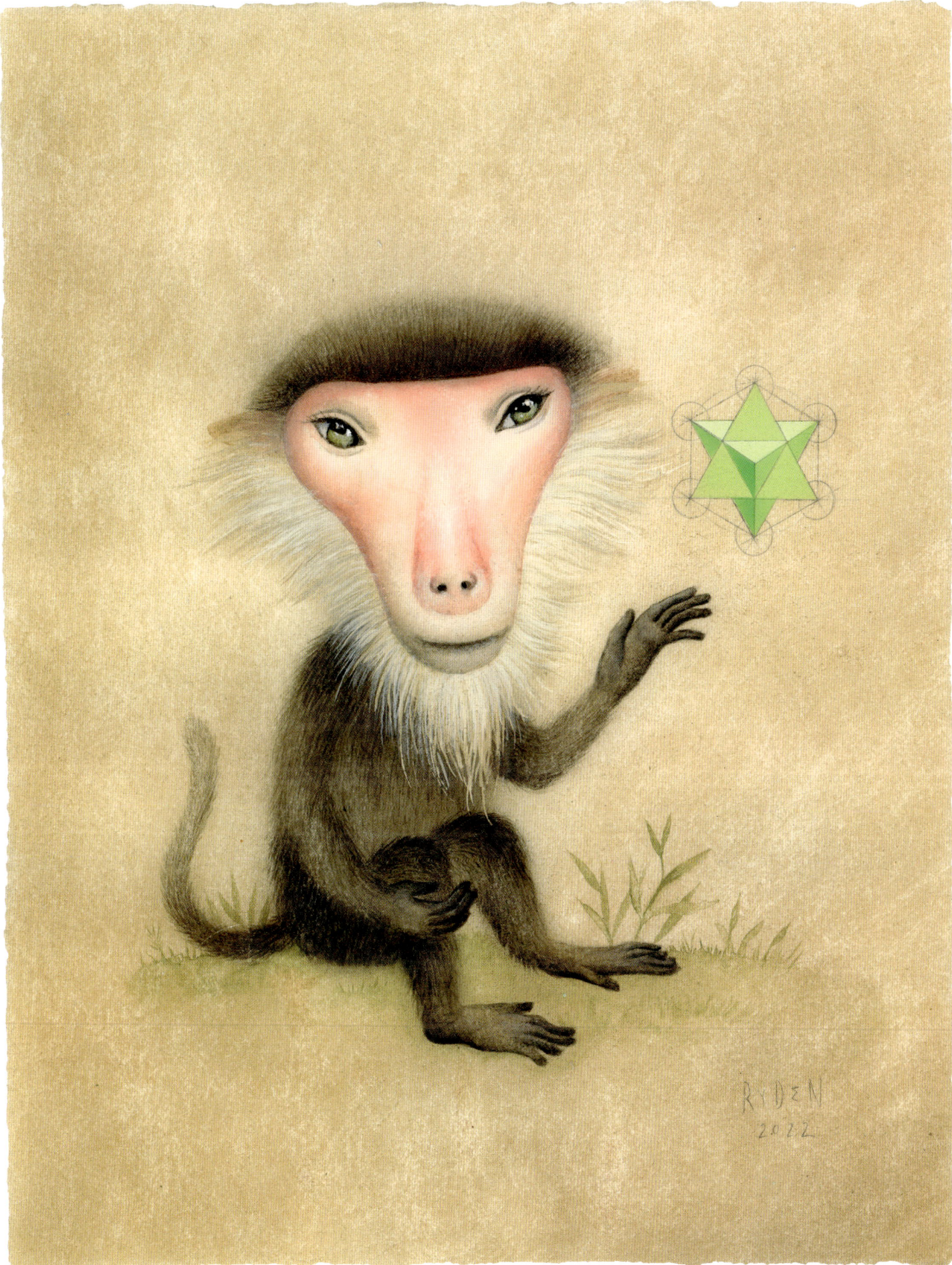

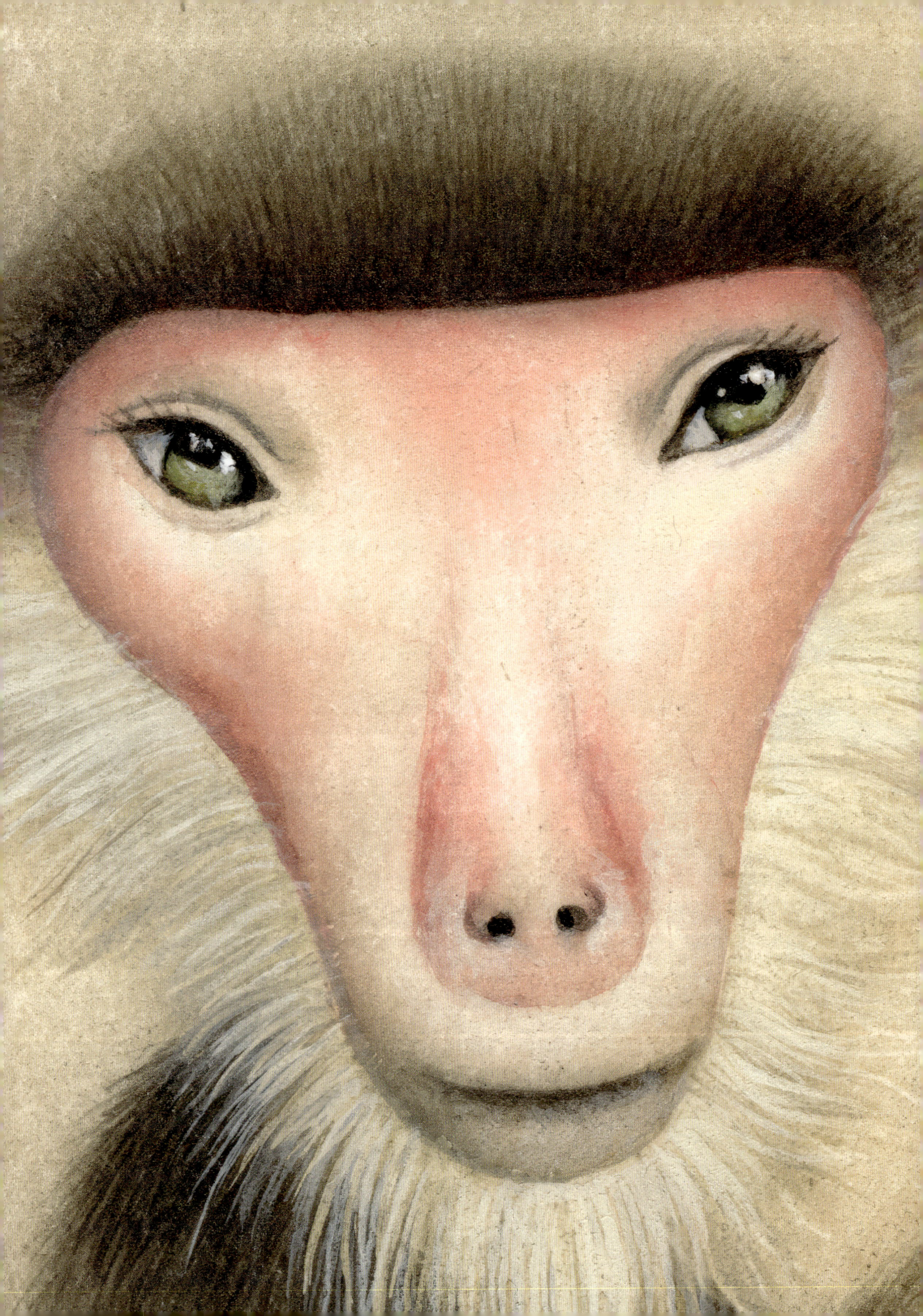

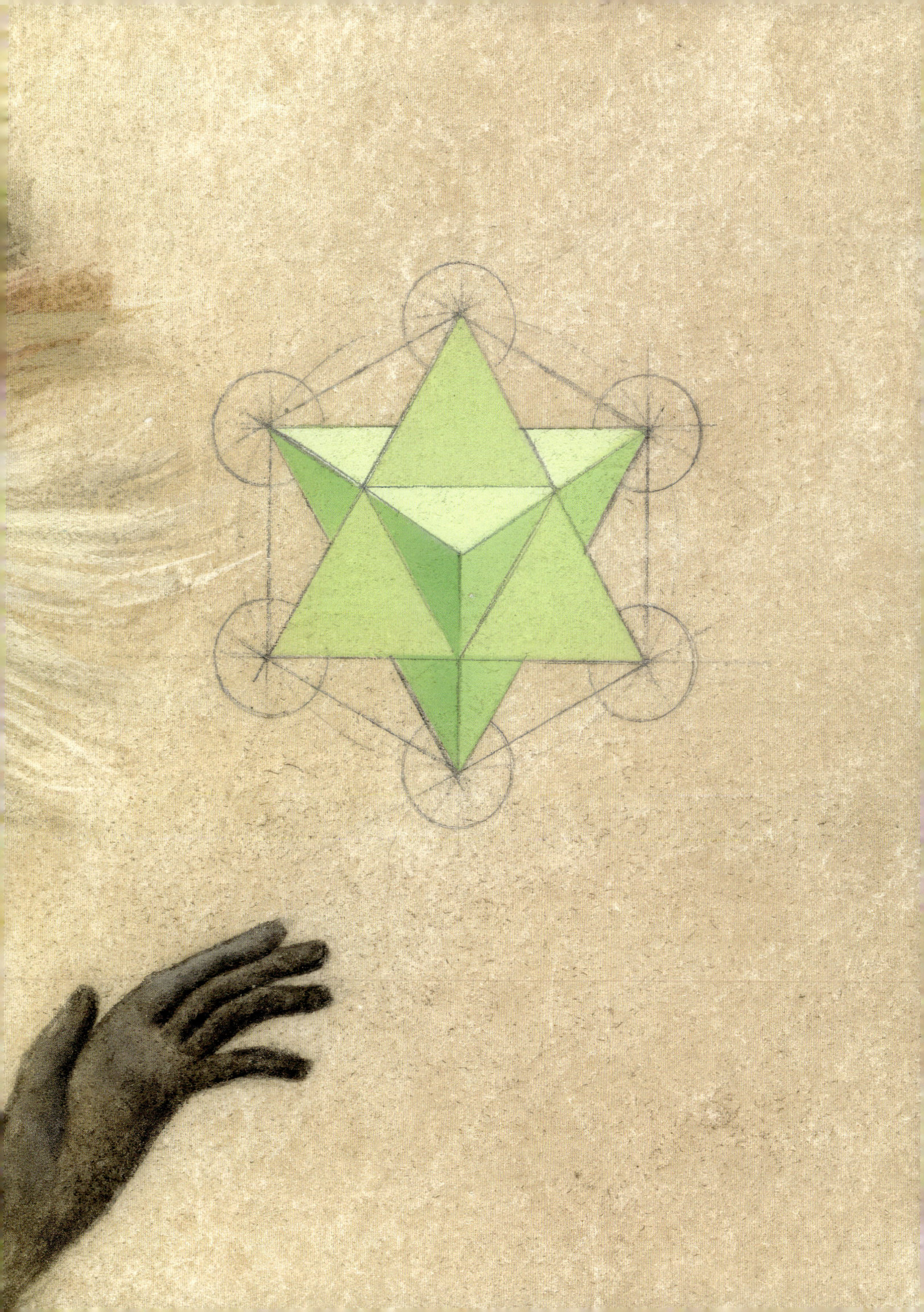

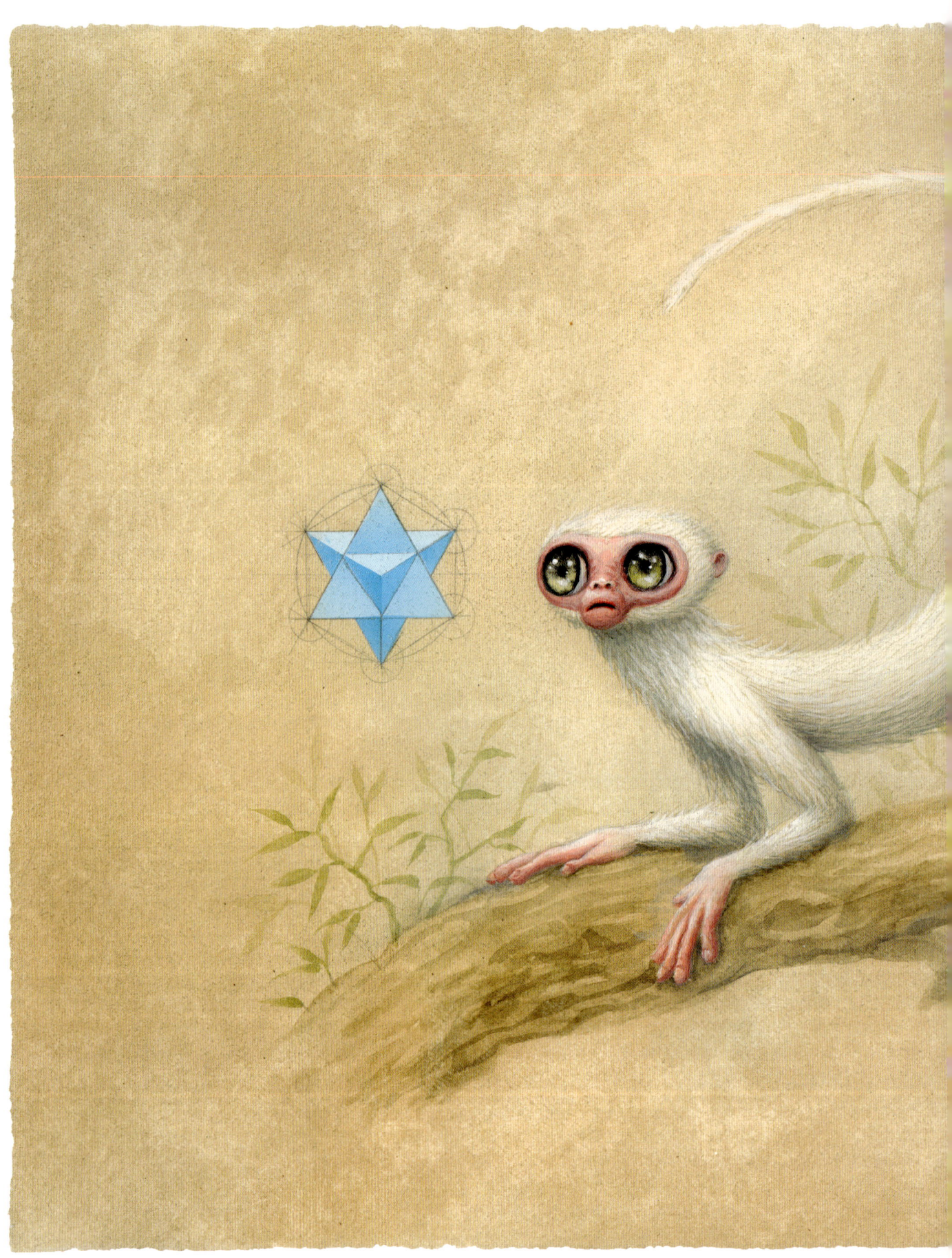

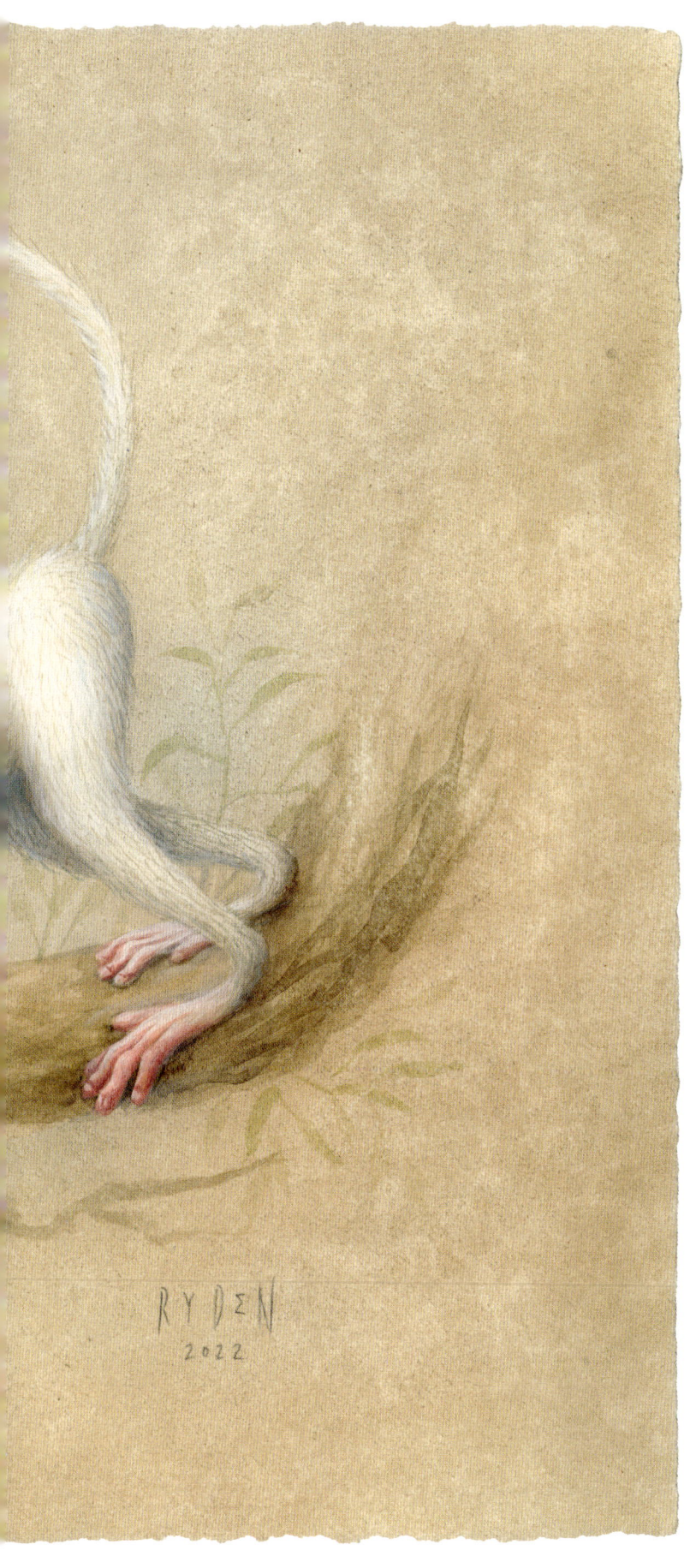

RYDƐN
2022

MERKABA CERULEAN

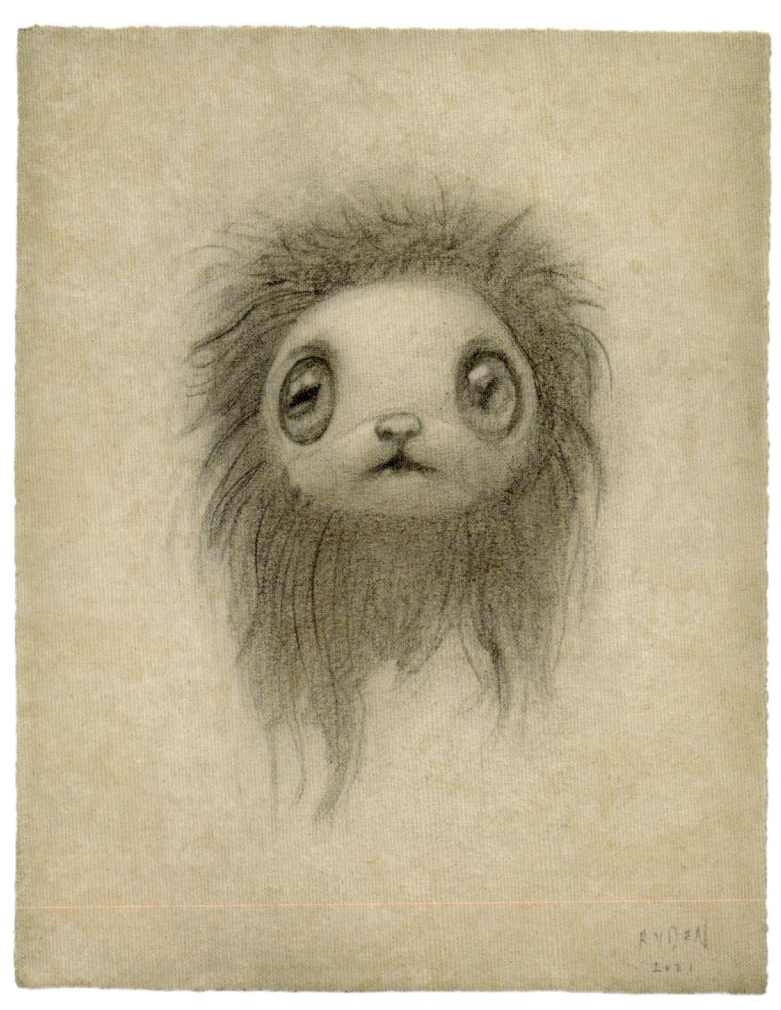

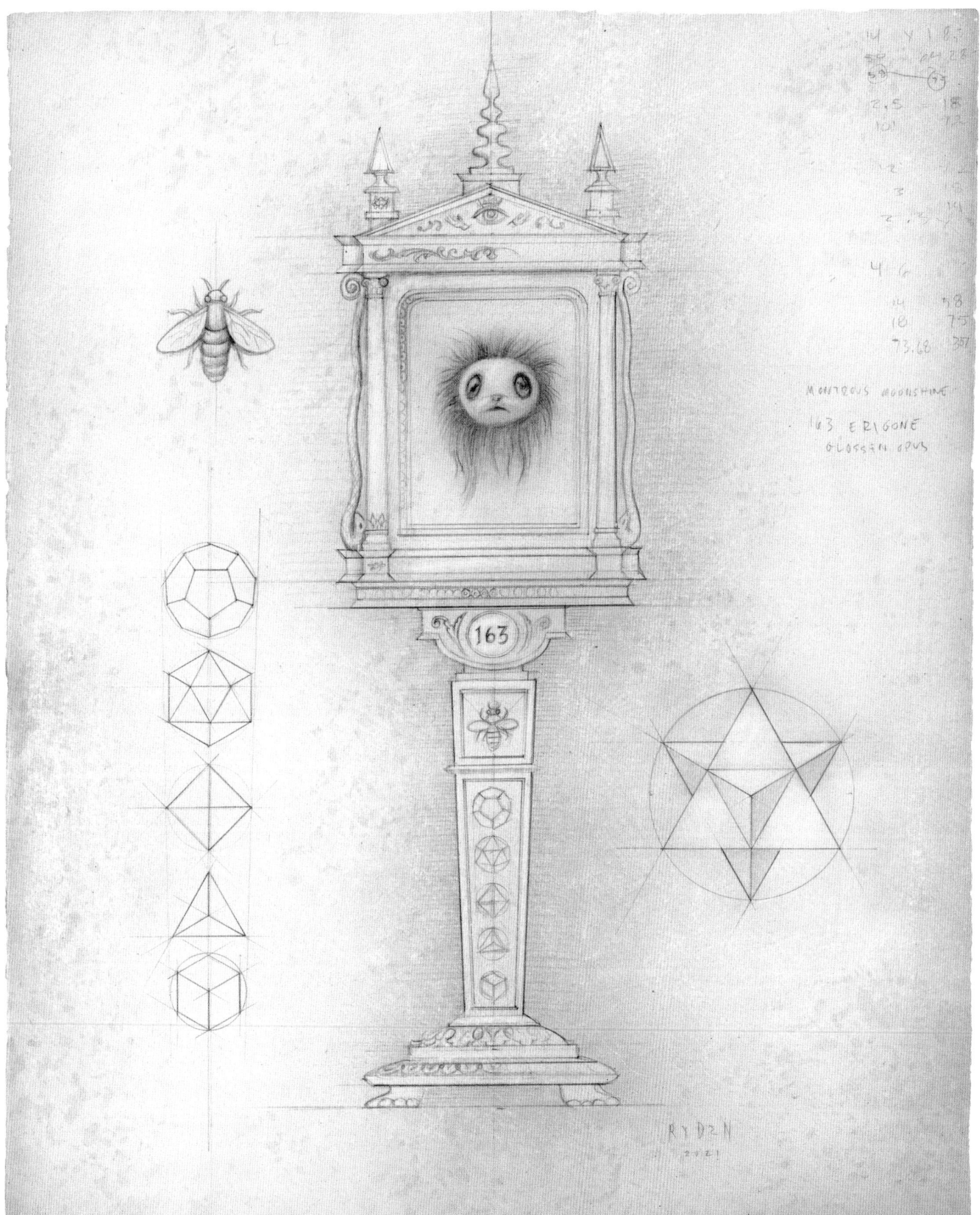

MONSTROUS MOONSHINE

163 ERIGONE
GLOSSEN OPUS

163

RYDEN
2021

FLOATING VISION

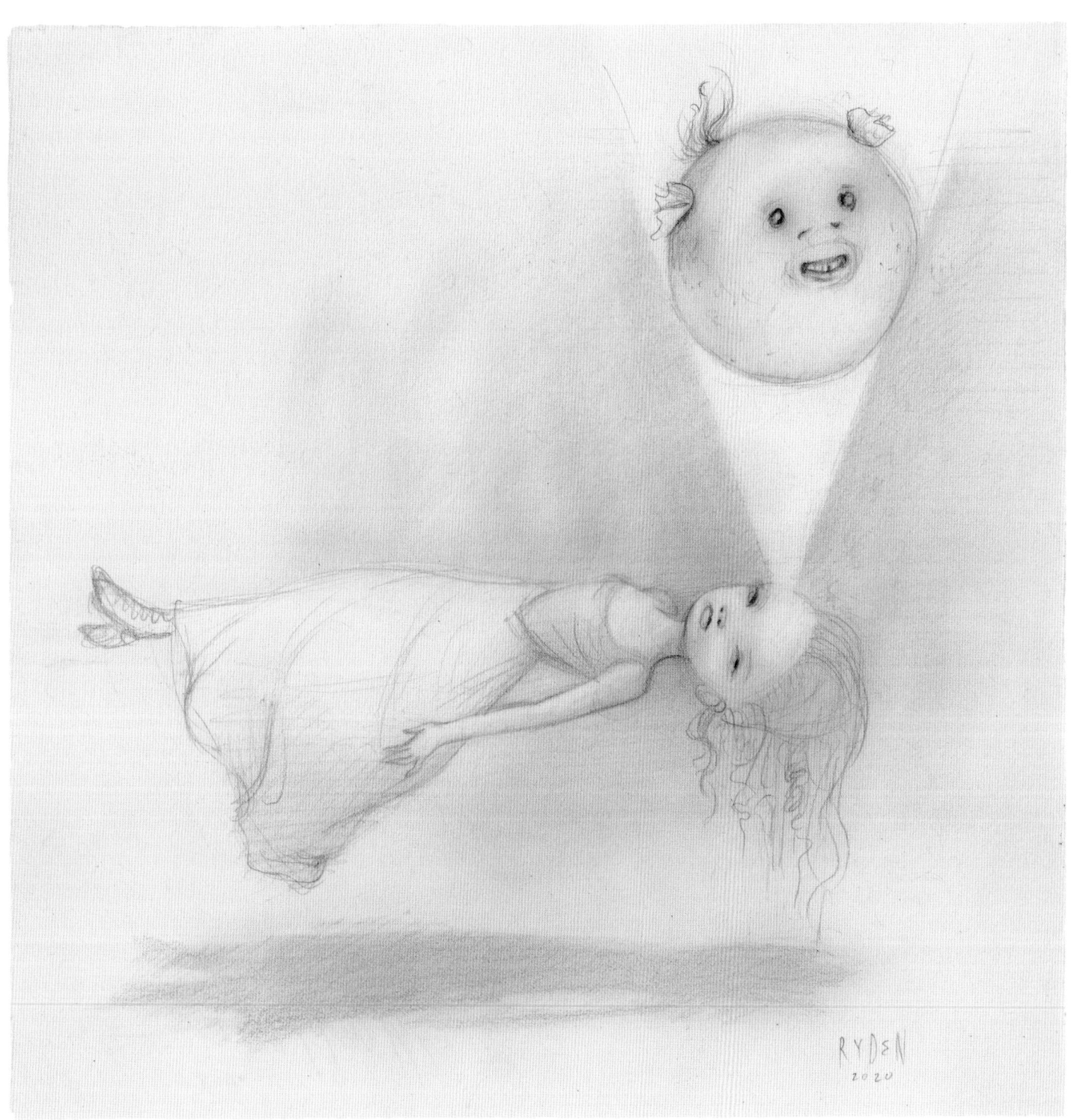

JELLY'S FRIEND

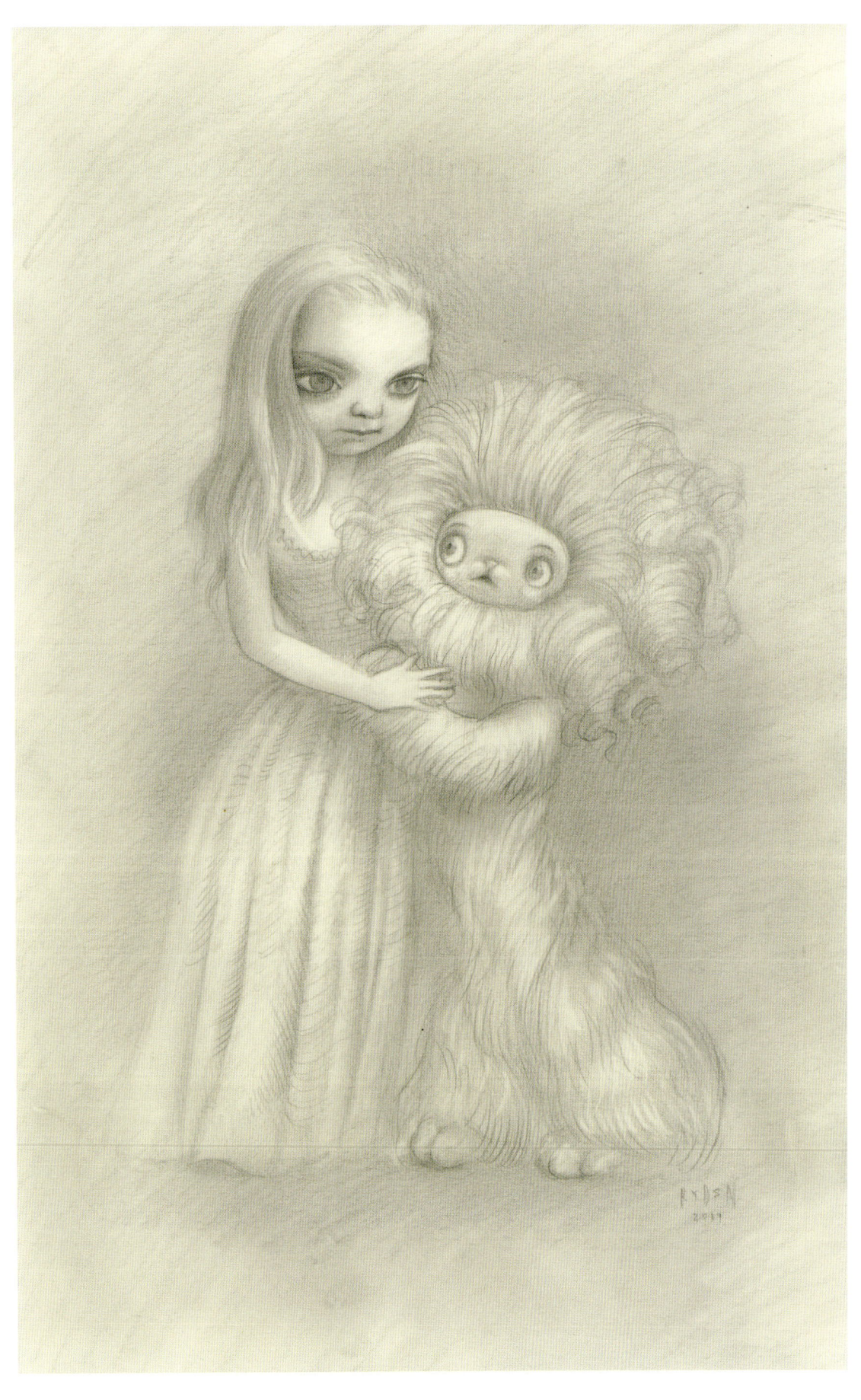

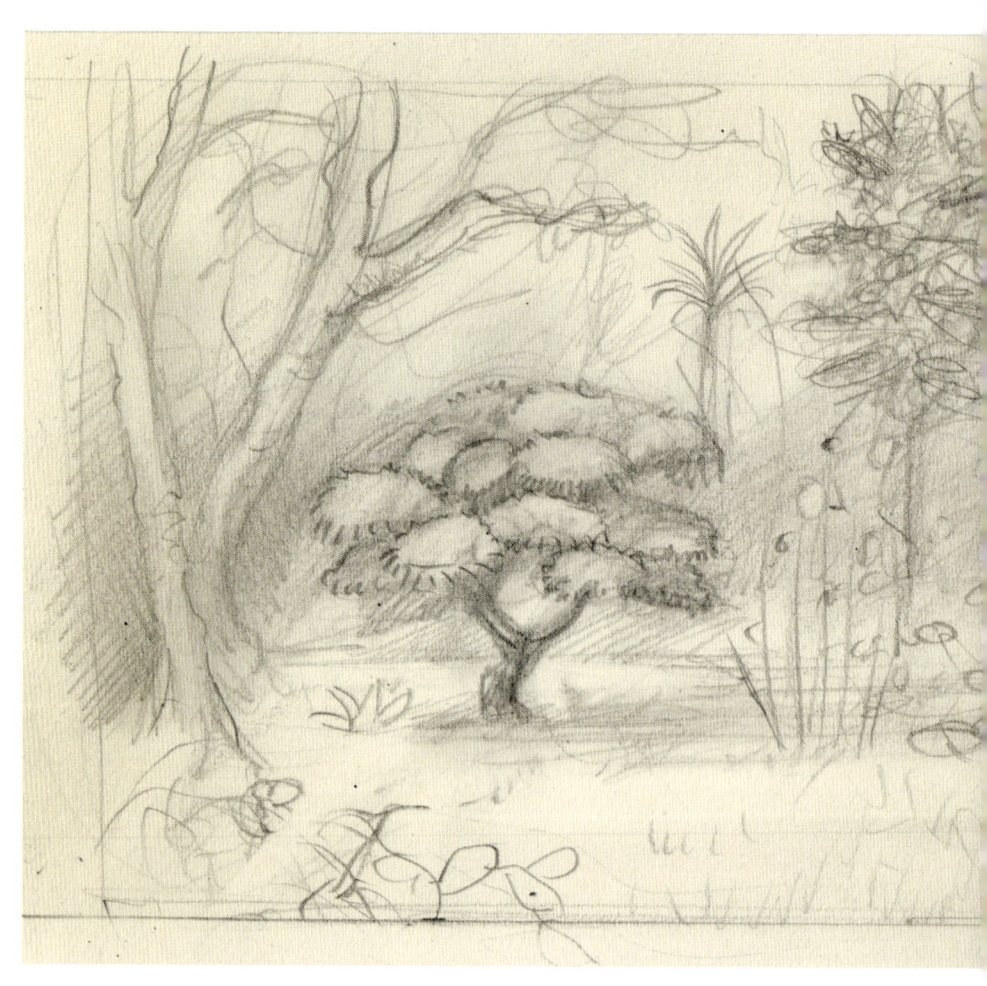

KAMI (DRAWING)

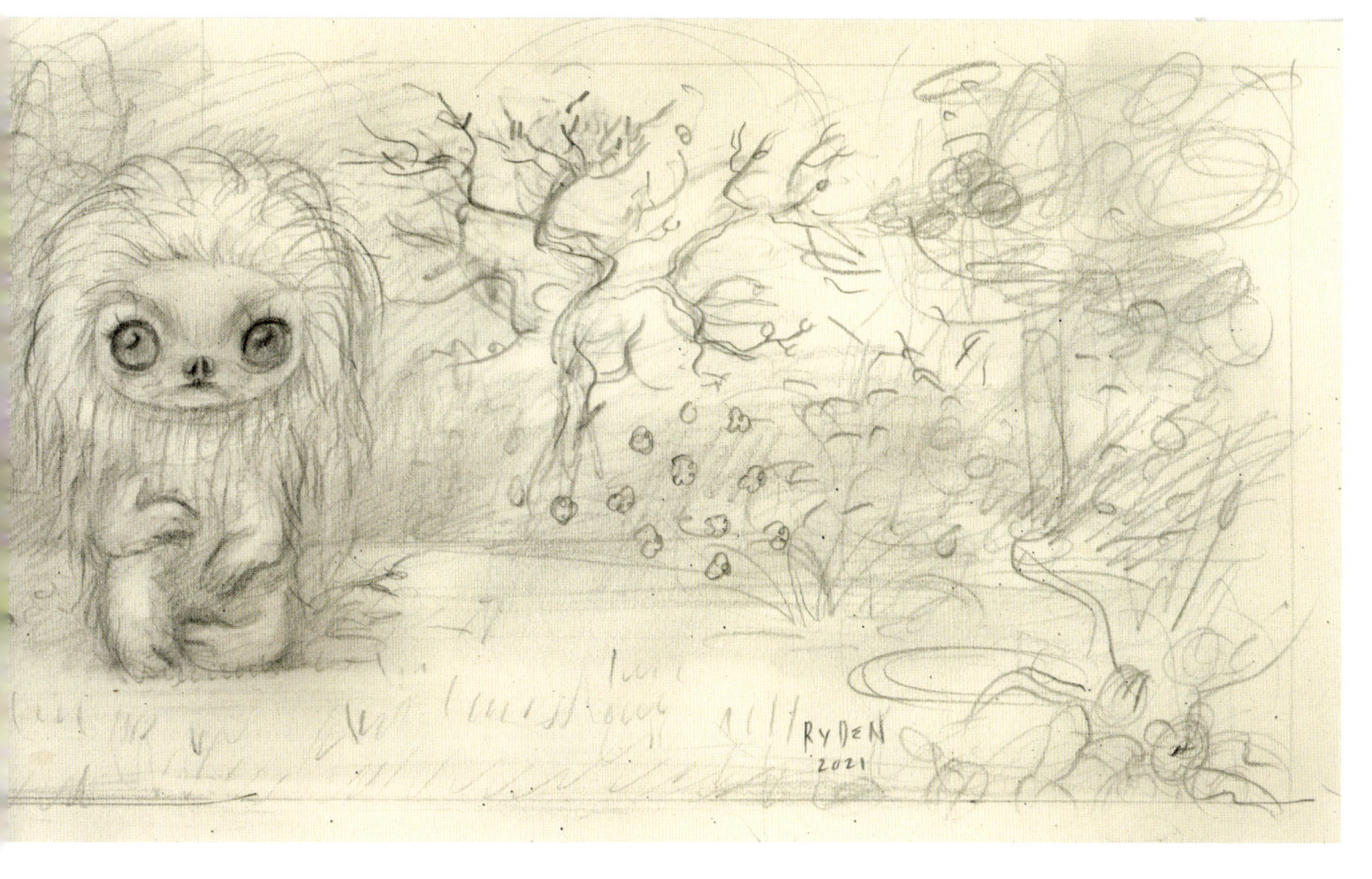
RYDEN
2021

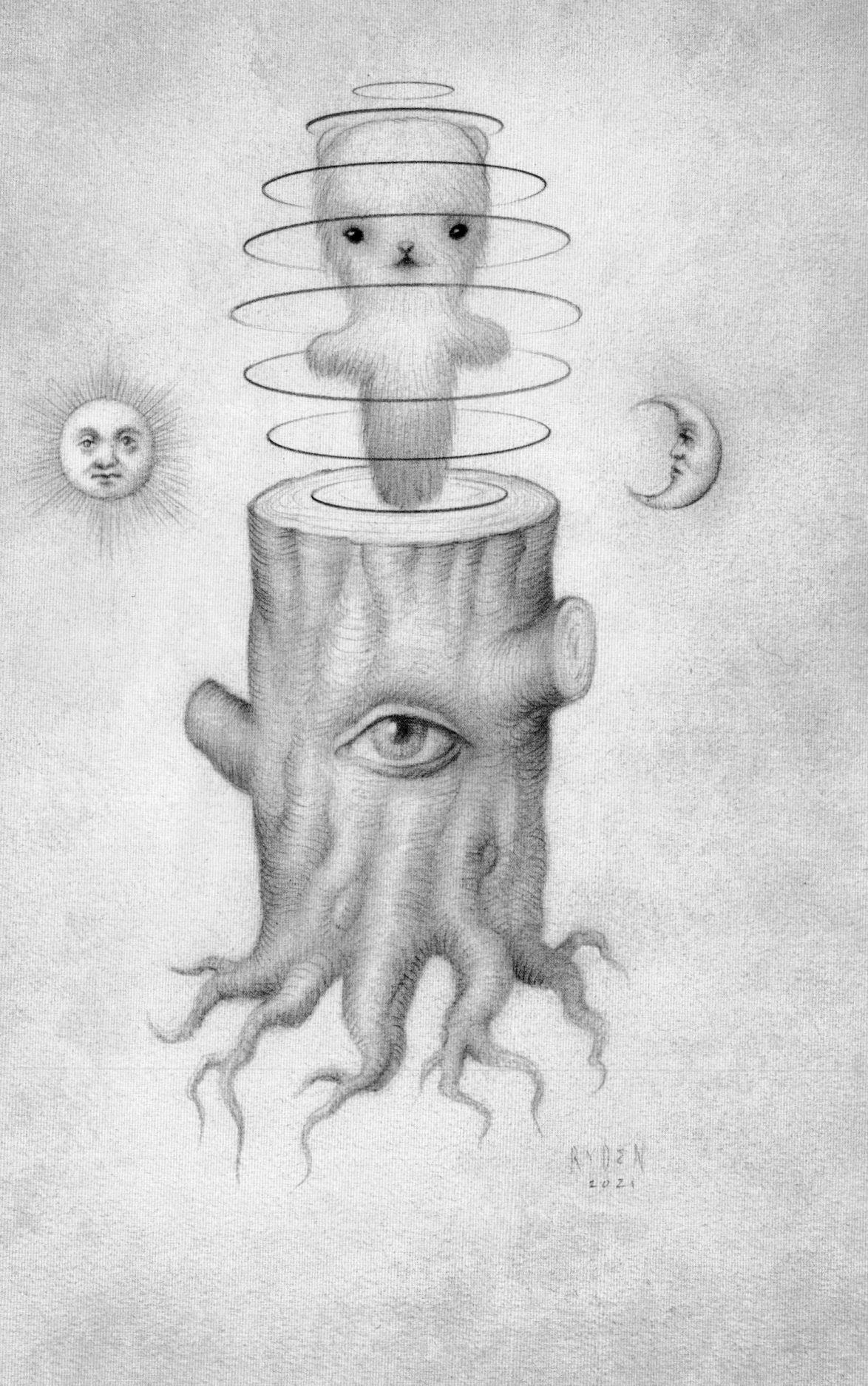

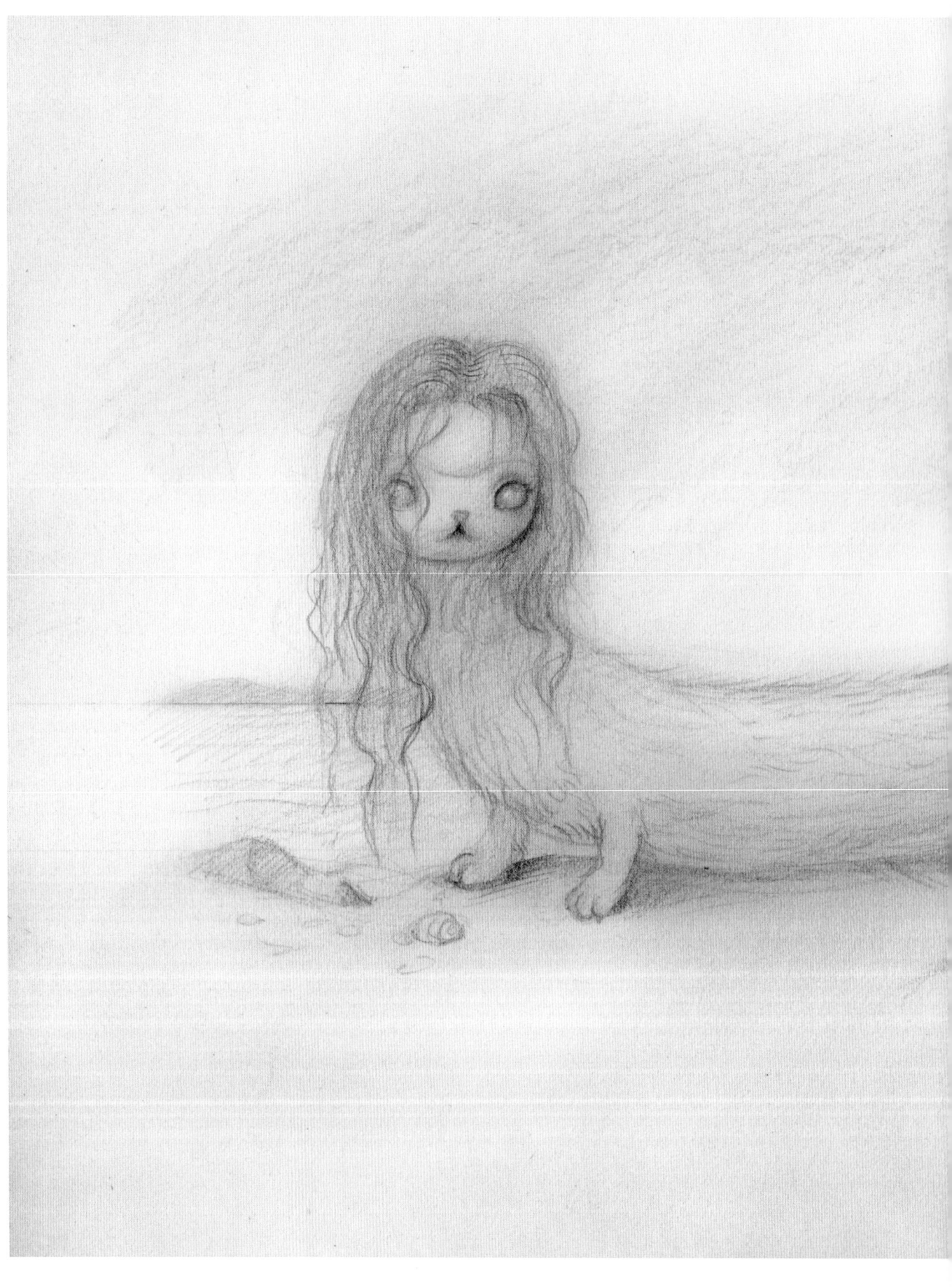

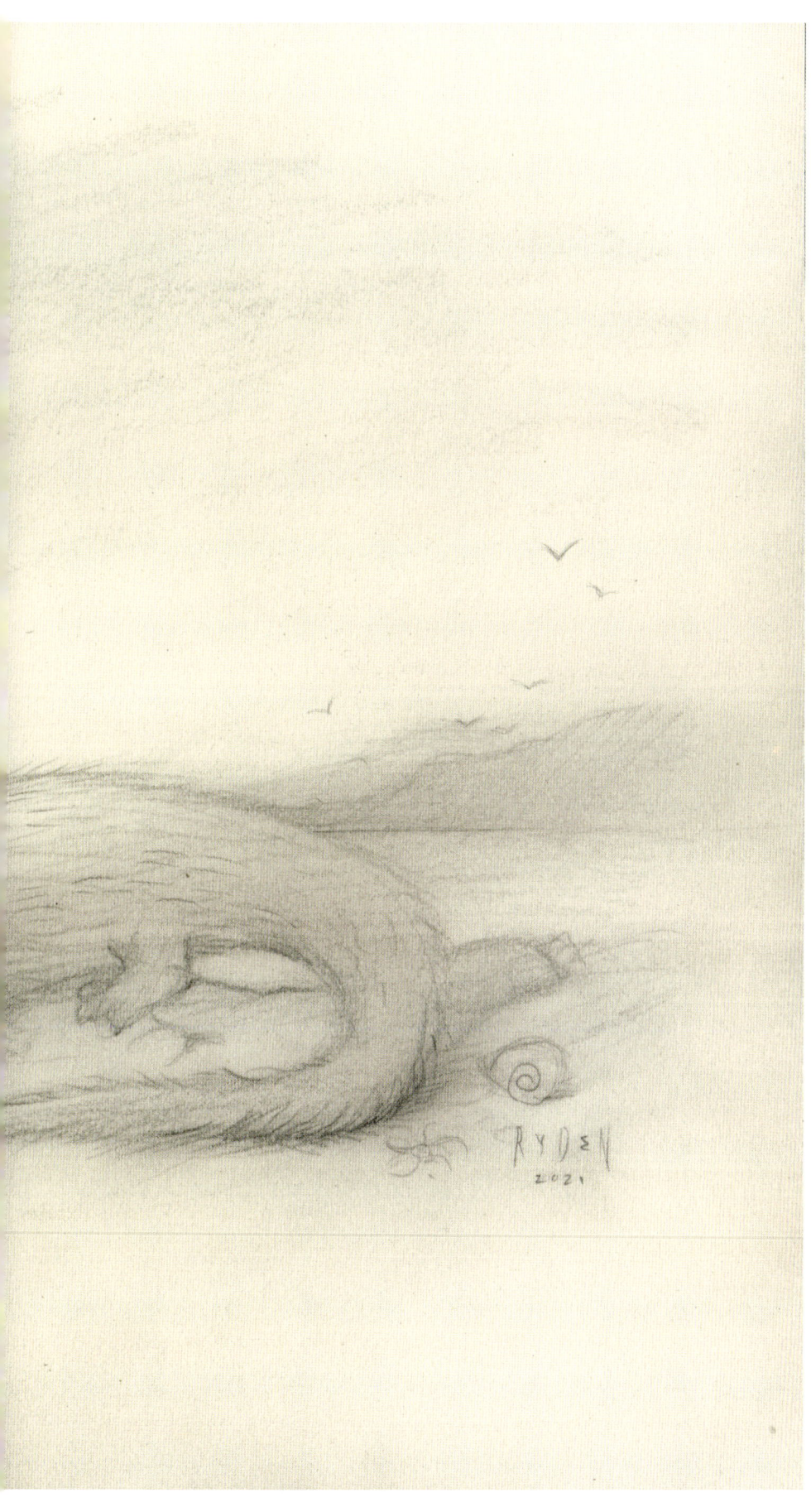

RED SIREN
(DRAWING)

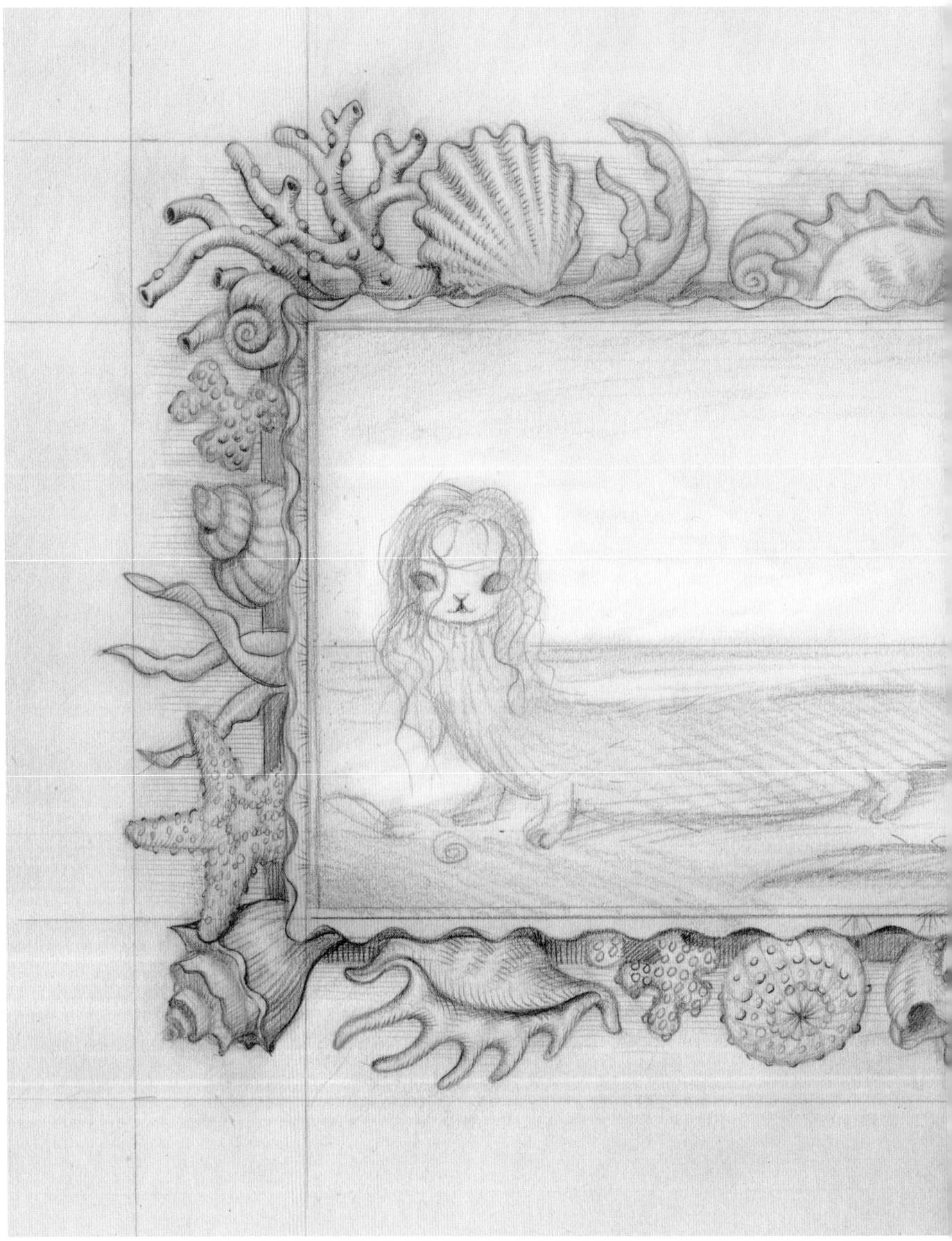

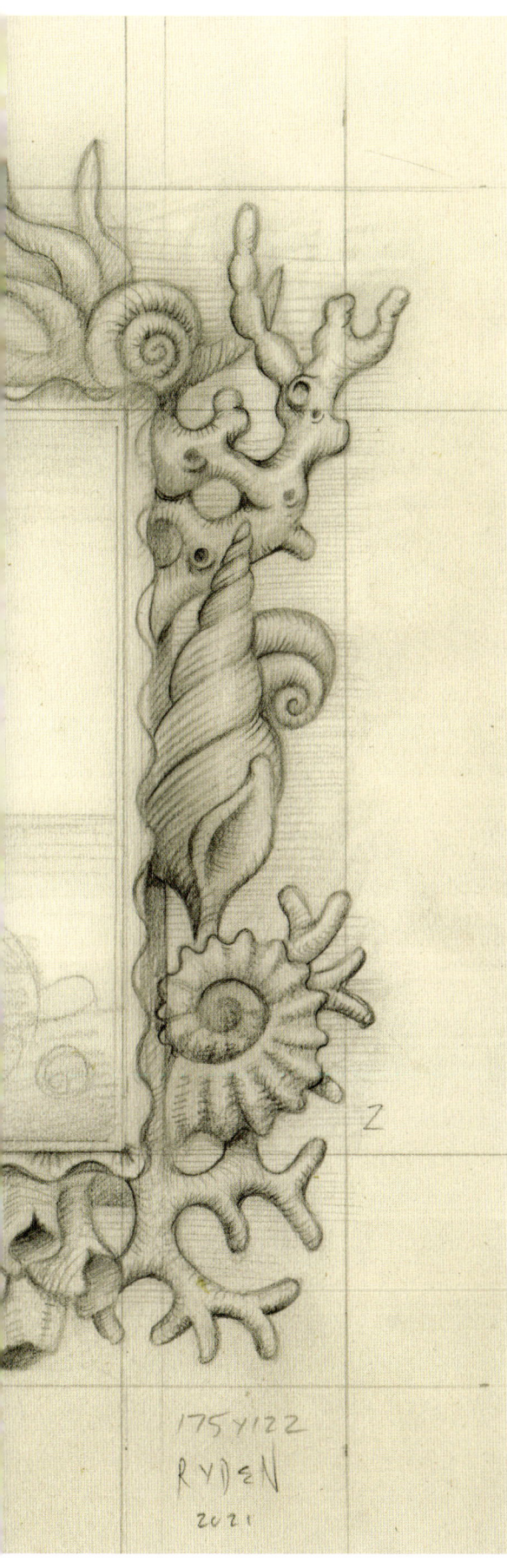

RED SIREN (FRAME STUDY)

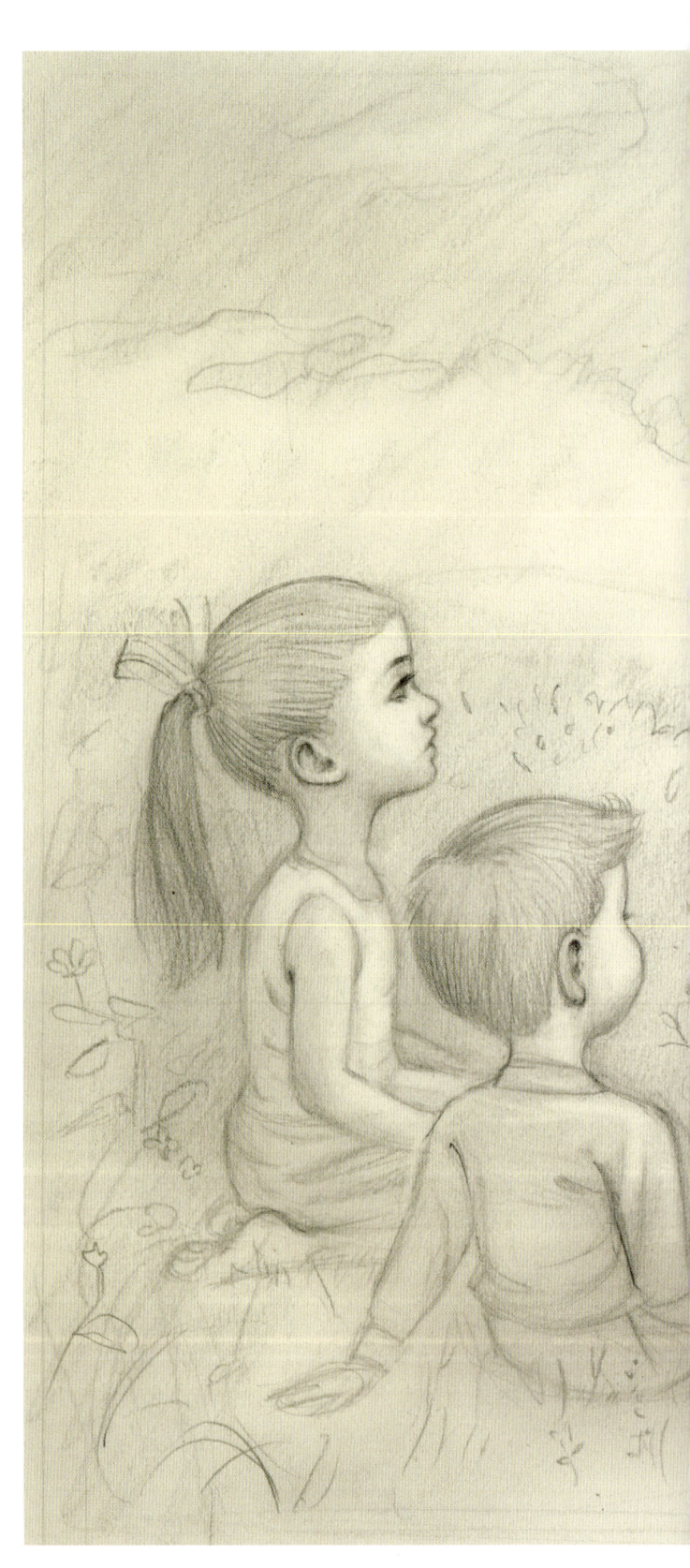

THE VISITATION
(DRAWING)

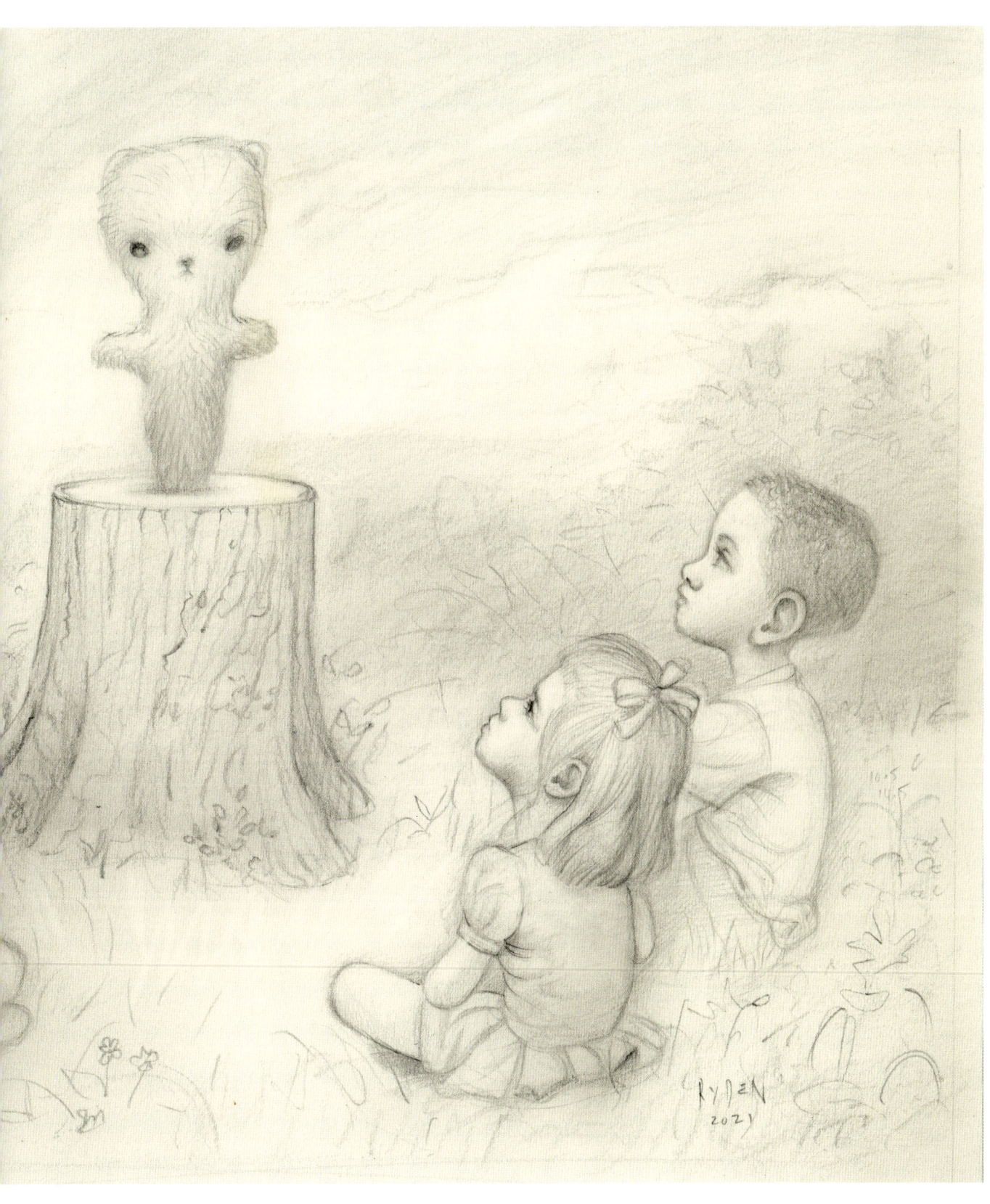

YUKI THE YOUNG YAK

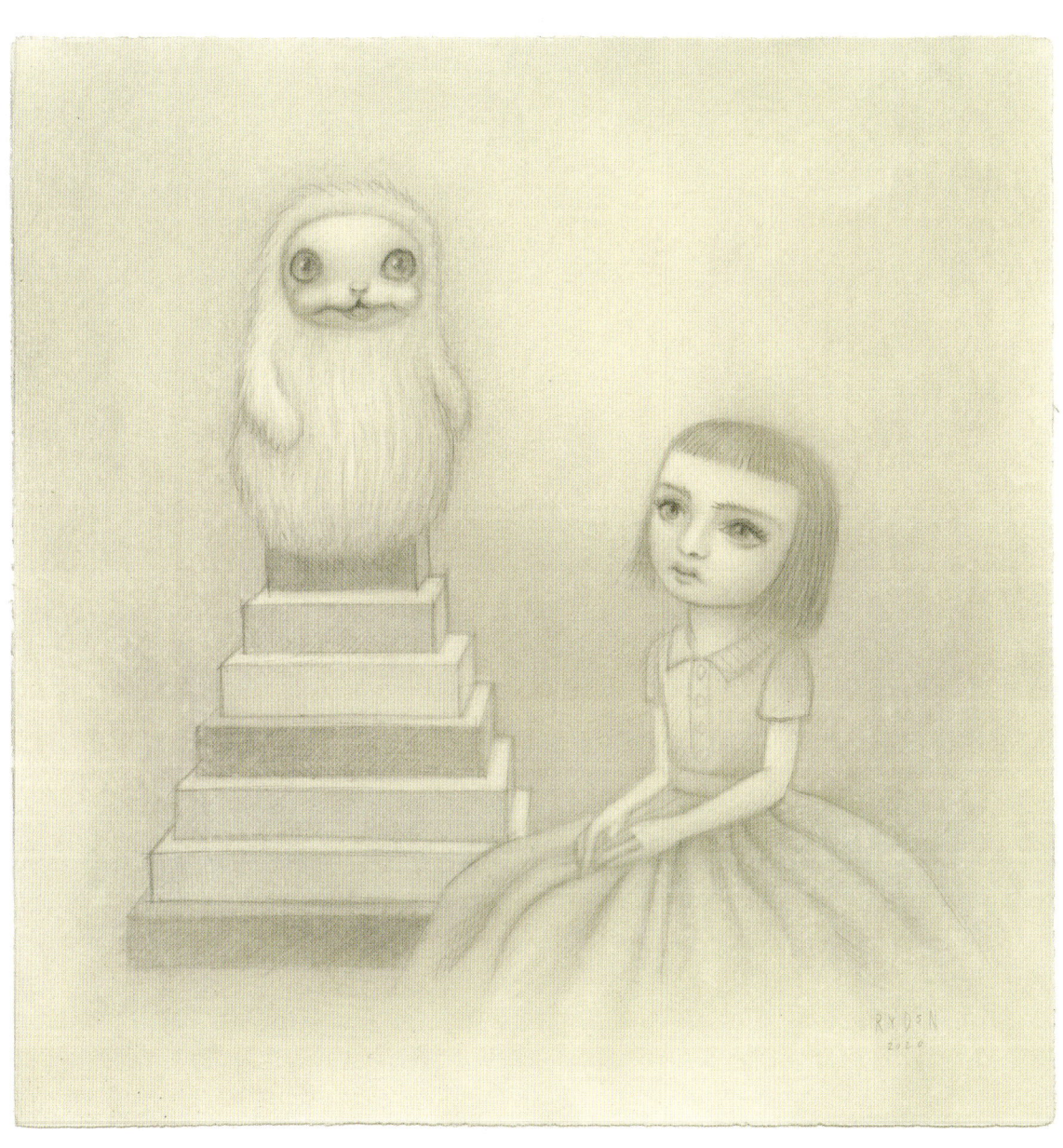

INSTALLATIONS

View of the exhibition *Mark Ryden: Animal Secrets* at Perrotin Paris, 2022.

Courtesy of the artist and Perrotin.

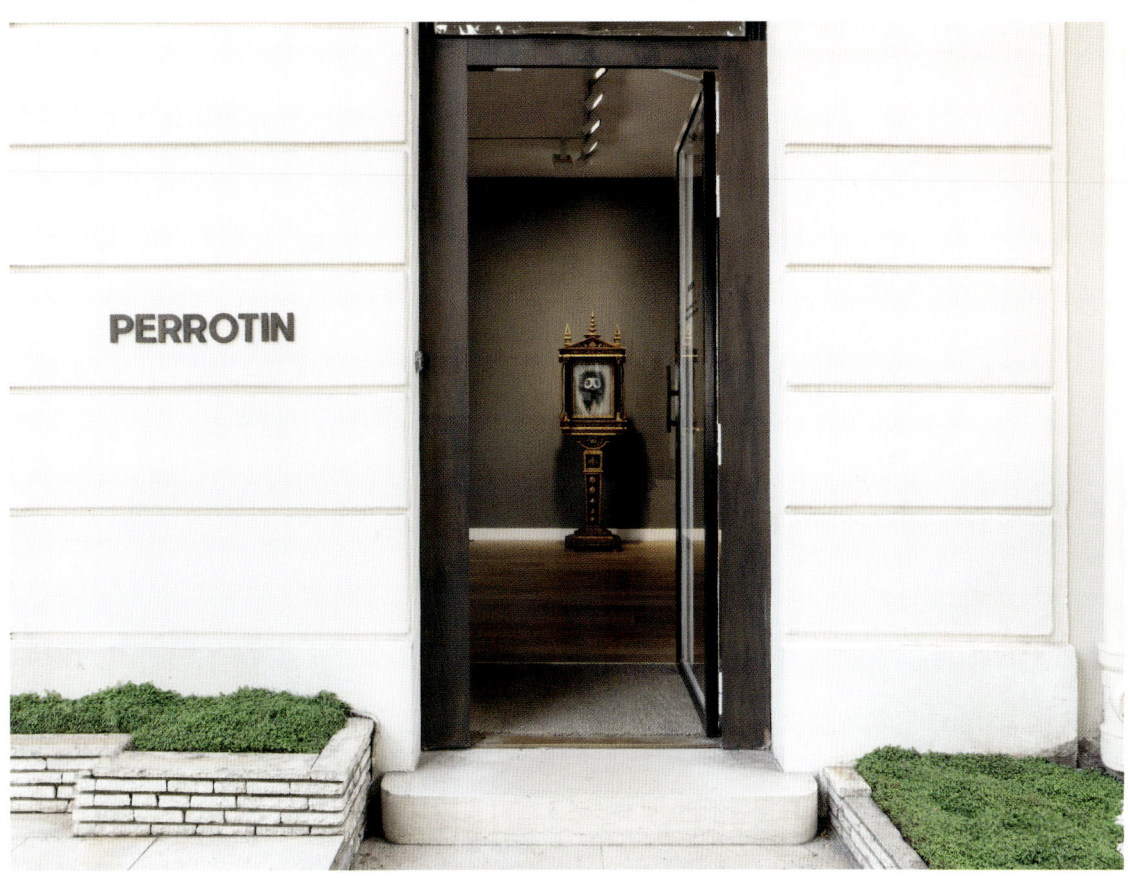

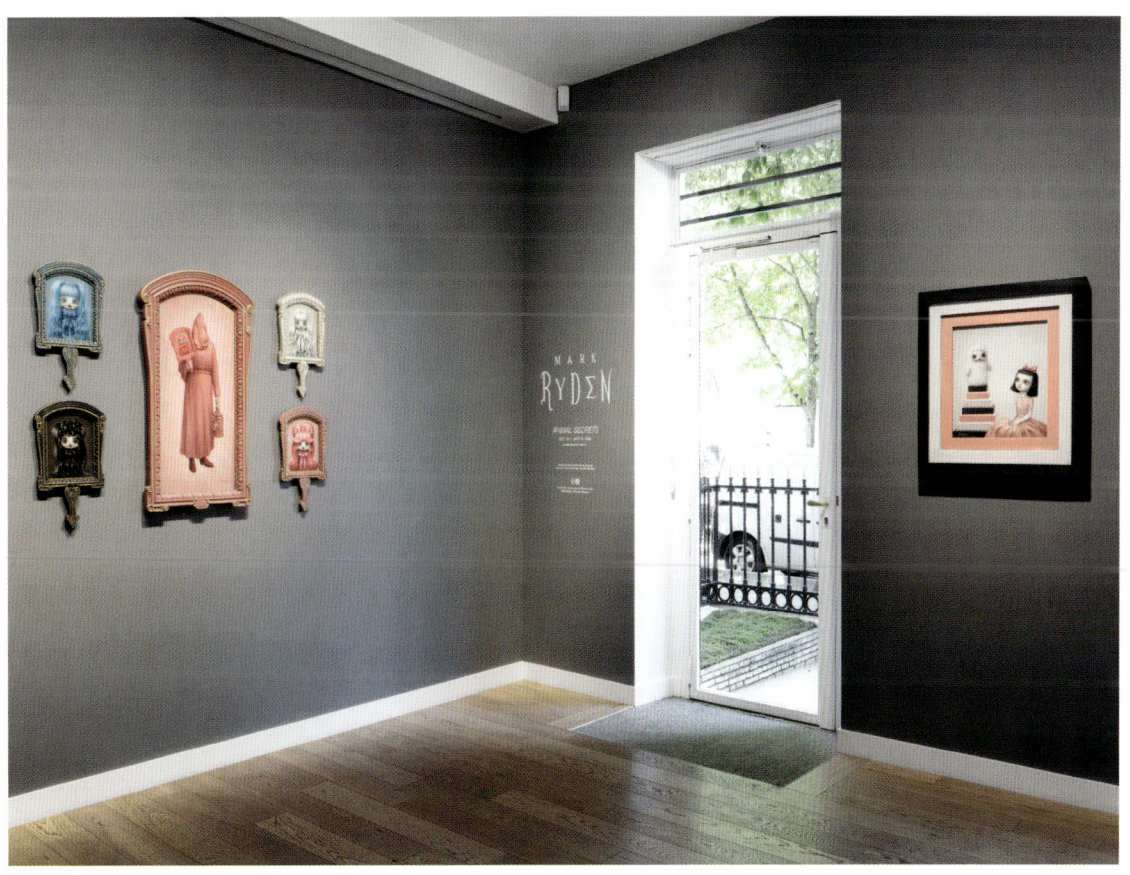

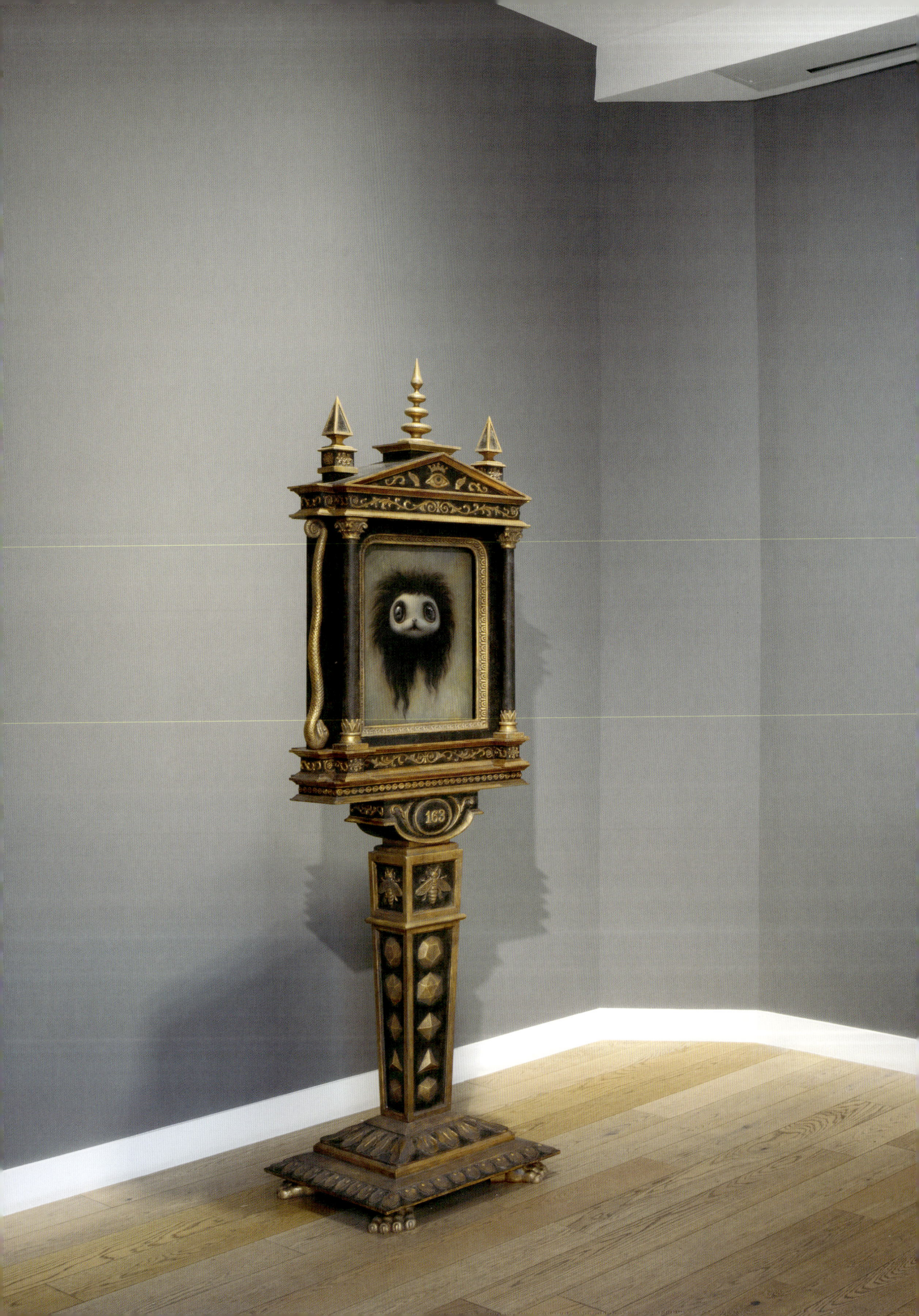

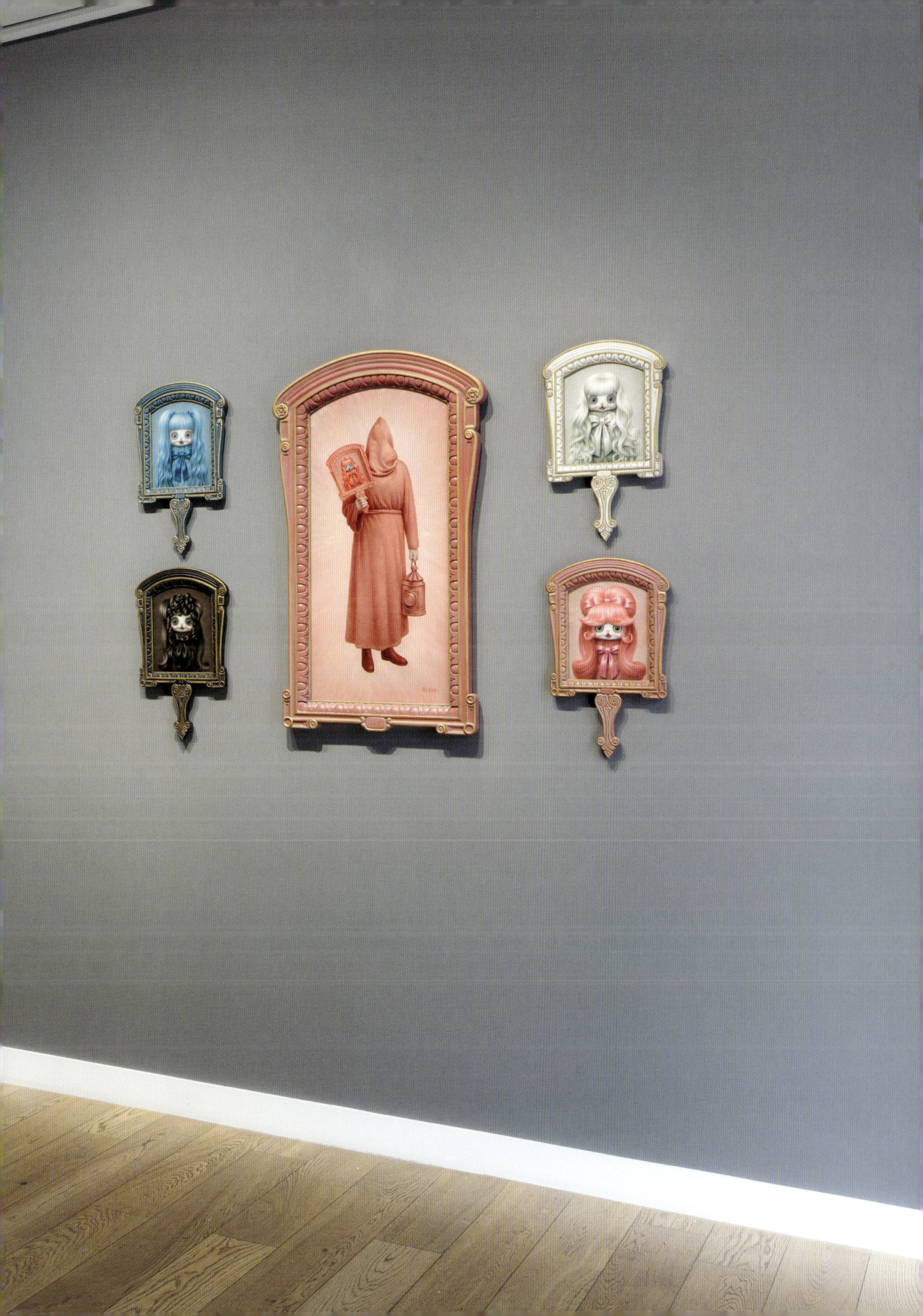

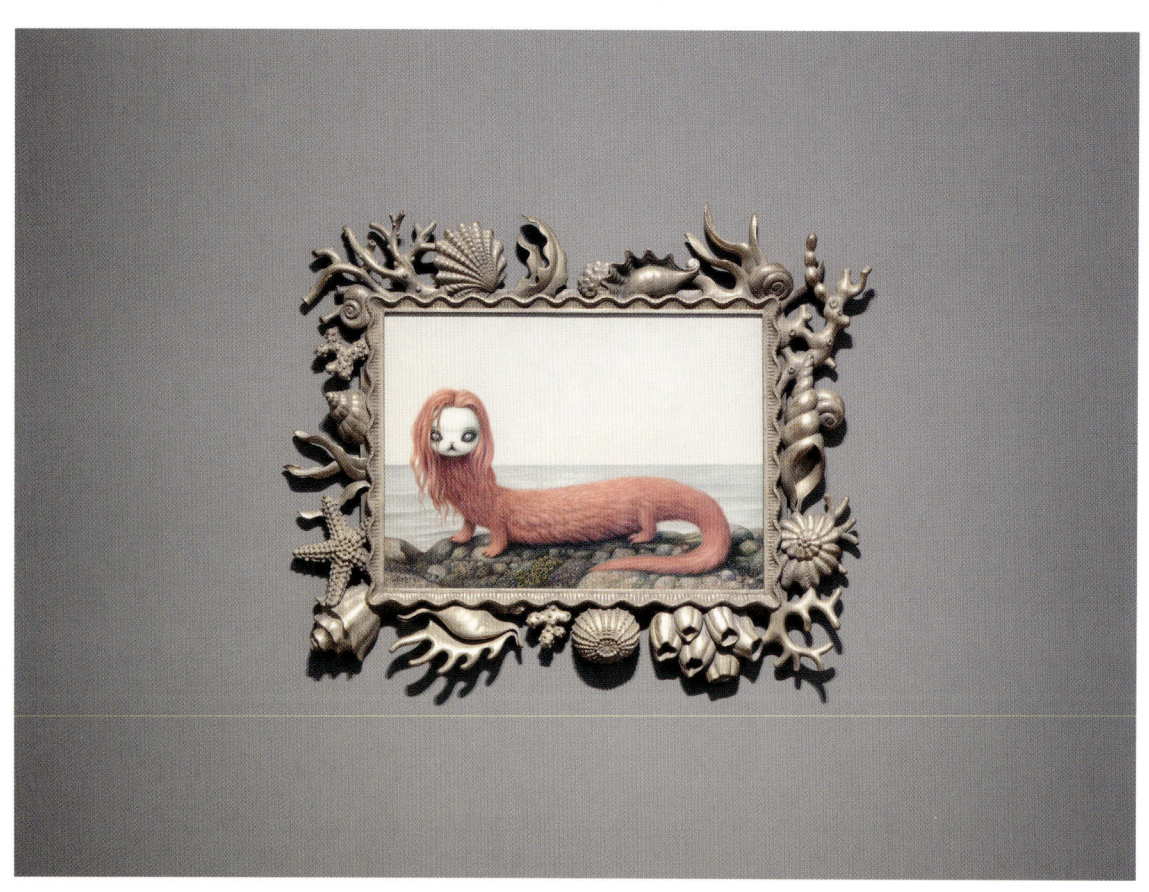

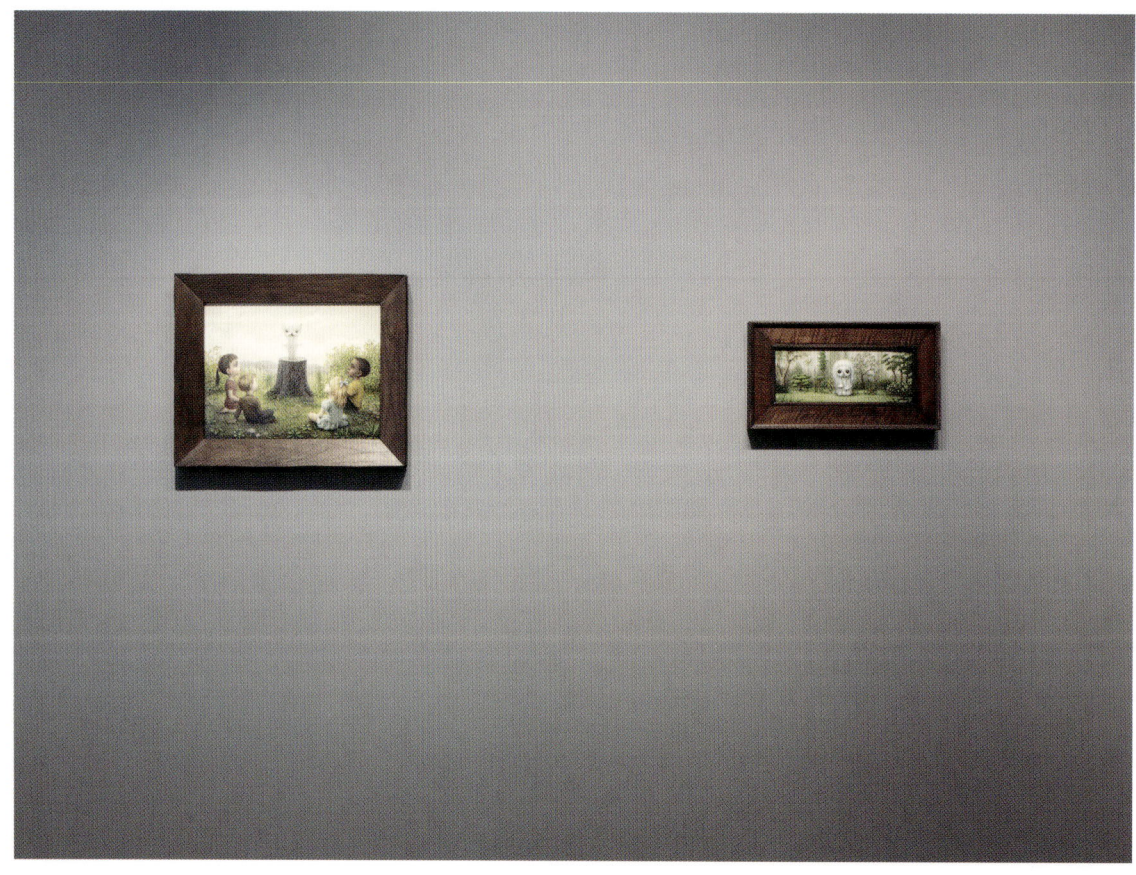

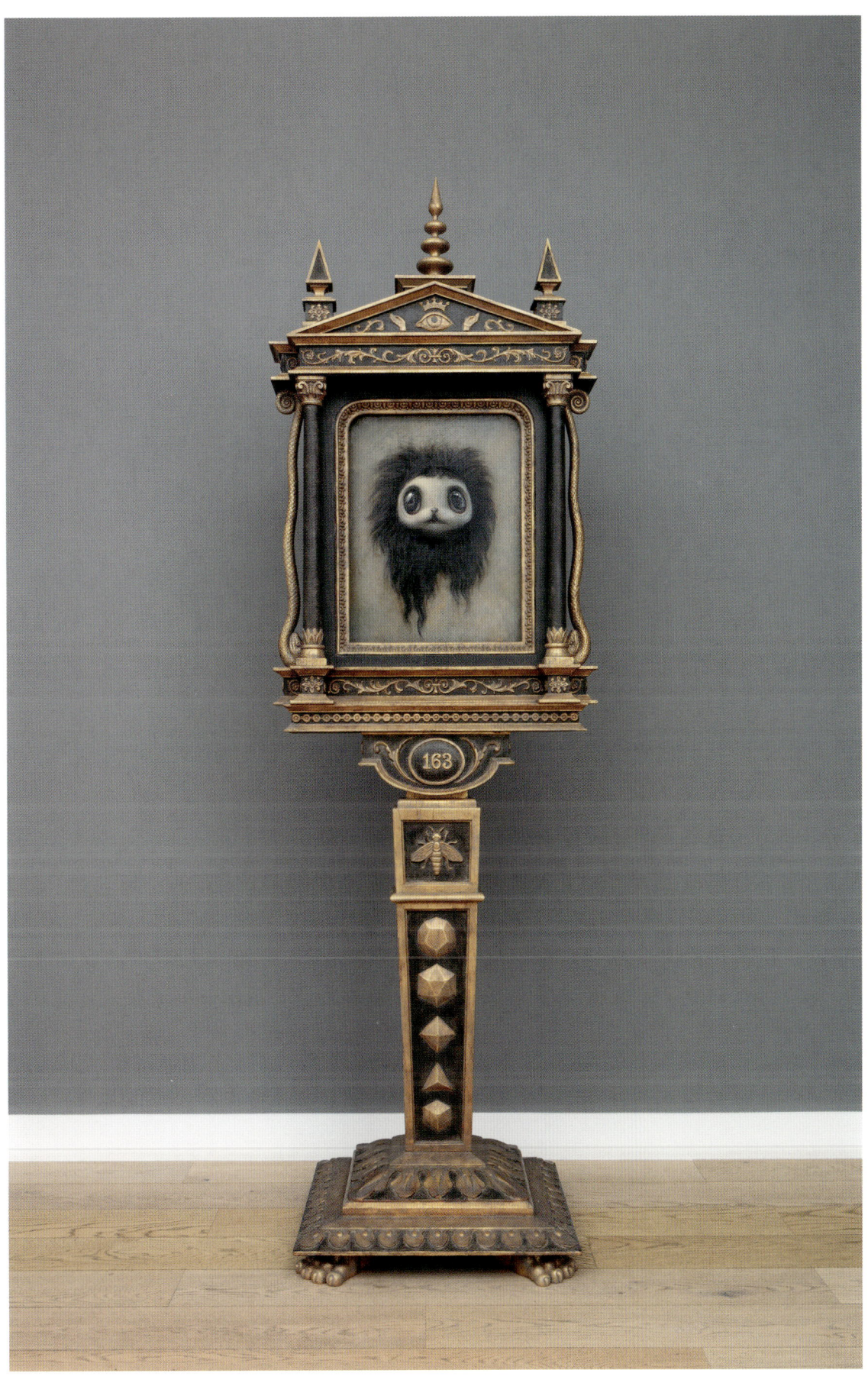

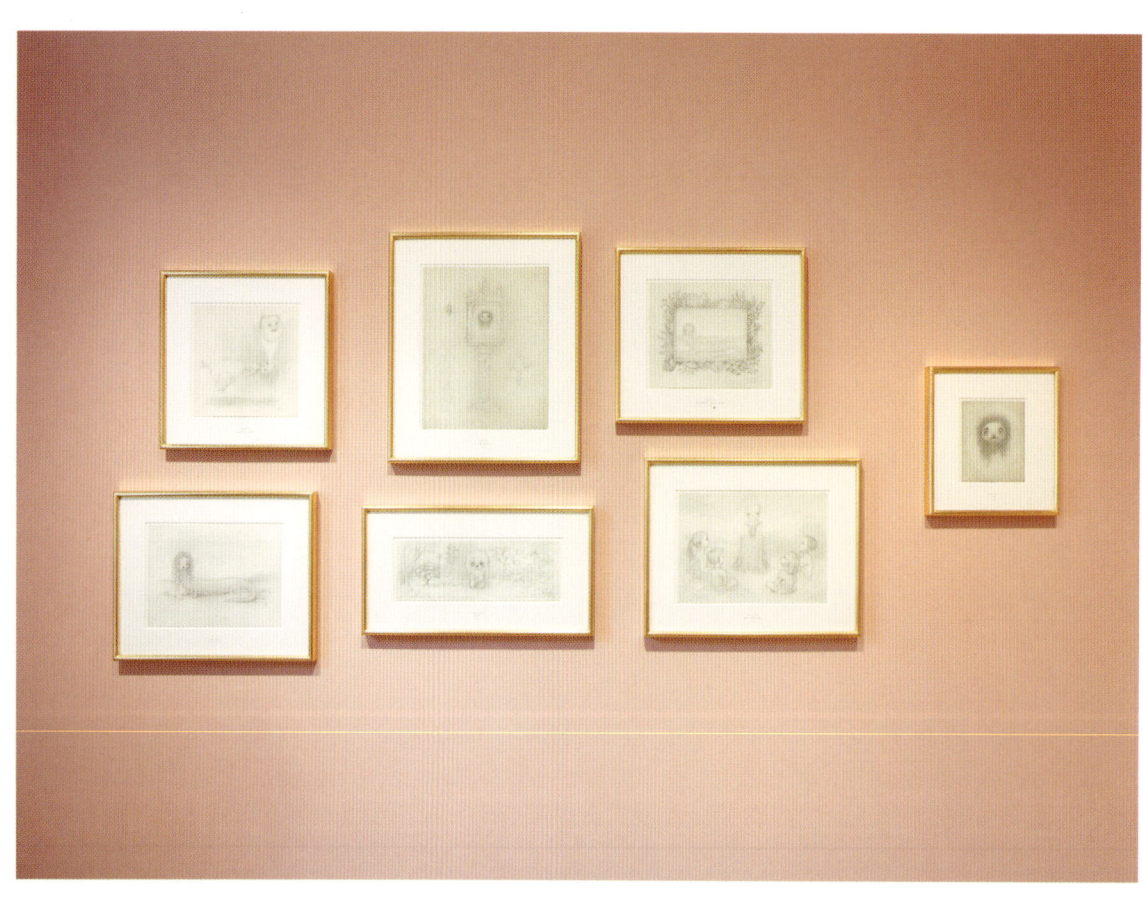

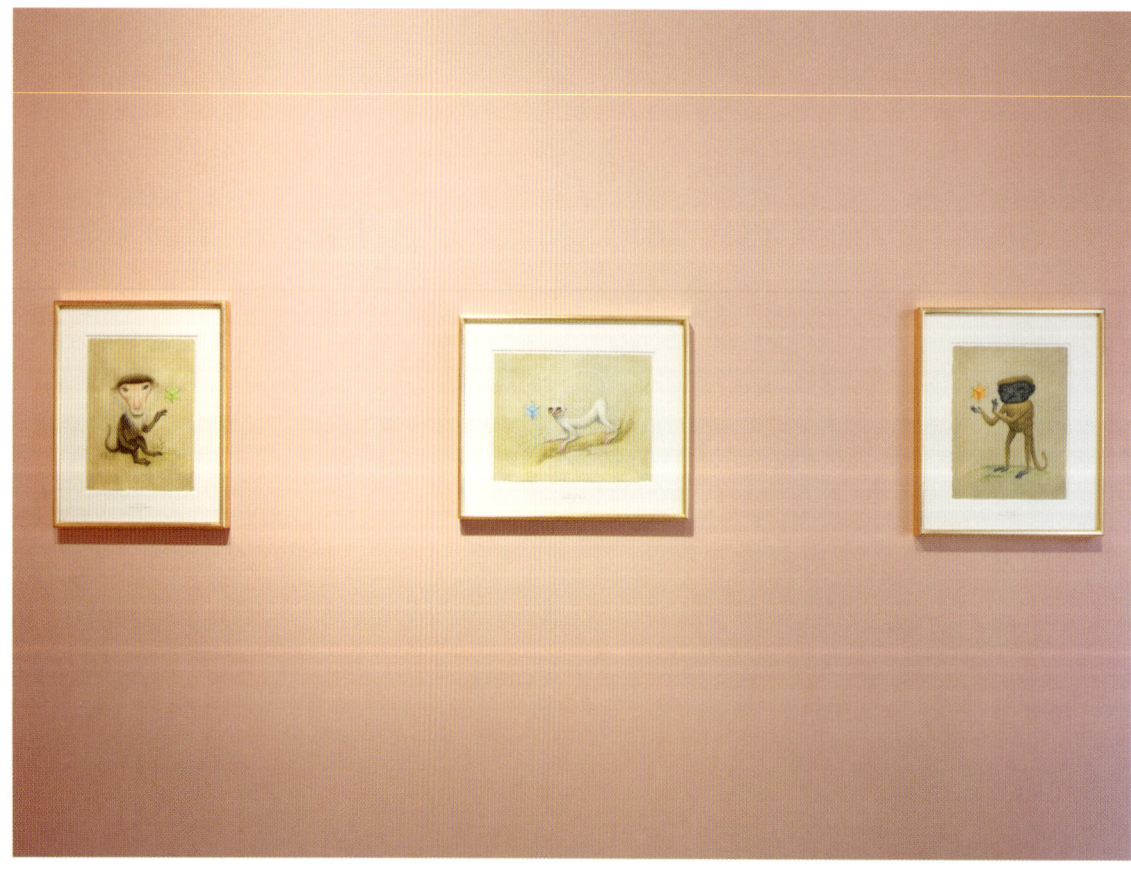

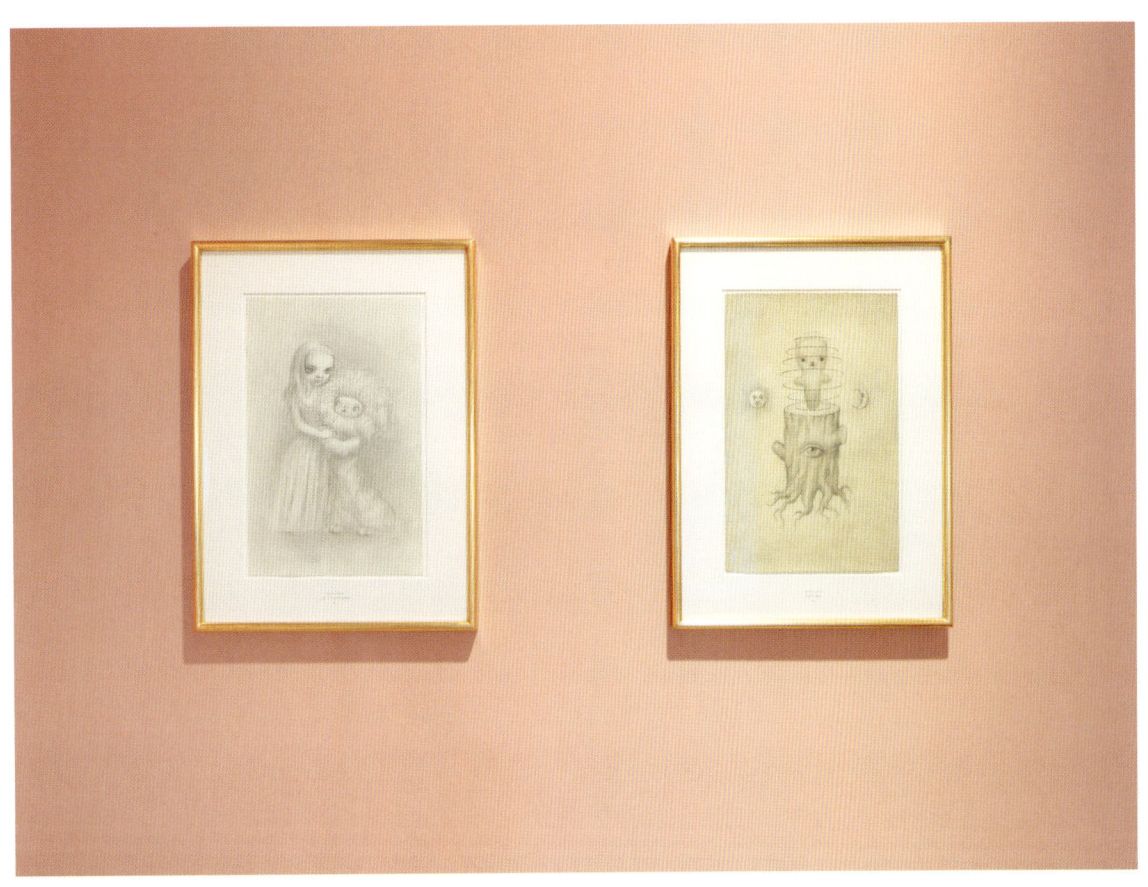

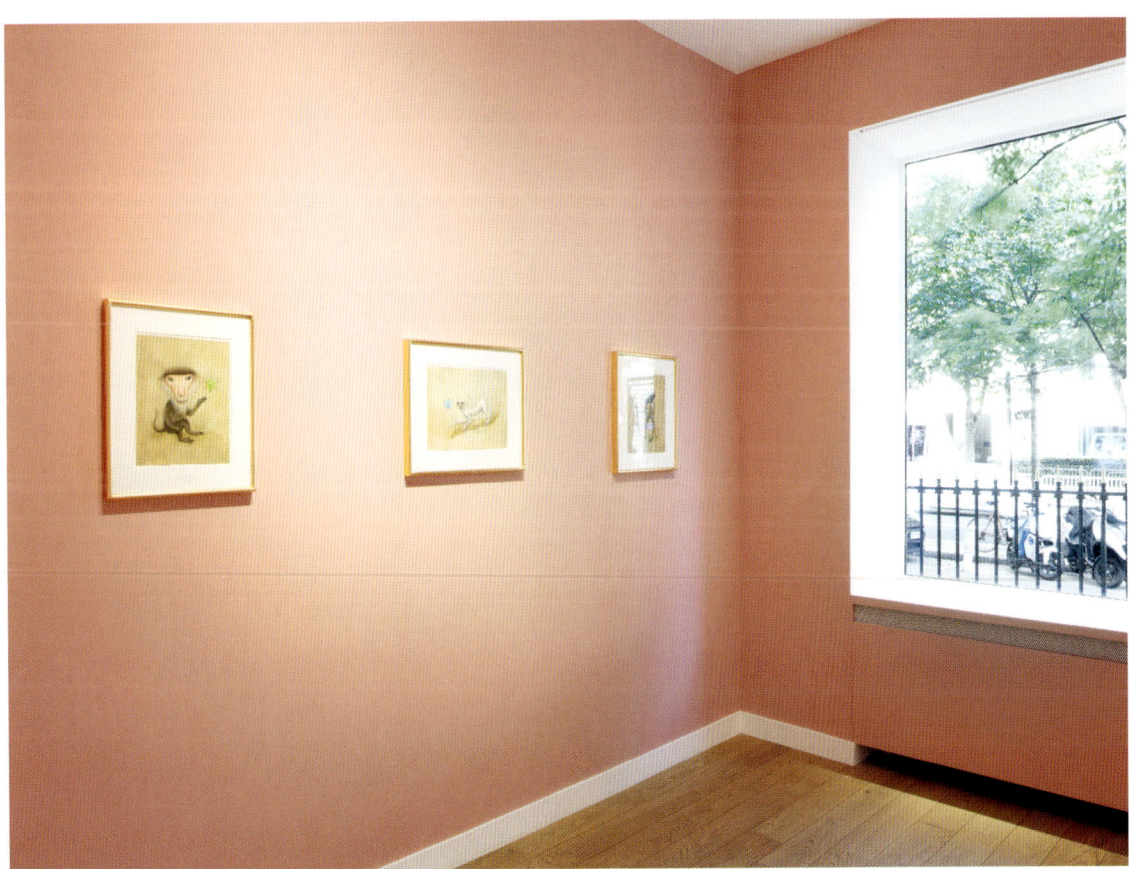

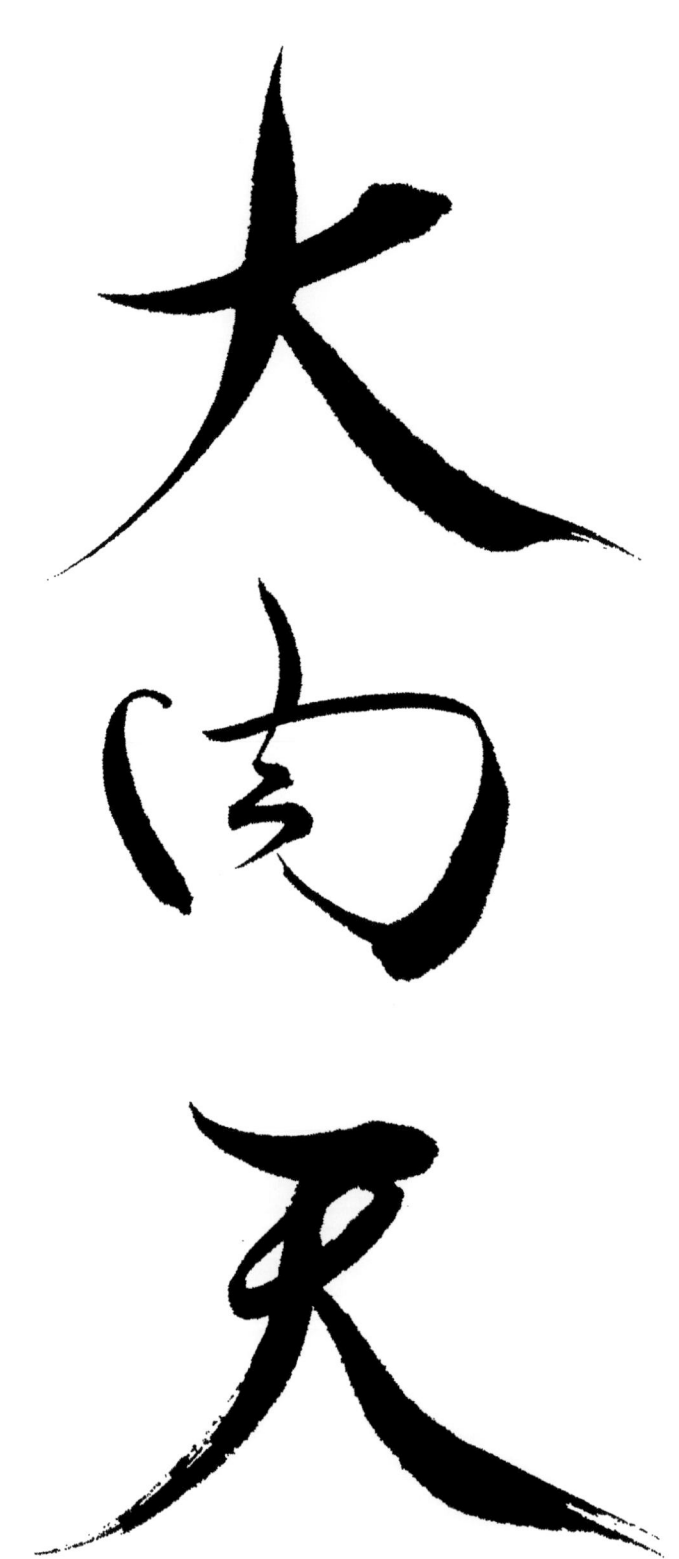

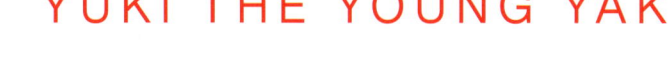

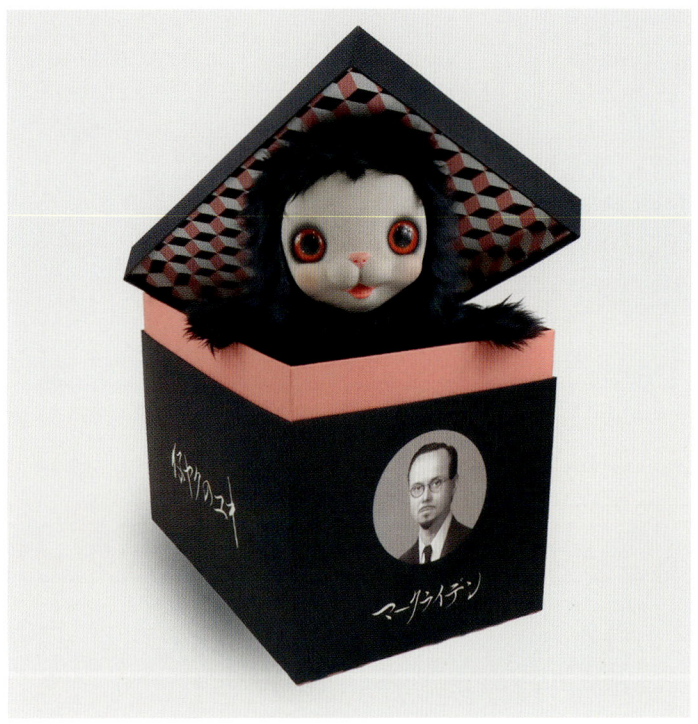

マークライデン

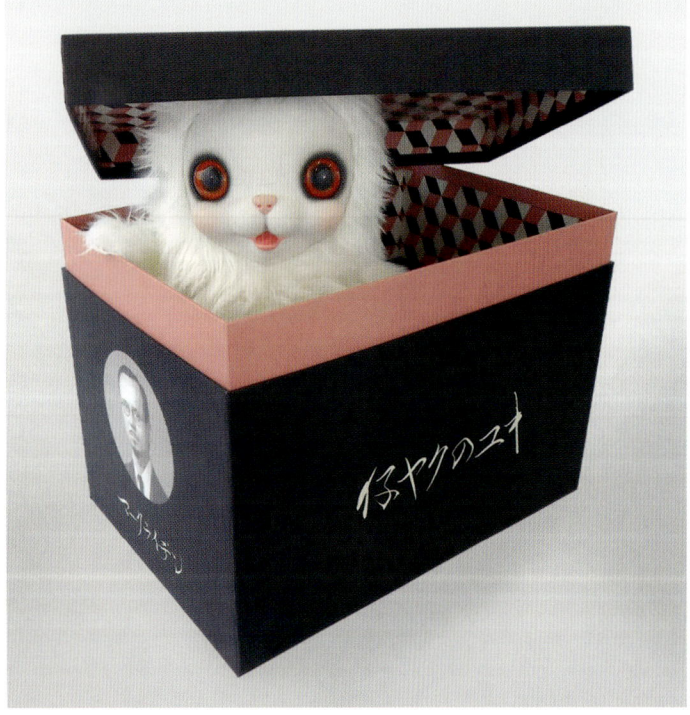

In 2022, Mark Ryden collaborated with Artoyz and its new imprint GOLEM to release *Yuki The Young Yak*.

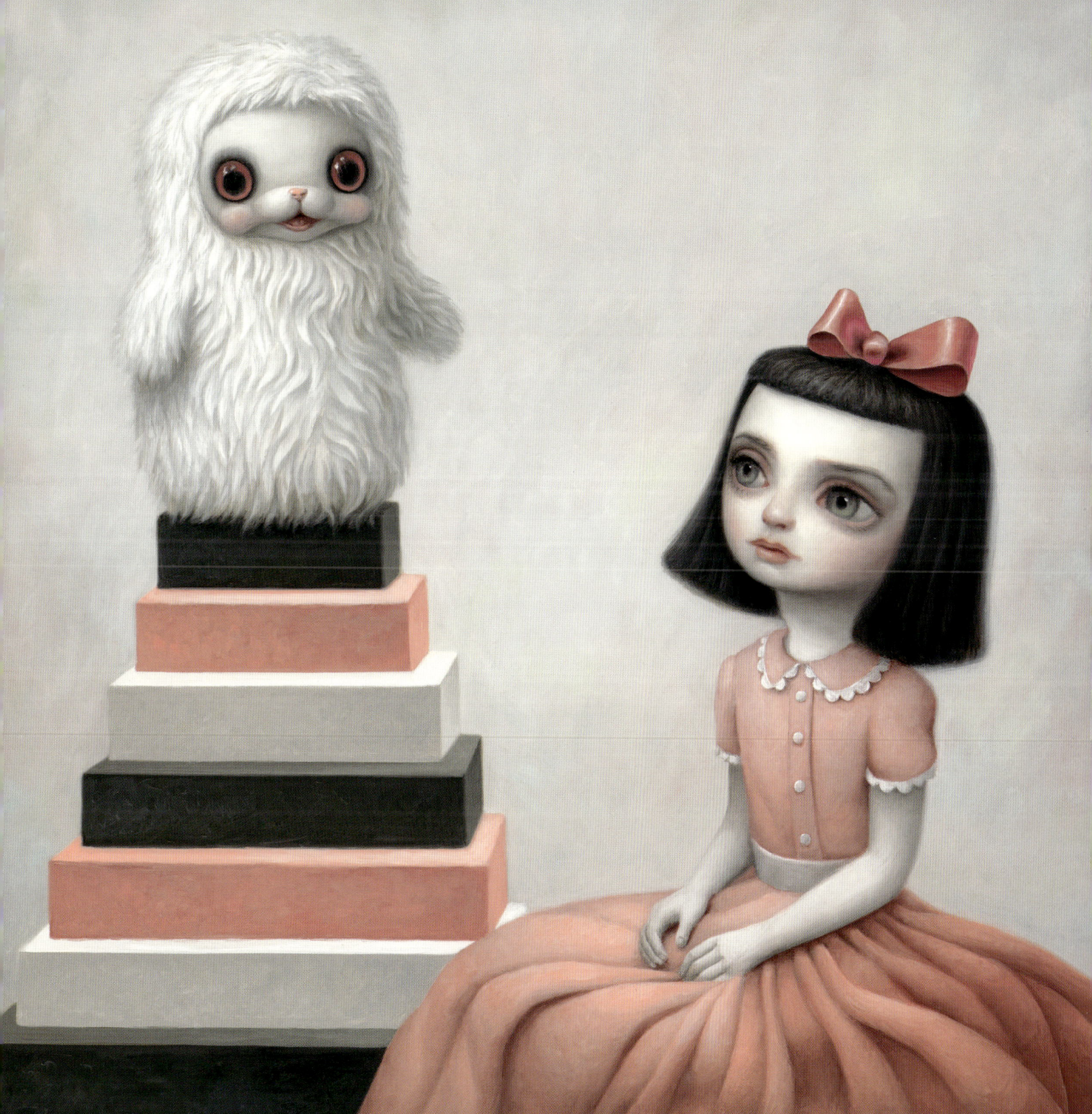

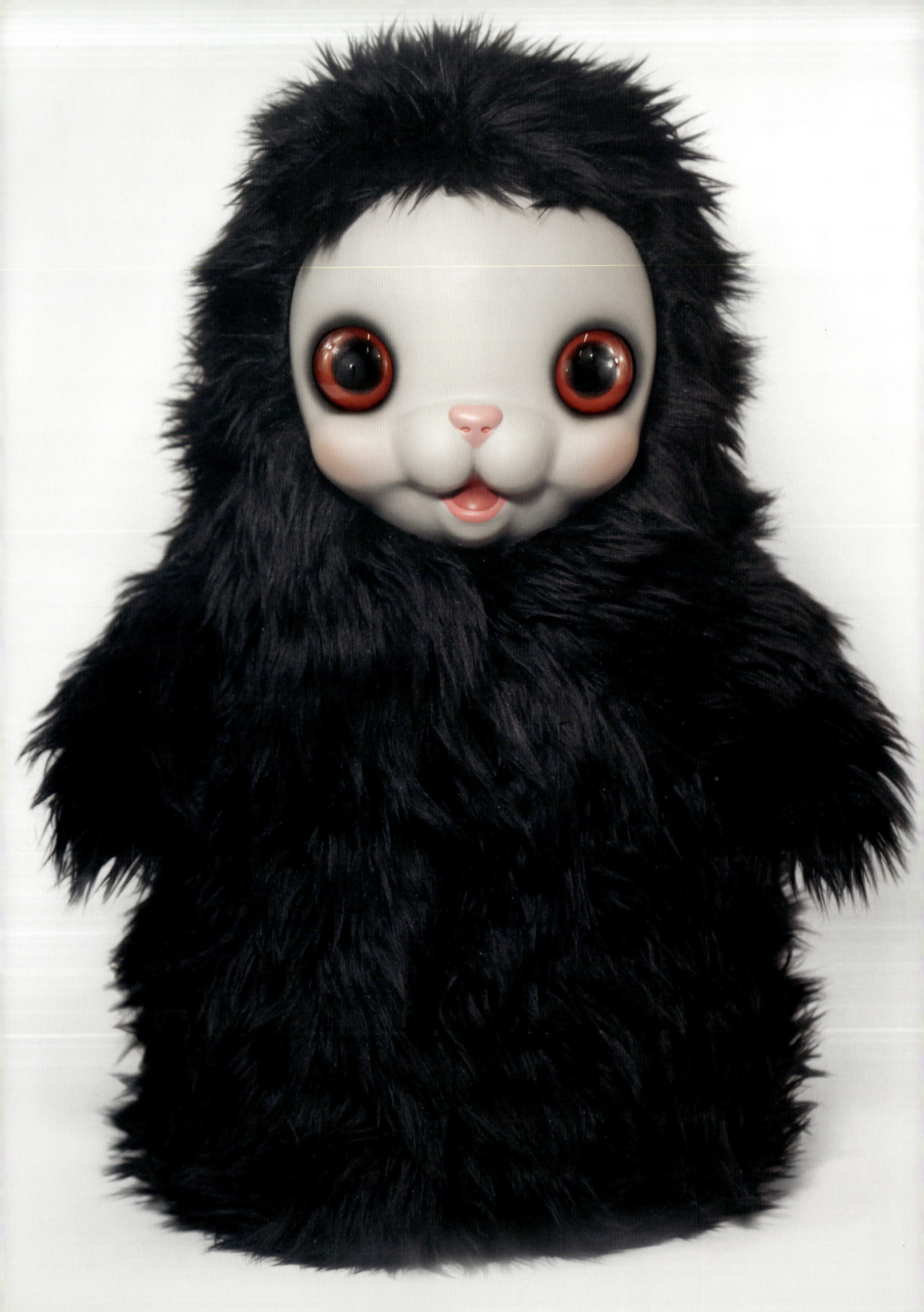

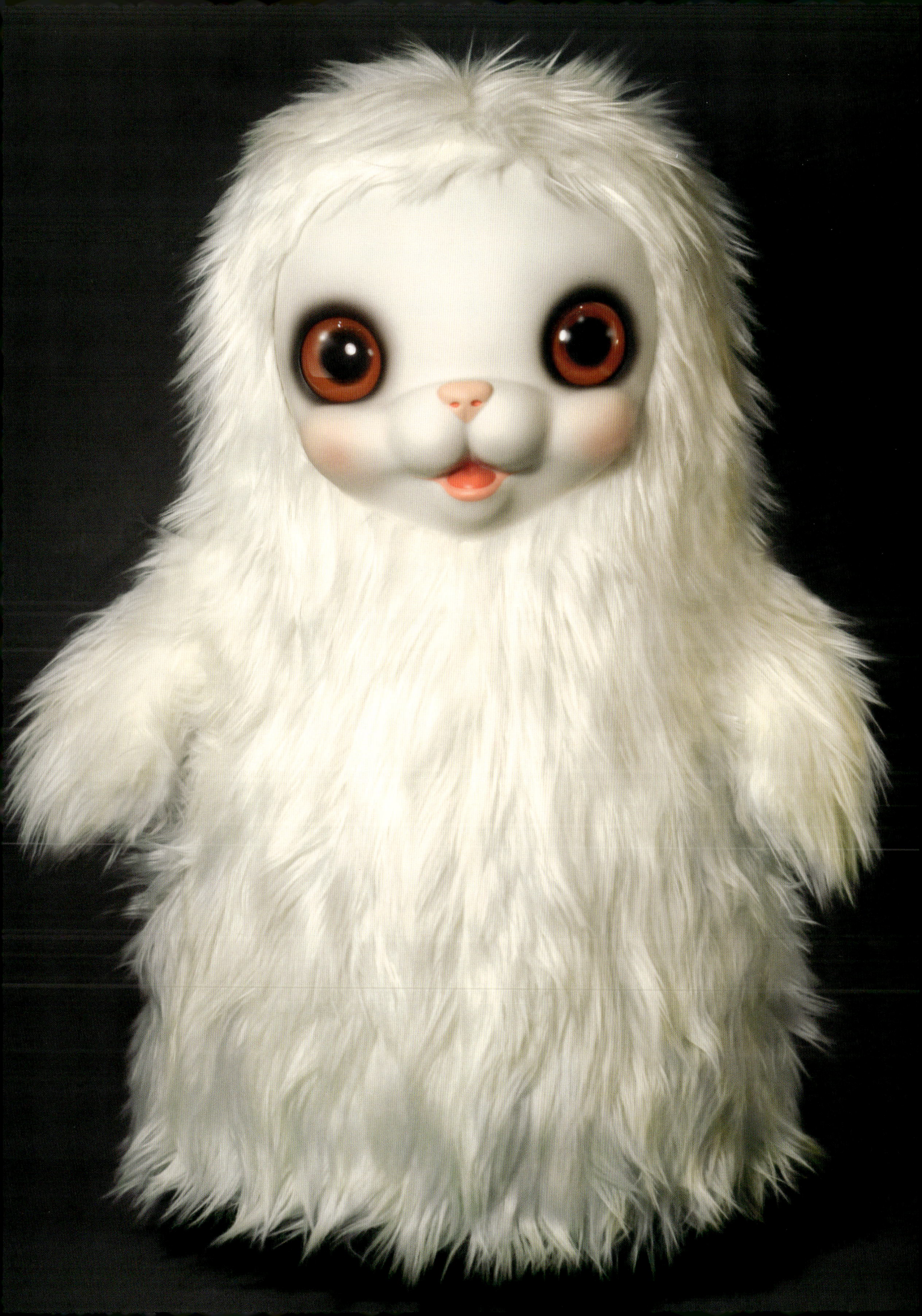

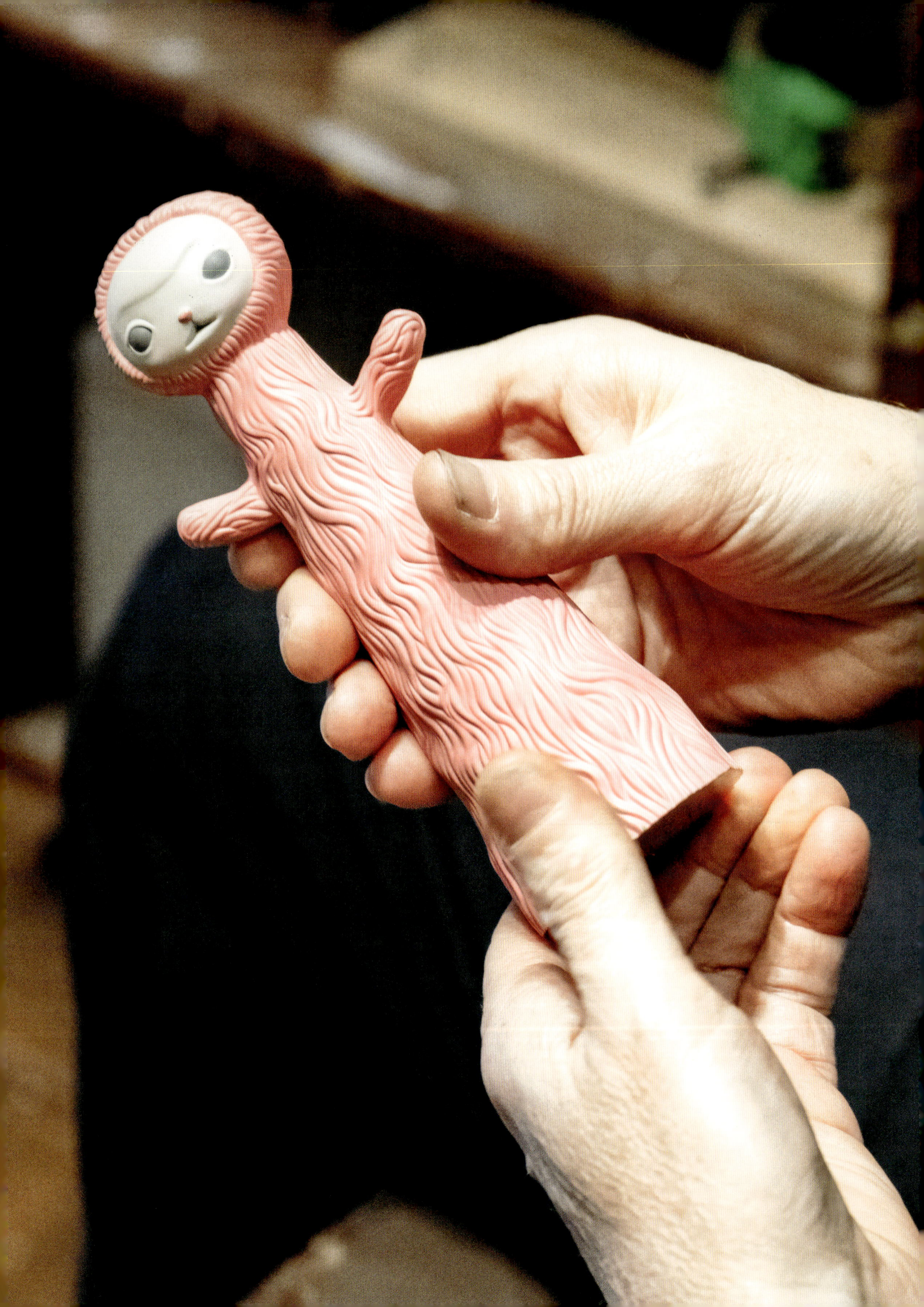

PICCOLINA YAKALINA ENNEAD

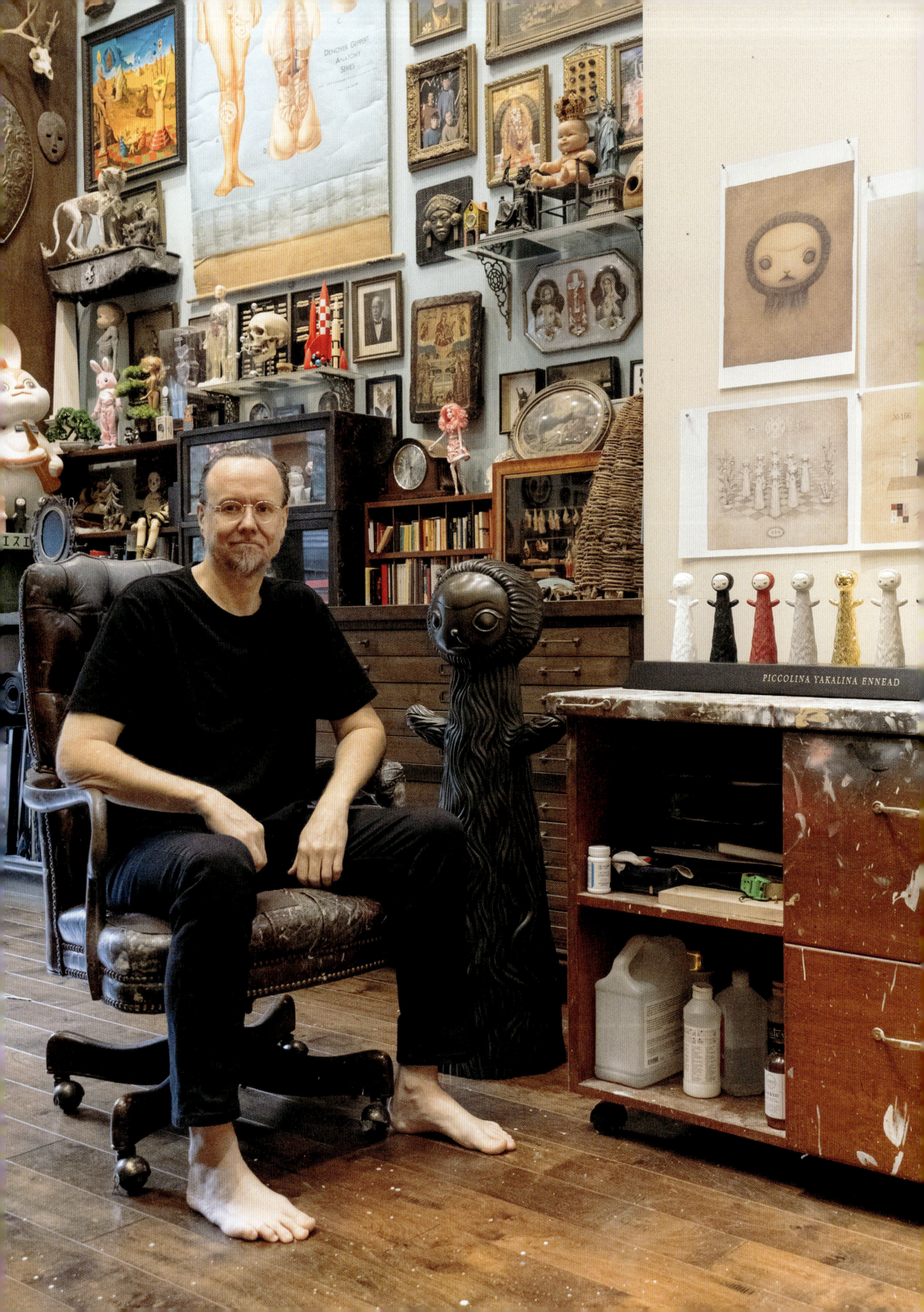

PICCOLINA YAKALINA ENNEAD

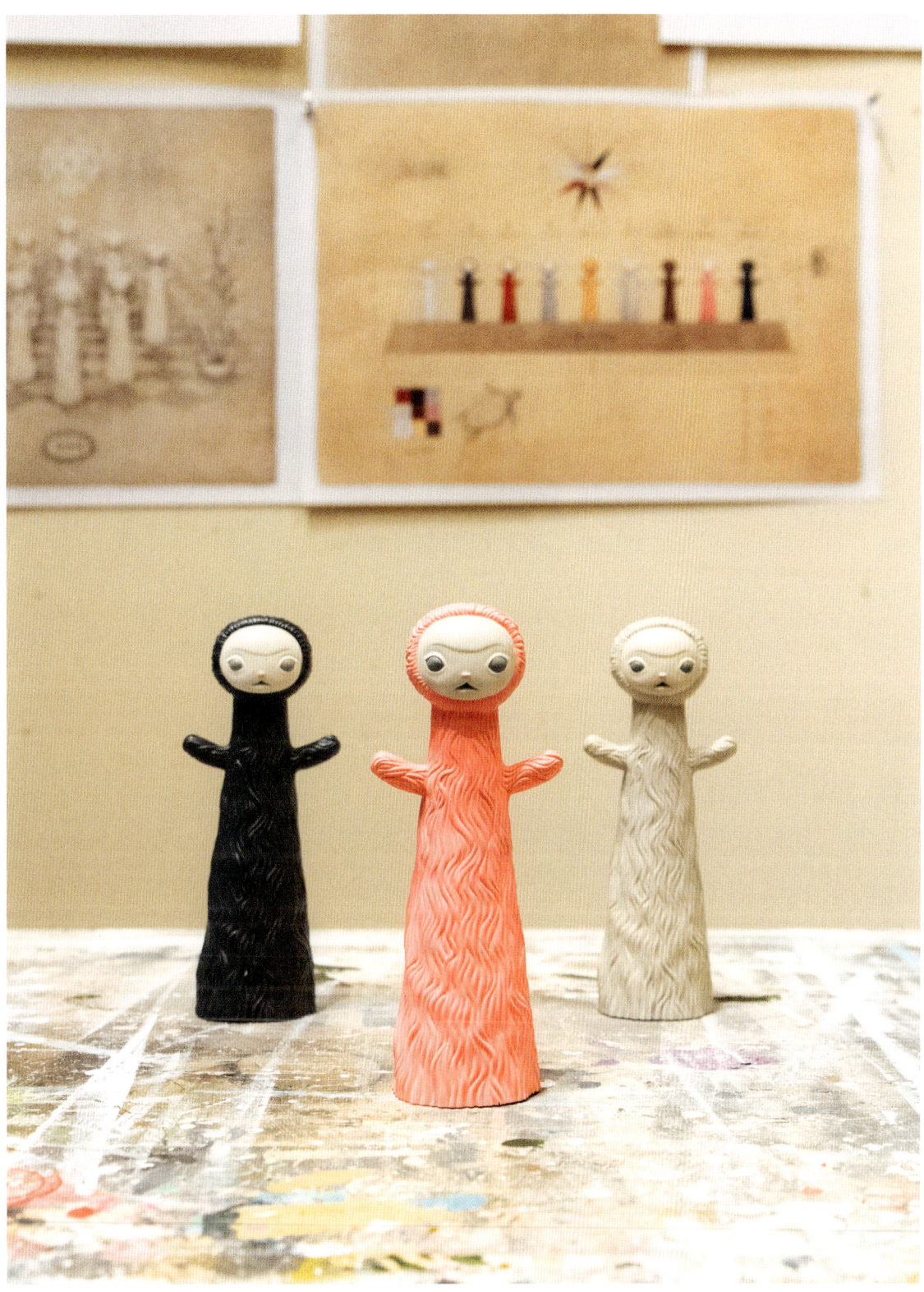

In 2023, Mark Ryden collaborated with DDT Store by AllRightsReserved to release *Piccolina Yakalina Ennead*.

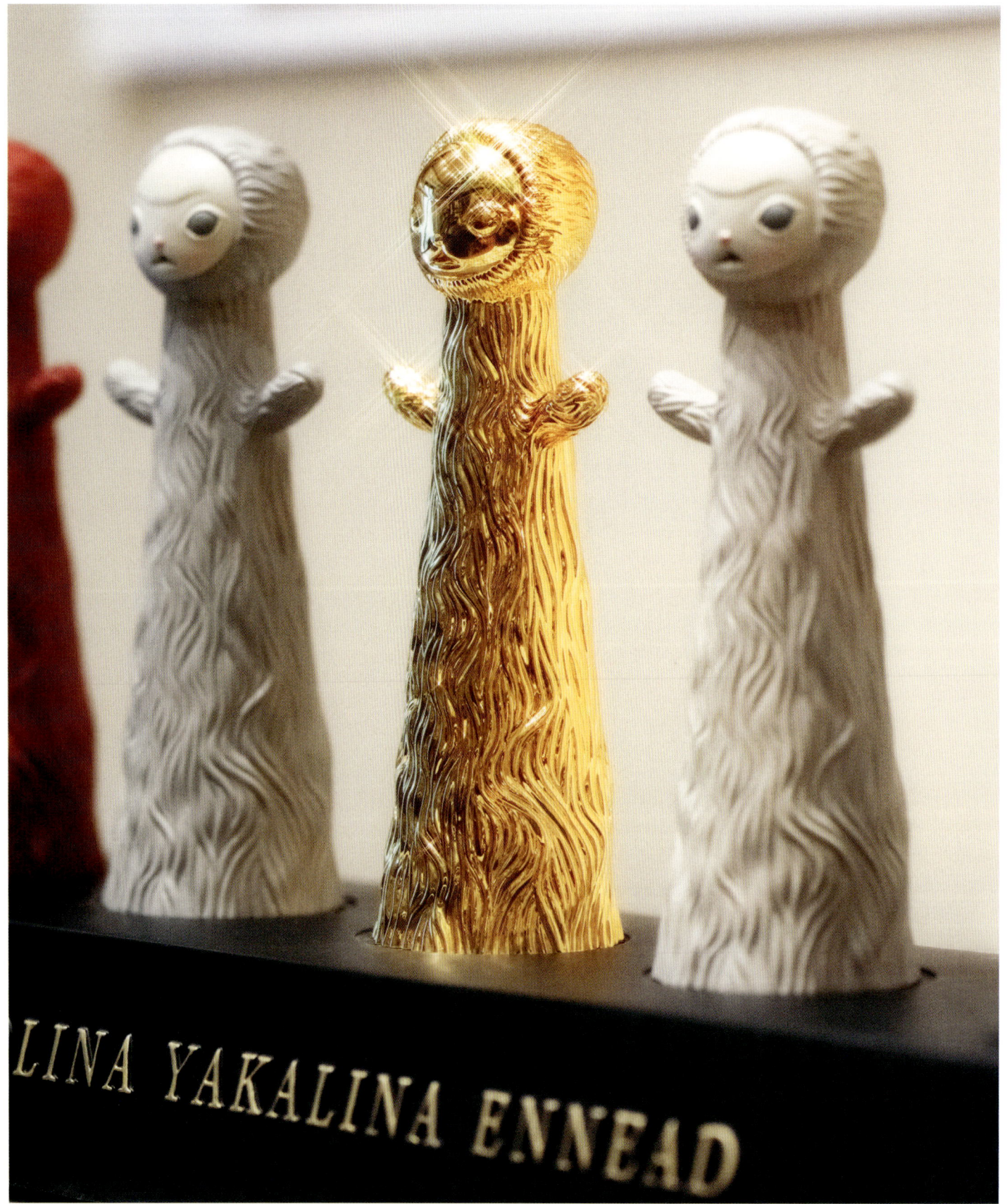

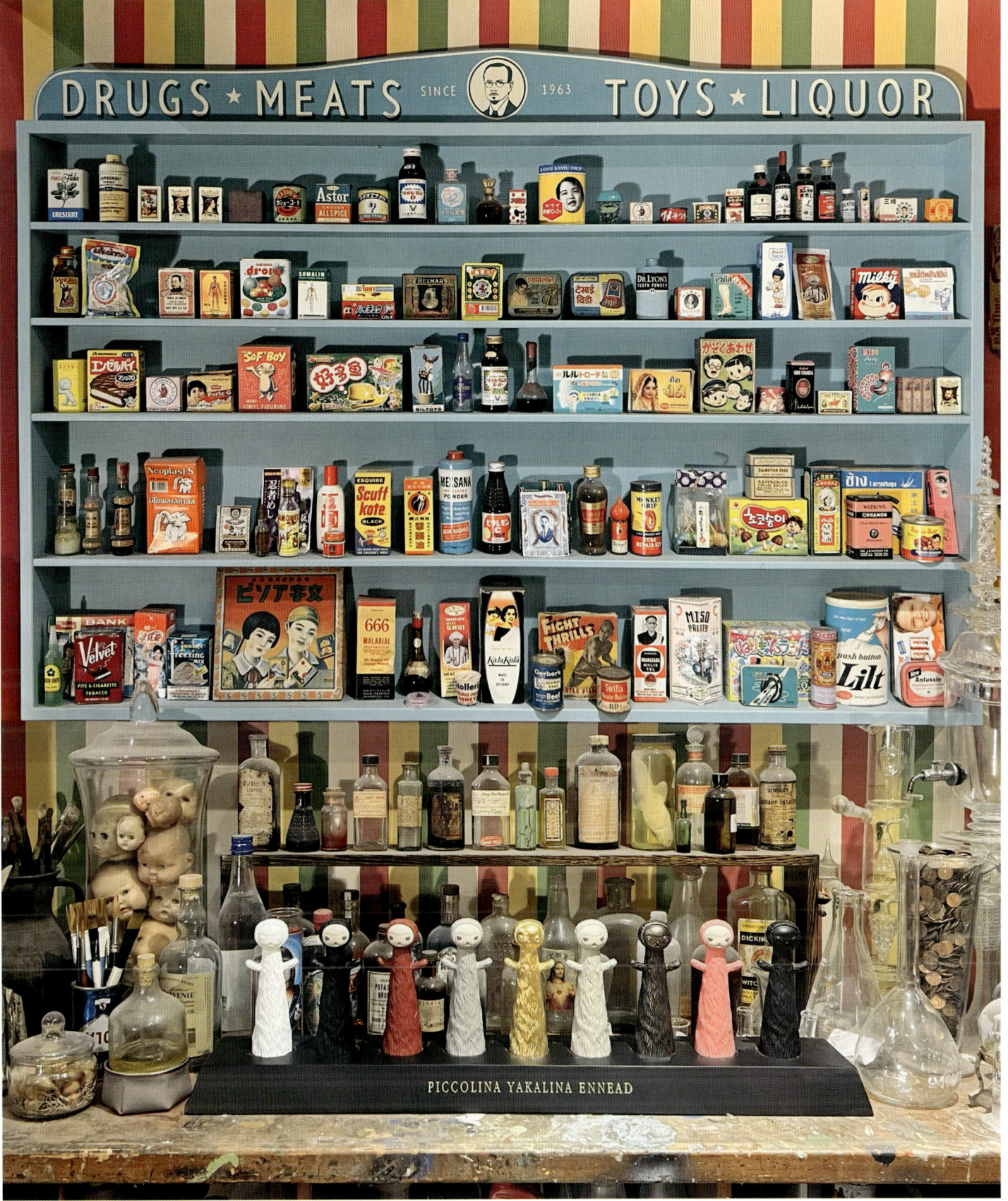

MARK RYDEN

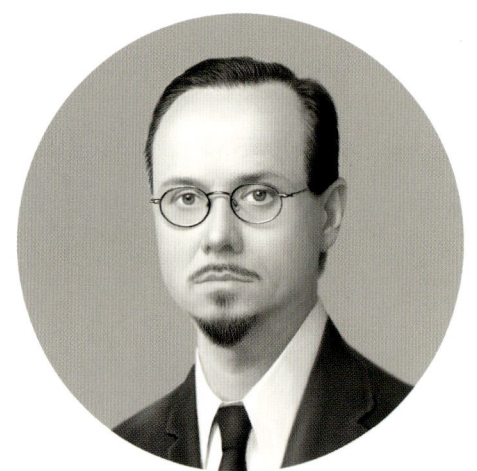

Born in Medford, Oregon, 1963.

Currently lives and works in Portland, Oregon.

Blending themes of pop culture with techniques reminiscent of the old masters, Mark Ryden has devised a singular style that blurs traditional boundaries. His work first garnered attention in the 1990s as he ushered in a new genre of painting, "Pop Surrealism," which developed the scope and spirit of the twentieth-century surrealism by embellishing its vocabulary with contemporary cultural references.

Ryden's work exquisitely renders a universe replete with fantastical characters amid enchanted landscapes that embody the artist's meticulously realized signature blend of archetype, kitsch, and narrative mysticism. Ryden's modern mythologies inseparably interweave twin senses of comfort and menace. "Most of my work engages with the relationship between the physical world and the spiritual world," he has said. His are scenes that exist in the ambiguous space between these two realms, in which nostalgia—and by extension memory, even death—are ever-present.

This time-honored, artistic craftsmanship elevates heavily sentimentalized elements of American tradition and antiquity, collected as though for a cabinet of wonders. The labor-intensive canvases deftly rework centuries of art history, combining the grandeur of Spanish and Italian religious painting with the decorative richness of Old Master compositions and the lush textures of French Neoclassicism. His ornately carved frames and meticulously glazed surfaces lend the paintings a baroque exuberance that adds gravity to their enigmatic themes.

Takashi Murakami has said: "Mark Ryden, Yoshitomo Nara, and I, among others, belong to a generation of artists who have been facing in the same general direction. What I mean by the 'same direction' is that as children, we were baptized in subculture and that experience remains intensely imprinted on each of our beings. When we subsequently began painting in our adolescent years, we also started to study art history while simultaneously developing our painting technique. Once we had full command of both of these, we succeeded in combining historical painting methods with subculture. That, in a nutshell, is our generation."

Ryden joined a rarified tradition of artists who have designed sets and costumes for the theater and ballet when he collaborated with American Ballet Theatre to create *Whipped Cream*, a reimagining of *Schlagobers*, a Richard Strauss ballet first performed at the Vienna State Opera in 1924. *Whipped Cream* had its New York debut at the Metropolitan Opera House in 2017. *The New Yorker* magazine called it "an extravaganza for the eyes and ears."

Mark Ryden received his BFA in 1987 from Art Center College of Design in Pasadena. His paintings have been exhibited in museums and galleries worldwide, including a career-spanning retrospective *Cámara de las maravillas* at The Centro de Arte Contemporáneo of Málaga, as well as an earlier retrospective *Wondertoonel* at the Frye Museum of Art in Seattle and Pasadena Museum of California Art. Mark Ryden currently lives and works in Portland, Oregon.

LINDA TESNER

Linda Tesner is a fine arts consultant and independent curator in Portland, Oregon. She was the interim director and curator of the Jordan D. Schnitzer Museum of Art at Portland State University. She was formerly the director and curator of the Ronna and Eric Hoffman Gallery of Contemporary Art at Lewis & Clark College, Portland, the assistant director of the Portland Art Museum, and the director of the Maryhill Museum of Art in Goldendale, Washington. She is the author of numerous exhibition catalogs and monographs.

EXHIBITIONS

SOLO EXHIBITIONS

2022 *Pink Pop - Ryden x Barbie*, Kasmin Gallery Pop Up,
Los Angeles, California

2022 *Animal Secrets*, Perrotin, Paris, France

2022 *Yakalina 9*, Perrotin, Tokyo, Japan

2020 *Anima Animals*, Perrotin and Kasmin Gallery, Shanghai, China

2018 *Quintessence 132*, Hong Kong Cultural Center and PMQ,
Hong Kong, China

2017 *The Art of Whipped Cream*, Paul Kasmin Gallery and Gallery Met
at the Metropolitan Opera House, New York, New York

2016 *Camara de las maravillas*, Centro de Arte Contemporáneo de Málaga,
Málaga, Spain

Diversaform, Hidari Zingaro Gallery, Tokyo, Japan

2015 *Dodecahedron*, Paul Kasmin Gallery, New York, New York

2014 *The Gay 90's West*, Michael Kohn Gallery, Los Angeles, California

2010 *The Gay 90's Olde Tyme Art Show*, Paul Kasmin Gallery, New York,
New York

2009 *The Snow Yak Show*, Tomio Koyama Gallery, Tokyo, Japan

2007 *The Tree Show*, Michael Kohn Gallery, Los Angeles, California

2005 *Wondertoonel*, Pasadena Museum of California Art, Pasadena,
California

2004 *Wondertoonel*, Frye Art Museum, Seattle, Washington

2003 *Blood*, Earl McGrath Gallery, Los Angeles, California

Insalata Mista, Mondo Bizzarro Gallery, Bologna, Italy

2002 *Bunnies and Bees*, Grand Central Art Center, Santa Ana, California

2001 *Bunnies and Bees*, Earl McGrath Gallery, New York, New York

Amalgamation, Outre Gallery, Melbourne, Australia

1998 *The Meat Show*, Mendenhall Gallery, Pasadena, California

GROUP EXHIBITIONS

2018 *Michael Jackson on the Wall*, National Portrait Gallery,
London, England, Jun 28 – Oct 1, 2018

Michael Jackson on the Wall, Paris Grand Palais,
Paris, France, Nov 23, 2018 – Feb 14, 2019

2016 *Turn the Page: the First Ten Years of Hi-Fructose*,
Virginia Museum Of Contemporary Art, Virginia Beach, Virginia

Juxtapoz x Superflat, Vancouver Art Gallery, Vancouver, Canada

Takashi Murakami's Superflat Collection, Yokohama Museum of Art,
Yokohama, Japan

2015 *HEY! modern art & pop culture / Act III*,
Musée de la Halle Saint Pierre, Paris, France

Fade to Black, Riverside Art Museum, Riverside, California

2014 *Lowbrow Insurgence: The Rise of Post-Pop Art*,
Harwood Museum of Art, Taos, New Mexico

2010 *The Artist's Museum, Los Angeles Artists 1980–2010*,
The Museum of Contemporary Art (MOCA), Los Angeles, California

Art Shack, Laguna Art Museum, Laguna Beach, California

2009 *Naked*, Paul Kasmin Gallery, New York, New York

Pictopia - Festival of New Character Worlds,
Haus der Kulturen der Welt, Berlin, Germany

2008 *Prints from the Cal State Fullerton University Collection II*,
Cal State Fullerton Main Art Gallery, Fullerton, California

In the Land of Retinal Delights, Laguna Art Museum,
Laguna Beach, California

2007 *Charity by Numbers*, Corey Helford Gallery, Culver City, California

El rey de la casa, Institut de Cultura de Barcelona, Spain

2006 *Drawn to Expression*, Art Center College of Design, Pasadena, California

2005 *Au Pays de Merveilles*, Galerie Magda Danysz, Paris, France

2004 *Innocence Found*, DFN Gallery, New York, New York

100 Artists See Satan, Grand Central Art Center, Santa Ana, California

Age of Aquarius, Copro-Nason Gallery, Culver City, California

Modern Love, M Modern Gallery, Palm Springs, California

From Your Valentine, Copro-Nason Gallery, Culver City, California

Juxtapoz 10th Anniversary Group Show, 111 Minna Gallery,
San Francisco, California

2003 *Dark Fairytales*, Roq La Rue Gallery, Seattle, Washington

Group Show, La Luz De Jesus Gallery, Los Angeles, California

Raising the Brow, Earl McGrath Gallery, Los Angeles, California

2002 *Hello*, PressPop Gallery, Tokyo, Japan

Gods and Monsters, Roq La Rue Gallery, Seattle, Washington

Group Show, La Luz De Jesus Gallery, Los Angeles, California

Draw, Roq La Rue Gallery, Seattle, Washington

Von Dutch an American Original, Northridge Art Galleries,
Northridge, California

2001 *Representing LA, Pictorial Currents in Southern CA Arts*,
Frye Art Museum, Seattle, Washington

Representing LA, Pictorial Currents in Southern CA Arts,
Laguna Art Museum, Laguna Beach, California

Group Show, La Luz De Jesus Gallery, Los Angeles, California

2000 *Margaret Keane and Keaneabilia*, Laguna Art Museum,
Laguna Beach, California

Luck of the Draw, La Luz De Jesus Gallery, Los Angeles, California

Retrospective, Mendenhall Gallery, Pasadena, California

Invitational III, La Luz De Jesus Gallery, Los Angeles, California

Up From the Underground, Hollywood Arts & Culture Center,
Hollywood, Florida

1999 *Group Show*, Copro-Nason Gallery, Culver City, California

Six Forms of Love and Despair, Merry Karnowsky Gallery,
Los Angeles, California

Tiki Group Show, Huntington Beach Arts Center,
Huntington Beach, California

Invitational II, La Luz De Jesus Gallery, Los Angeles, California

1998 *Kittens'n'Kads*, Merry Karnowsky Gallery, Los Angeles, California

Custom II, Acme Gallery, San Francisco, California

No Red Ribbons, Julie Rico Gallery, Santa Monica, California

Tribute to La Luz de Jesus, Track 16 Gallery, Los Angeles, California

Group Show, La Luz De Jesus Gallery, Los Angeles, California

1997 *Calivera Kustom*, Merry Karnowsky Gallery, Los Angeles, California

The Secret Society of Dog Art, Random Gallery, Los Angeles,
California

1996 *21st Century Tiki*, La Luz De Jesus Gallery, Los Angeles, California

1994 *Side Show*, Tamara Bane Gallery, Los Angeles, California

INDEX

YAKALINA 9

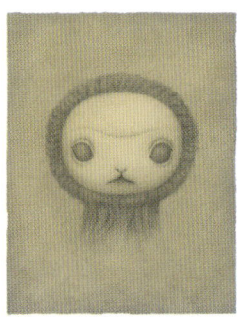

YAKALINA PORTRAIT

2022

Mixed media on paper

Unframed: 54.6 × 43.2 cm | 21 ½ × 17 inches
Framed: 70.5 × 59.2 × 3.3 cm | 27 ¾ × 23 ⁵⁄₁₆ × 1 ⁵⁄₁₆ inches

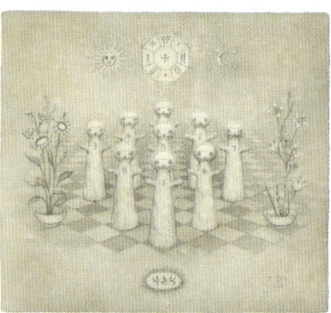

YAKALINA 9

2022

Mixed media on paper

Unframed: 31.8 × 35.6 cm | 12 ½ × 14 inches
Framed: 47.6 × 51.4 × 3.3 cm | 18 ¾ × 20 ¼ × 1 ⁵⁄₁₆ inches

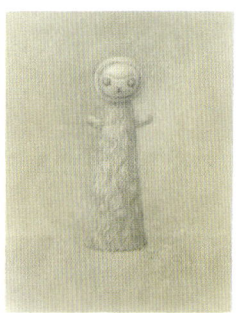

YAKALINA

2022

Mixed media on paper

Unframed: 41.9 × 33 cm | 16 ½ × 13 inches
Framed: 59.2 × 49 × 3.3 cm | 23 ⁵⁄₁₆ × 19 ⁵⁄₁₆ × 1 ⁵⁄₁₆ inches

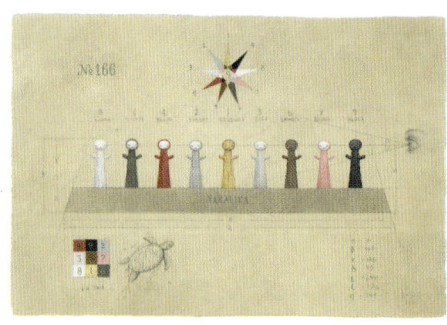

YAKALINA ARRAY

2022

Mixed media on paper

Unframed: 31.8 × 39.4 cm | 12 ½ × 15 ½ inches
Framed: 48 × 63 × 3.3 cm | 18 ⅞ × 24 ¹³⁄₁₆ × 1 ⁵⁄₁₆ inches

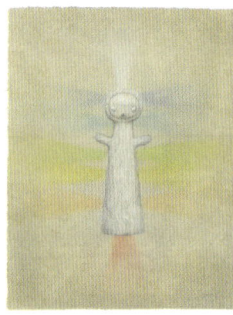

YAKALINA VISIBLE AND INVISIBLE

2022

Mixed media on paper

Unframed: 41.9 × 33 cm | 16 ½ × 13 inches
Framed: 58 × 49 × 3.3 cm | 22 ¹³⁄₁₆ × 19 ⁵⁄₁₆ × 1 ⁵⁄₁₆ inches

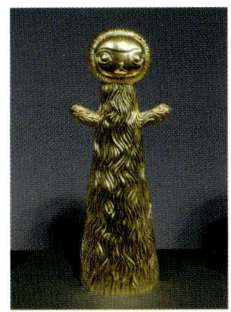

YAKALINA (BRILLIANT)

2022

Bronze with gold leaf

41 5/16 × 16 15/16 × 13 inches
Base: 13 3/8 × 13 inches

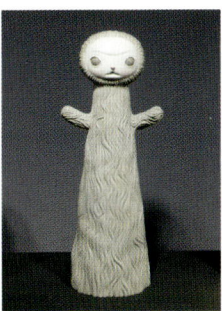

YAKALINA (BOMBAY)

2022

Bronze with patina

41 5/16 × 16 15/16 × 13 inches
Base: 13 3/8 × 13 inches

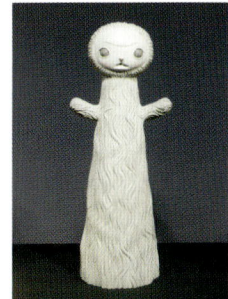

YAKALINA (BUFF)

2022

Bronze with patina

41 5/16 × 16 15/16 × 13 inches
Base: 13 3/8 × 13 inches

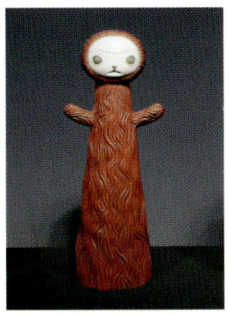

YAKALINA (BLOOD)

2022

Bronze with patina

41 5/16 × 16 15/16 × 13 inches
Base: 13 3/8 × 13 inches

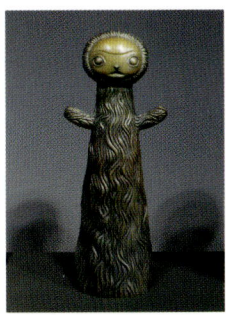

YAKALINA (BRONZE)

2022

Bronze with patina

41 5/16 × 16 15/16 × 13 inches
Base: 13 3/8 × 13 inches

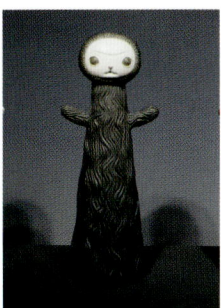

YAKALINA (BISTRE)

2022

Bronze with patina

41 5/16 × 16 15/16 × 13 inches
Base: 13 3/8 × 13 inches

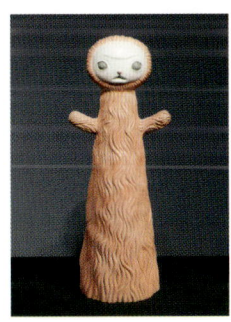

YAKALINA (BLUSH)

2022

Bronze with patina

41 5/16 × 16 15/16 × 13 inches
Base: 13 3/8 × 13 inches

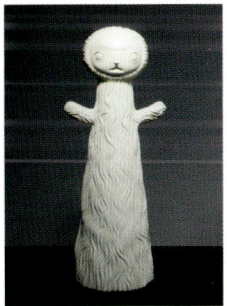

YAKALINA (BIANCA)

2022

Bronze with patina

41 5/16 × 16 15/16 × 13 inches
Base: 13 3/8 × 13 inches

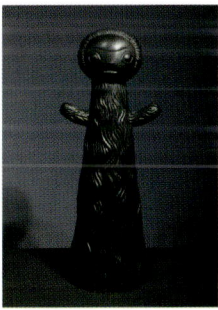

YAKALINA (BLACK)

2022

Bronze with patina

41 5/16 × 16 15/16 × 13 inches
Base: 13 3/8 × 13 inches

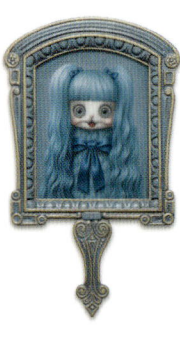

INDEX

ANIMAL SECRETS

TAVOLETTA AZZURRI (BLUE) (#161)
2021
Oil on panel and hand-carved wood frame
Size: 26.7 × 20.3 cm | 10 ½ × 8 ½ inches
Framed: 48.3 × 27.9 × 3.2 cm | 19 × 11 × 1 ¼ inches

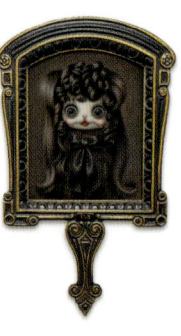

TAVOLETTA BRUNA (BRUNETTE) (#158)
2021
Oil on panel and hand-carved wood frame
Size: 26.7 × 21.6 cm | 10 ½ × 8 ½ inches
Framed: 48.3 × 27.9 × 3 cm | 19 × 11 × 1 ¼ inches

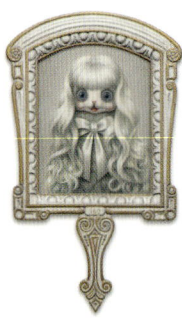

TAVOLETTA BIONDA (BLONDE) (#160)
2021
Oil on panel and hand-carved wood frame
Size: 26.7 × 20.3 cm | 10 ½ × 8 ½ inches
Framed: 48.3 × 27.9 × 2.5 cm | 19 × 11 × 1 ¼ inches

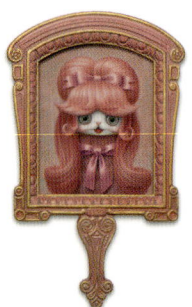

TAVOLETTA ROSA (PINK) (#159)
2021
Oil on panel and hand-carved wood frame
Size: 26.7 × 22.9 cm | 10 ½ × 8 ½ inches
Framed: 48.3 × 27.9 × 2.5 cm | 19 × 11 × 1 ¼ inches

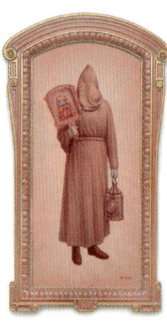

FRATELLO DELLA TAVOLETTA (#162)
2021
Oil on panel and hand-carved wood frame
Size: 82.6 × 38.1 cm | 32 ½ × 15 ½ inches
Framed: 99.1 × 39.4 × 5.1 cm | 39 × 15 ½ × 2 inches

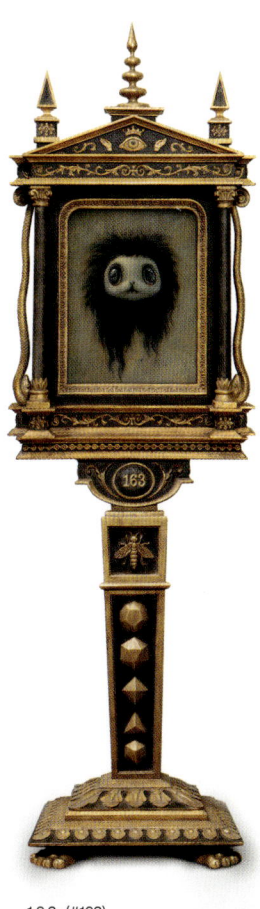

163 (#163)

2021

Oil on panel and hand-carved wood frame

Size: 45.7 × 35.6 cm | 18 × 14 inches
Framed: 208.3 × 66 × 53.3 cm | 82 × 26 × 21 inches

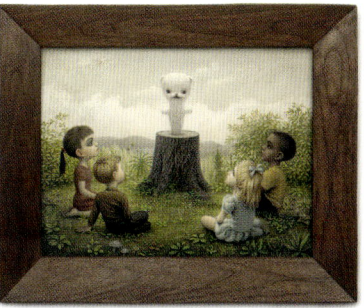

THE VISITATION (#164)

2021

Oil on panel and hand-carved wood frame

Size: 38.1 × 50.8 cm | 15 × 20 inches
Framed: 52.7 × 65.4 × 5.1 cm | 20 ¾ × 25 ¾ × 2 inches

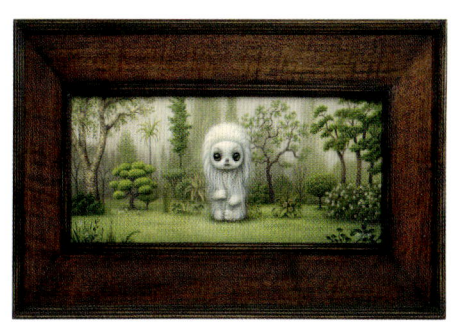

KAMI (#165)

2021

Oil on panel and hand-carved wood frame

Size: 15.2 × 40 cm | 6 × 15 ¾ inches
Framed: 29.8 × 54.6 × 5.1 cm | 11 ¾ × 21 ½ × 2 inches

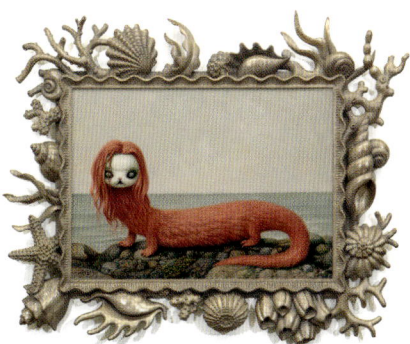

RED SIREN (#156)

2021

Oil on panel with carved and gilded wood frame

Size: 43.2 × 61 cm | 17 × 24 inches
Framed: 71.1 × 91.4 × 5.1 cm | 28 × 36 × 2 inches

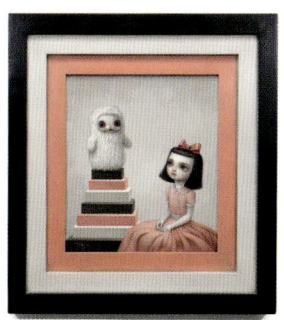

YUKI THE YOUNG YAK (#157)

2021

Oil on panel and hand-carved wood frame

Size: 45.7 × 40.6 cm | 18 × 16 inches
Framed: 76.2 × 71.1 × 5.1 cm | 30 × 28 × 2 inches

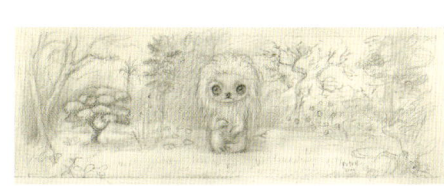

KAMI (DRAWING)

2021

Graphite on paper

Size: 15.2 × 43.2 cm | 6 × 17 inches
Framed: 32.1 × 60.1 cm | 12 ⅝ × 23 ¹¹⁄₁₆ inches

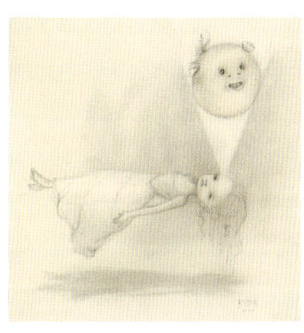

FLOATING VISION

2020

Graphite on paper

Size: 27.9 × 27.9 cm | 11 × 11 inches
Framed: 44.6 × 44.5 cm | 17 ⁹⁄₁₆ × 17 ½ inches

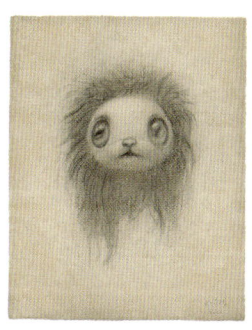

163 (DRAWING)

2021

Graphite on paper

Size: 20.3 × 16.5 cm | 8 × 6 ½ inches
Framed: 37 × 33.6 cm | 14 ⁹⁄₁₆ × 13 ¼ inches

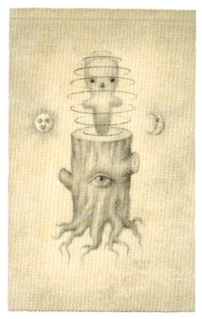

KODAMA

2021

Graphite on paper

Size: 43.2 × 27.9 cm | 17 × 11 inches
Framed: 60.1 × 44.6 cm | 23 ¹¹⁄₁₆ × 17 ⁹⁄₁₆ inches

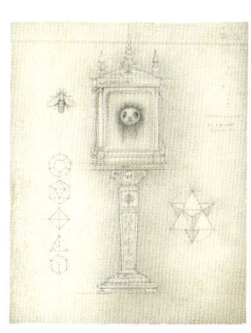

163 (FRAME STUDY)

2021

Graphite on paper

Size: 40.6 × 33 cm | 16 × 13 inches
Framed: 57.5 × 50.1 cm | 22 ⅝ × 19 ¾ inches

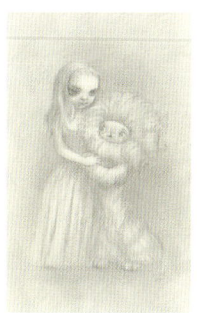

JELLY'S FRIEND

2019

Graphite on paper

Size: 43.2 × 27.9 cm | 17 × 11 inches
Framed: 60.1 × 44.6 cm | 23 ¹¹⁄₁₆ × 17 ⁹⁄₁₆ inches

INDEX

ANIMAL SECRETS

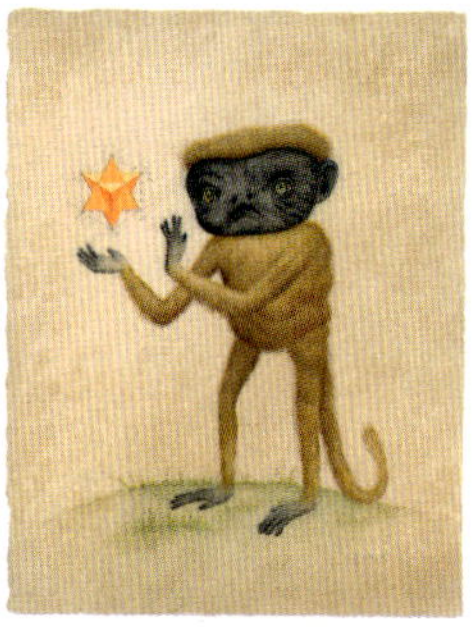

MERKABA GAMBOGE

2022

Mixed media on paper

Size: 34 × 26.7 cm | 13 3/8 × 10 1/2 inches
Framed: 51.1 × 43.6 cm | 20 1/8 × 17 3/16 inches

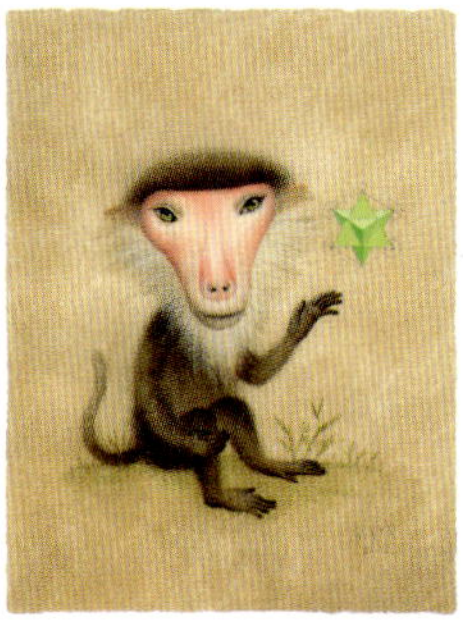

MERKABA EMERALD

2022

Mixed media on paper

Size: 34 × 25.4 cm | 13 3/8 × 10 3/8 inches
Framed: 51.5 × 42.1 cm | 20 1/4 × 16 9/16 inches

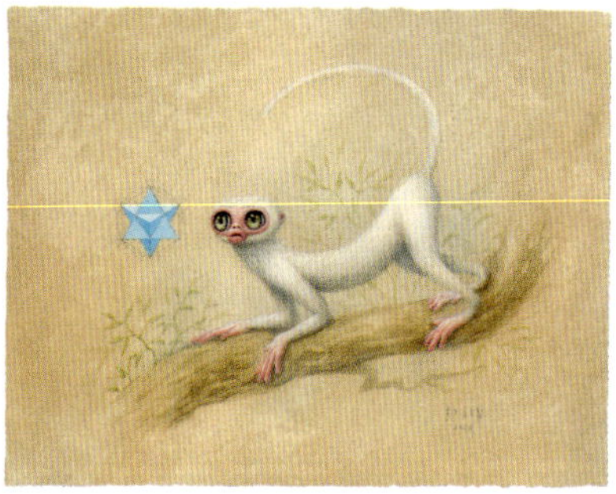

MERKABA CERULEAN

2022

Mixed media on paper

Size: 28.6 × 37.1 cm | 11 1/4 × 14 5/8 inches
Framed: 45.5 × 54.2 cm | 17 15/16 × 21 5/16 inches

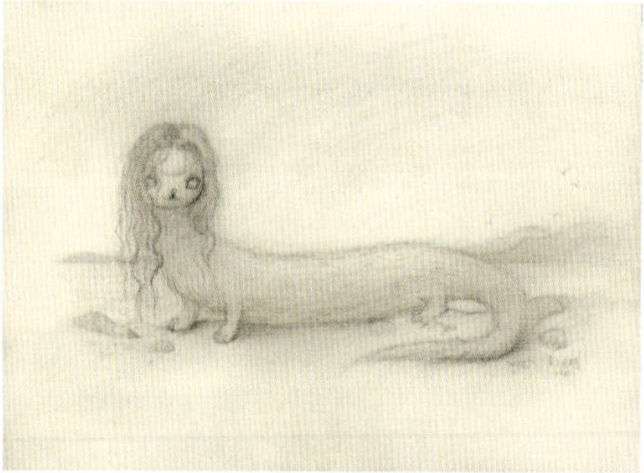

RED SIREN (DRAWING)

2021

Graphite on paper

Size: 25.4 × 35.6 cm | 10 × 14 inches
Framed: 41.9 × 52.6 cm | 16 1/2 × 20 11/16 inches

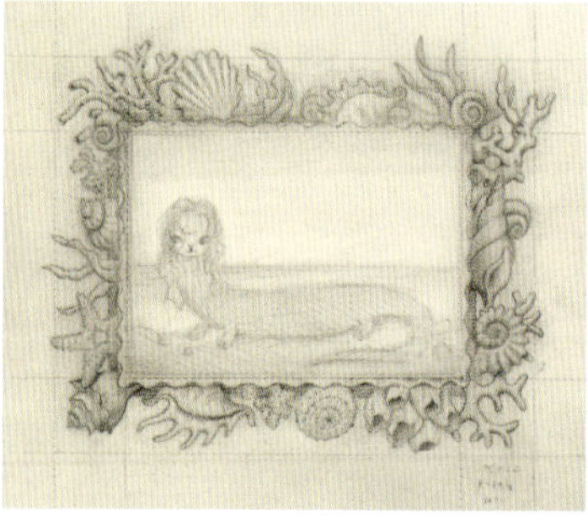

RED SIREN (FRAME STUDY)

2021

Graphite on paper

Size: 26.7 × 31.8 cm | 10 1/2 × 12 1/2 inches
Framed: 43.6 × 48.7 cm | 17 3/16 × 19 3/16 inches

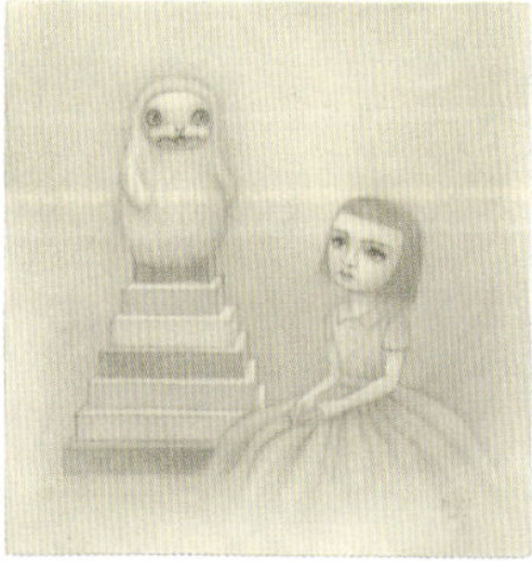

YUKI THE YOUNG YAK

2020

Graphite on paper

Size: 35.6 × 35.6 cm | 14 × 14 inches

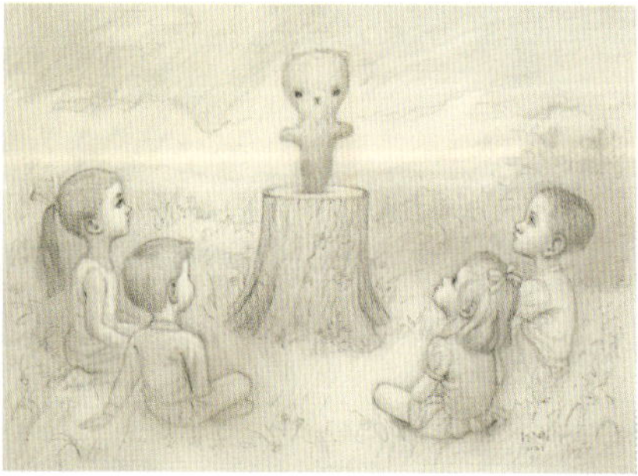

THE VISITATION (DRAWING)

2021

Graphite on paper

Size: 27.3 × 38.1 cm | 10 3/4 × 15 inches
Framed: 44.1 × 55.1 cm | 17 3/8 × 21 11/16 inches

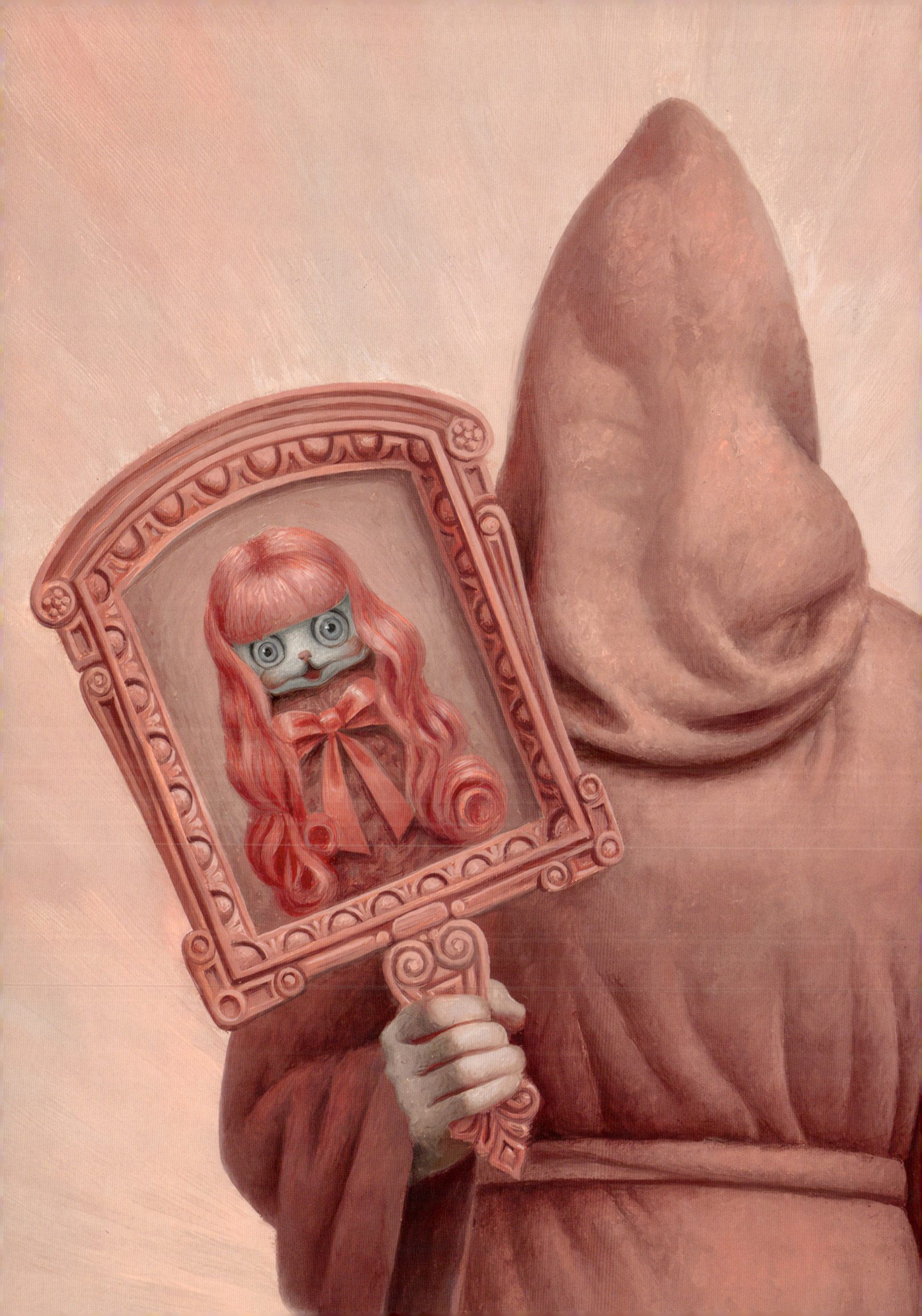

MARK RYDEN
YAKALINA SECRETS

ISBN: 978-1-4197-7190-3
Library of Congress Control Number: 2023945557

Copyright © 2024 Mark Ryden
www.markryden.com

Printed and bound in China
10 9 8 7 6 5 4 3 2 1

Text credits: respective authors
Yuki The Young Yak Japanese calligraphy © Tamayo Takamoto
Exhibition views for *Animal Secrets* © Tanguy Beurdeley /
images courtesy of Perrotin
Exhibition views and cropped artwork photos for *Yakalina 9* ©
Keizo Kioku / images courtesy of Perrotin
Photographs on pages 132, 133, 134 © Silas Lee &
AllRightsReserved
All other photographs © Christopher French
Cernunnos logo design: Mark Ryden
Book design: Benjamin Brard

Abrams books are available at special discounts when
purchased in quantity for premiums and promotions as
well as fundraising or educational use. Special editions
can also be created to specification. For details, contact
specialsales@abramsbooks.com or the address below.

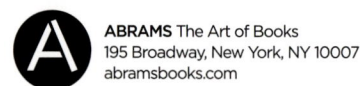

ABRAMS The Art of Books
195 Broadway, New York, NY 10007
abramsbooks.com

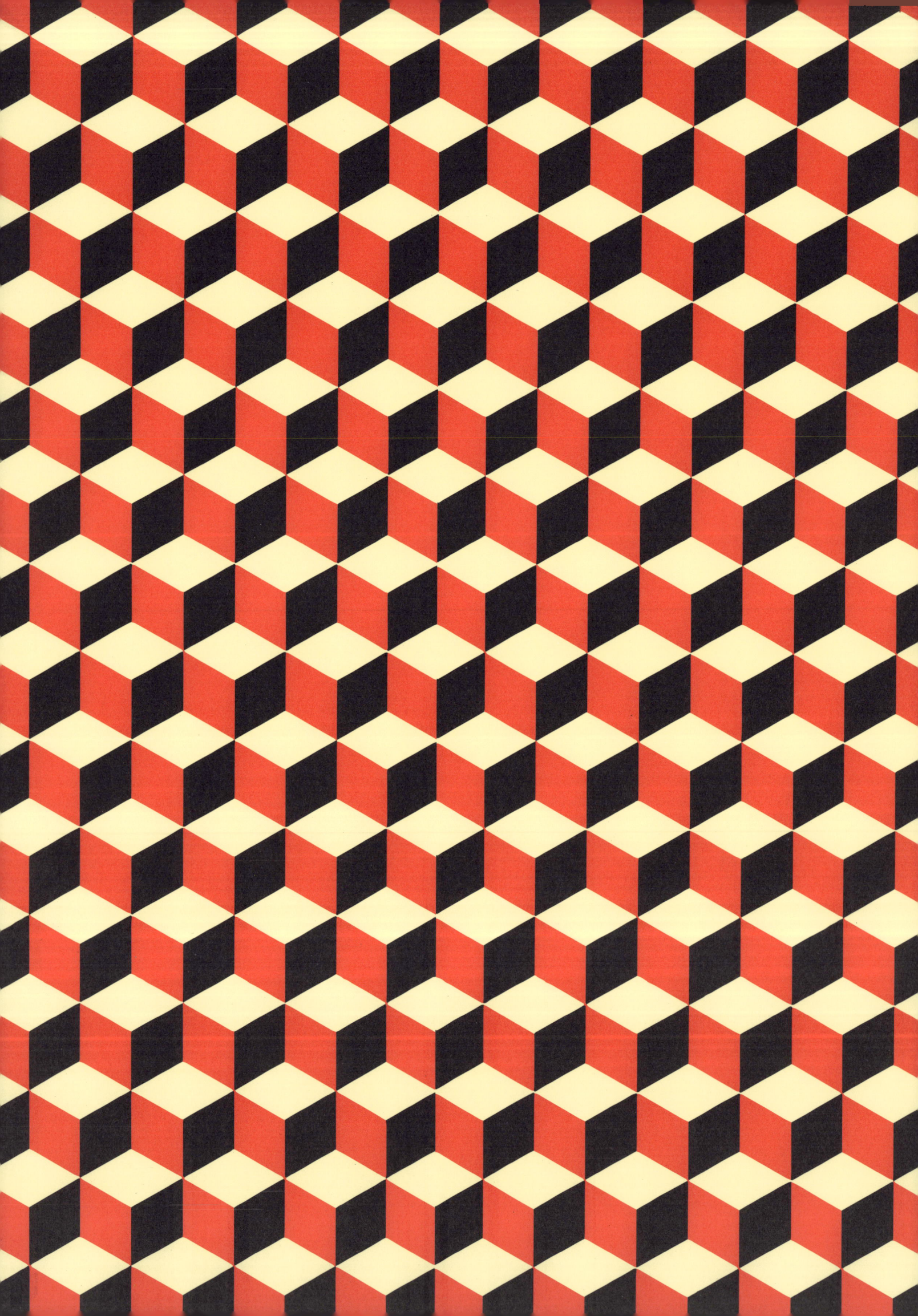